Public Speaking For Dummies, 2nd Edition

Preparing your speech

1. Resist making a speech that you don't want to make.
2. Organize your information in a simple pattern that the audience can easily recognize.
3. Use various types of material — examples, stories, statistics, quotes — to maintain audience interest.
4. Use your introduction to set the audience's expectations.
5. Have a special conclusion ready that you can go right into if you run out of time. Never omit a conclusion.
6. Anticipate the questions you'll be asked and have answers ready.
7. Practice out loud.

Perfecting your delivery

1. Try to establish eye contact with your entire audience.
2. Vary the rate, pitch, and volume of your voice, as well as its tone.
3. Use your hands to gesture instead of keeping them clasped in front of your crotch.
4. Look at the audience more than your notes.
5. Don't pace back and forth, jingle change in your pocket, or play with your hair.
6. Stand behind a podium if it makes you feel more comfortable.
7. Convey enthusiasm for your subject — it's contagious.

Readying the room

1. Get to the room early so that you have time to make changes if it's set up improperly.
2. Close the curtains so that the audience can't stare out the windows.
3. Control audience seating. Make sure that chairs and tables are arranged in the configuration that you want. Remove extra chairs.
4. Check the microphone and sound system while you're standing exactly where you'll be using them.
5. Make sure that the room isn't too cold or too stuffy.
6. Find out exactly where the room is located and how long it takes you to get there.

For Dummies: Bestselling Book Series for Beginners

BESTSELLING BOOK SERIES

Public Speaking For Dummies, 2nd Edition

Cheat Sheet

Using great visual aids

1. Make slides and overheads easy to read by avoiding too many words per line, too many colors, and designs that are too busy or too small.

2. Check text for spelling errors.

3. Take advantage of computer software templates that help you design visual aids.

4. You know you need time to design slides and overheads.

5. Number all your slides and overheads.

6. You can't check the working condition of the slide or overhead projector too many times.

7. Bring an extension cord and adapter.

Managing stage fright

1. Avoid alcohol and pills — they don't work. If they wear off before you speak, you'll be even more nervous. If they don't, you'll be incoherent.

2. Channel nervous tension into your performance.

3. Work off nervous energy by taking a few deep breaths.

4. Leave time to go to the bathroom shortly before you speak.

5. Remember that the audience wants you to succeed.

Checking Out Helpful Web Sites

Task	Web Site
Find great links for public speakers.	www.kushnergroup.com
Start here if you're researching a topic.	www.refdesk.com
Try a Web ring if you're tired of using traditional search engines to research a topic.	www.webring.org
Check out several links to humor for use in speeches.	www.museumofhumor.com
Discover a gold mine of government information.	www.fedworld.gov
Find a visual aid.	http://images.google.com
Go here to download the Real Player, and then listen to speeches on your computer.	www.real.com

For more information about Wiley Publishing, call 1-800-762-2974.

For Dummies: Bestselling Book Series for Beginners

Public Speaking

FOR

DUMMIES®

2ND EDITION

by Malcolm Kushner

WILEY

Wiley Publishing, Inc.

Public Speaking For Dummies,® 2nd Edition

Published by
Wiley Publishing, Inc.
111 River St.
Hoboken, NJ 07030-5774
www.wiley.com

Copyright © 2004 by Wiley Publishing, Inc., Indianapolis, Indiana

Published by Wiley Publishing, Inc., Indianapolis, Indiana

Published simultaneously in Canada

Library of Congress Control Number: 2004103139

ISBN: 0-7645-5954-0

Manufactured in the United States of America

10 9 8 7 6 5 4 3 2

2B/SQ/QU/QU/IN

WILEY

About the Author

Malcolm Kushner, "America's Favorite Humor Consultant," is an internationally acclaimed expert on humor and communication and a professional speaker. Since 1982, he has trained thousands of managers, executives and professionals how to gain a competitive edge with humor. His clients include IBM, Hewlett-Packard, AT&T, Chevron, Aetna, Motorola, and Bank of America.

A popular speaker, his Leading With Laughter presentation features rare video clips of U.S. presidents using humor intentionally and successfully. He has performed the speech at many corporate and association meetings, as well as at the Smithsonian Institution.

A Phi Beta Kappa graduate of the University of Buffalo, Kushner holds a BA in Speech-Communication. His MA in Speech-Communication is from the University of Southern California, where he taught freshman speech. He also has a JD from the University of California Hastings College of the Law. Prior to becoming a humor consultant, he practiced law with a major San Francisco law firm.

Kushner is the author of *The Light Touch: How to Use Humor for Business Success* and *Vintage Humor for Wine Lovers*. He is also a co-creator of the humor exhibit at the Ronald Reagan Presidential Library.

Frequently interviewed by the media, Kushner has been profiled in *Time Magazine, USA Today, The New York Times,* and numerous other publications. His television and radio appearances include CNN, National Public Radio, CNBC, *Voice of America,* and *The Larry King Show*. His annual "Cost of Laughing Index" has been featured on *The Tonight Show* and the front page of *The Wall Street Journal*.

Need a great speaker for your next meeting or event? Contact Malcolm at P.O. Box 7509, Santa Cruz, CA 95061, call 831-425-4839, or e-mail him at mk@kushnergroup.com. Visit his Web site at www.kushnergroup.com.

Dedication

This book is dedicated to my parents — Pauline, Hank and Helen. Thank you for all of your love and support

Author's Acknowledgments

Let's start with the people at Wiley. My thanks go to Marc Mikulich for talking me into writing this book and to Kathy Cox for making this edition happen. And to Jennifer Connolly who provided superb editing and listened to me kvetch.

Speaking of special thanks, I must shower praise upon my wife Christine Griger who looked at the pages as they came out of the printer. (Jennifer, if you think *your* job was tough, you should have seen what the stuff looked like *before* Chris's corrections!) And I must thank my son Sam for his encouragement.

Special thanks go to the late San Francisco comedy coach John Cantu. He was a good friend and teacher. And he is greatly missed by everyone who knew him. Loyd Auerbach, Allatia Harris and N.R. Mitgang also received repeated calls to tap into their expertise — and came through every time.

I also want to thank all the other people who were interviewed for this book. They include John Austin, Neil Baron, Donna Bedford, J.E. Aeliot Boswell, Rachael Brune, Joe DiNucci, Steve Fraticelli, James Harris III, Barbara Howard, Joyce Lekas, Marcia Lemmons, Jim Luckaszewski, Chuck McCann, Jeff Raleigh, Steve Resnick, Jackie Roach, Zack Rss, David Schmidt, Ken Sereno, Allen Weiner, Bill Zachmeier, Patty White, Russell Feingold, David Bartlett, Scott Fivash, Kare Anderson, Shawn Whalen, Rich Johnson, and Martin Gonzales Bravo.

Thanks for support and encouragement go to Rich Herzfeld, Bob Reed, Jack Burkett, Stu Silverstein, Linda Mead, Debra DeCuir, Karen Kushner, Barbara Nash, Corwin and Tyler Sparks, and Arthur, Karen, Heather and Amy Tamarkin. Special thanks go to Tom Daly IV at Vital Speeches for granting permission to use so many of the quotes contained in the book.

Publisher's Acknowledgments

We're proud of this book; please send us your comments through our Dummies online registration form located at www.dummies.com/register/.

Some of the people who helped bring this book to market include the following:

Acquisitions, Editorial, and Media Development

Project Editor: Jennifer Connolly

(Previous edition: Stacey Mickelbart, Ryan Rader)

Acquisitions Editor: Kathy Cox

Copy Editor: Jennifer Connolly

(Previous edition: Rowena Rappaport)

Assistant Editor: Holly Grimes

Technical Editor: Loyd Auerbach

Editorial Manager: Michelle Hacker

Editorial Assistant: Melissa Bennett, Elizabeth Rea

Cover Photo: © Don Klumpp/Getty Images/ The Image Bank

Cartoons: Rich Tennant, www.the5thwave.com

Production

Project Coordinator: Courtney MacIntyre

Layout and Graphics: Amanda Carter, Andrea Dahl, Denny Hager, Heather Ryan, Julie Trippetti,

Proofreaders: David Faust, Carl William Pierce, TECHBOOKS Production Services

Indexer: TECHBOOKS Production Services

Publishing and Editorial for Consumer Dummies

    Diane Graves Steele, Vice President and Publisher, Consumer Dummies

    Joyce Pepple, Acquisitions Director, Consumer Dummies

    Kristin A. Cocks, Product Development Director, Consumer Dummies

    Michael Spring, Vice President and Publisher, Travel

    Brice Gosnell, Associate Publisher, Travel

    Kelly Regan, Editorial Director, Travel

Publishing for Technology Dummies

    Andy Cummings, Vice President and Publisher, Dummies Technology/General User

Composition Services

    Gerry Fahey, Vice President of Production Services

    Debbie Stailey, Director of Composition Services

Contents at a Glance

Table of Contents

Introduction

* *

*W*elcome to *Public Speaking For Dummies,* 2nd Edition, the
book that gives a new meaning to the term "influence ped-
dling." No, I don't show you anything illegal, but you do figure out
how to use basic speaking skills to influence your boss, coworkers,
relatives, loved ones, butcher, baker, candlestick maker, and anyone
else who matters in your life. You can even influence people who
don't matter — like your senator.

This book provides all the tools you need to master public speaking. And that doesn't mean just formal speeches. Some of the most
important speeches you ever give may not involve a microphone
or a podium, like an impromptu talk about your strategy to some
customers; an answer that defuses a hostile question at a business
meeting; an impassioned plea to a police officer not to issue the
ticket. Success or failure in all of these situations, as well as in
formal speeches, depends on how you speak.

Why You Need This Book

Whether you're dealing with one person or one thousand, the ability to transmit ideas in a coherent and compelling fashion is one of
the most important skills you can ever develop. It's a basic survival
skill, and it always has been. From the earliest caveman who yelled
"Fire!" to the latest Web surfer who flamed someone on the Internet,
people have made speeches to motivate, persuade, and influence
each other.

Want to get a good job? Want to get promoted? Want to command
the respect of your peers? Want to get a date? The key to success
is what you say. To get what you want in life, you have to present
yourself forcefully, credibly, and convincingly. Sure, you can speak
softly and carry a big stick, but the real winner is the person who
talks you out of the stick.

In the information age, public speaking skills are even more important than ever before. We live in a society of sound bites. Communication is the currency of the realm. In survey after survey, public

speaking skills are cited as a key factor in hiring and promotion decisions. The days when you could rise to the top just by being good at your job are over. Boards of directors, executive committees, and customers want more. You have to know how to get your message across.

Now let's admit it. Many people get nervous about giving speeches, particularly in a formal setting. My goal in writing this book is to rid you of those fears forever. If you simply apply the techniques described in *Public Speaking For Dummies,* 2nd Edition, you'll be able to give a talk more competently than many Oscar-winning performers. (You don't believe me? Just watch the Academy Awards and listen to the acceptance speeches.) I'm not saying you'll be the next Cicero, but you will see how to deliver a speech in an organized and engaging manner.

And don't fall for the big myth that you have to be "a born speaker." Nothing could be further from the truth. Some of the greatest orators in history were anything but "naturals." Demosthenes — the famous speaker of ancient Greece — was a shy, stammering introvert when he decided to become a successful orator. He taught himself to speak by rehearsing with rocks in his mouth. If all you have in your mouth is your foot, then you're way ahead of the game.

If you already have the "gift of gab," you can still pick up many tips and tricks from *Public Speaking For Dummies,* 2nd Edition. For example, you wouldn't believe how often experienced speakers completely undermine their entire speech with poorly designed slides and overheads. If you read nothing more than the chapter on how to correct this common mistake (Chapter 10, by the way), this book is well worth what you paid for it.

Let's talk straight. There are lots of books about public speaking, and they're written by people who have various credentials. But how many of them taught speech at the University of Southern California, practiced law with an international law firm, ghost-wrote speeches for leading business executives, traveled the lecture circuit as a keynote speaker at major corporate and association meetings, and appeared on *The Gong Show* — without being gonged?

I've done all that stuff and more, and that's what's unique about this book. It contains a treasure trove of nuts-and-bolts information based on real-life experience. You see what really works and what doesn't. Because if there are mistakes to be made, I've already made them. Now you don't have to repeat them.

About This Book

If you want to improve the full range of your public speaking skills, then read the entire book. You will become an expert communicator.

Too busy to read a whole book? Don't worry. *Public Speaking For Dummies,* 2nd Edition is designed with your time constraints in mind. The book is divided into easy-to-read segments that cover very specific topics. Choose an area of interest, such as dealing with hecklers, and turn directly to it.

You can also use the book to accent the design of your home or office. Just put it on a bookshelf in full view. The bold yellow and black of the cover contrast nicely with the muted brown tones of many bookcases. (And anyone seeing the book on your shelf will assume you read it and will think you're smart.)

Conventions Used in This Book

So you can navigate through this book better, I use the following conventions:

- ✔ *Italic* is used for emphasis and to highlight new words or terms that are defined.
- ✔ **Boldfaced** text is used to indicate keywords in bulleted lists.
- ✔ Monofont is used for Web addresses.
- ✔ Sidebars, which are shaded gray boxes with text enclosed in them, consist of information that is interesting to know but not necessarily critical to your understanding of the chapter or section's topic.

Foolish Assumptions

While writing this book, I've made some assumptions about you and your knowledge of public speaking. Here are the assumptions I've made about you:

- ✔ You may be fretting about your next speaking engagement because you don't understand how to engage the audience.
- ✔ You may know nothing about public speaking but would like to be prepared in case you're ever asked to speak — impromptu or otherwise.

✔ You may know quite a bit about public speaking and have a lot of experience, but you may want to polish your speech development and delivery more.

✔ You may know how to give a formal speech but you would like to improve your speaking skills in special situations — question-and-answer sessions, panels, roundtables or debates.

✔ You may know the basics of public speaking but you want to learn some advanced techniques like using humor successfully or adding some style.

✔ You may know that there's no reason to fear public speaking, but you fear it anyway and you want to know how to overcome your anxiety.

How This Book Is Organized

Public Speaking For Dummies, 2nd Edition has six major parts, each of which is divided into chapters covering specific topics. The chapters are self-contained units of brilliant insight, so you don't have to plow through them in sequence. You can read them separately or together in any order you wish. Don't worry about missing any gems of wisdom. The book is thoroughly cross-referenced and guides you to related items of information.

Each part covers a major area of public speaking skills. The following is brief tour of what you can find.

Part 1: Getting Started

You've been asked to give a speech, now what? How do you decide what to talk about? What if you've been given a topic you don't like? Can you change it? How do you find out detailed information about your audience? Where can you get interesting material for your speech? These are some of the questions that I address in this section. Discover how to get your speech research off to a fast, productive start.

Part 11: Preparing Your Speech

In today's fast-paced, competitive environment, fortunes can rise or fall on the basis of a single speech. So it better be good. That means informative, to the point, attention grabbing, and memorable. And your speech doesn't get that way by luck or accident. Careful preparation — from topic selection to outline structure to choice of material to writing the actual speech — is the key. In this section, I show you how to develop a speech that commands an audience's attention, influences their thinking, and achieves your goals.

Part III: Making Your Speech Sparkle

Powerful public speakers are not that different from run-of-the-mill speakers. Both use words. Both use visual aids. And both stand in front of an audience. But really good speakers use really good words. They polish their speech until it's a gem. They also make sure that their visual aids communicate not confound. And when they stand in front of an audience, they appear confident and in control. This part of the book tells you how to give your speech that "something extra" that transforms it into an exciting event.

Part IV: Delivering Your Speech

There's more to think about when it comes to giving a speech than just your topic. You have to make decisions about whether you should use a podium; what you should wear; what gestures you should use; how fast you should speak; how you should handle the audience and their questions. And these are just a few of the issues involved in transforming your written message into a masterful oral performance. In this section, I show you how to deliver a presentation that wows your audience. Simple, proven techniques guarantee your success. If you're nervous, shy, or disorganized, don't worry. I also explain how to handle any fears you have about public speaking.

Part V: Common Speaking Situations

Even if you're not a professional speaker, the odds are that you'll have to give a speech every so often. You may have to speak to a meeting of your city council or address a group of businesspeople from another country. Or you may serve as a panelist at an event sponsored by your club, association, or religious organization. And in this age of technology and globalism, this part is essential to discover how to speak internationally as well as over a variety of different mediums in the virtual world. In this section, I address these types of common speaking situations, and I tell you how to anticipate them and prepare for them. You even discover how to give a speech "off the top of your head."

Part VI: The Part of Tens

In this part, you can find simple types of humor that anyone can use to polish off a speech. And I give you a list of things to check before you speak so you don't leave out any of those important details that can stunt the effectiveness of your speech.

Icons Used in This Book

This icon signals important advice about how to maximize the effectiveness of your speech.

An elephant never forgets, but people do. This icon alerts you to information you'll want to remember (unless you're subpoenaed by a Senate subcommittee).

This icon points to information that justifies your purchase of this book — brilliant advice that you can't readily find anywhere else. Most of it's based on the personal experience, knowledge, and insight of myself as well as several of my colleagues.

To indicate potential problems, I use this icon.

Where Do I Go from Here?

You hold in your hands a powerful tool — a guide to increasing your influence through the sheer force of your speeches. This tool can be used for good or evil. That's up to you. Consider yourself warned. To begin your journey, turn to the Table of Contents or Index, pick a topic of interest, and turn to the page indicated. Good luck in your travels. You're now ready to dive into this book, unless you plan to wait for the movie version.

Part I
Getting Started

In this part . . .

The toughest part of preparing a speech, or doing anything, is getting started. In these chapters, I show you how to take the first steps toward doing what has to be done. You can also find out what information you need to know about your audience to craft a successful speech. I even cover how to get started researching what you're going to say.

Chapter 1

Giving a Speech

• •

In This Chapter

▶ Examining the contents of this book

▶ Exploring what you need to know

• •

Whether you're giving your first speech or your five hundredth, this book can show you how to improve your speaking skills. Crammed full of nuts-and-bolts ideas, techniques, and suggestions, beginners can benefit just from discovering and avoiding basic mistakes, and experienced speakers may appreciate the expert tips and techniques sprinkled throughout these pages. Because this book isn't designed to be read from cover to cover (of course, you can if you want to), you can skip chapters and even sections within chapters, focusing only on the material that suits your needs. So if you're looking for an idea of where to start or an idea of what chapters may benefit you the most, just check out the sections that follow to find out what each chapter has to offer.

Finding Out What You Need to Know

Before you give your speech, or even write it, there's a lot of basic information that you need to know. Chapters 2 and 3 tell you how to get started researching the basics.

Getting down the preliminaries

Getting asked to speak begins the process of making a lot of decisions. The first decision is exactly what to talk about. Even when you're assigned a topic, there's usually still room for you to shape it. How you do this depends on the audience — not just their age and sex, but also their education, attitudes, and much more. Chapter 2 tells you what you need to know and how to find it out.

Doing research

No matter what you talk about, you can improve it by doing a little research. I don't mean just locating facts and statistics. You can also find quotes, jokes, and stories to spice up your remarks. Chapter 3 puts a wealth of research tools and techniques at your disposal, such as using traditional library sleuthing, logging onto cool Web sites, and getting other people to do your research for you — for free.

Organizing your speech

After you've got a topic and you've done some research, it's time to get organized. To make your speech flow, you can choose from several patterns: problem and solution; past, present, and future; and cause and effect. Chapter 4 gives you lots of ideas for organizational patterns and shows you how to create a speech outline that's actually useful and conforms to your time limits.

Developing Your Speech

Giving a speech scares a lot of people. Writing one is just perceived as a hassle. And doing it right can take a lot of time. But calm down. This part of the book will show you everything you need to know to write a speech quickly and effectively.

Selecting the right material

You've done research and you've got an outline. Now it's time to put some meat on those bones. (Or leaves on those branches if you're a vegetarian.) If you're looking for the key to captivating an audience with statistics quotes, stories, and examples, you're in luck. I unlock all kinds of potential speech material in Chapter 5.

Starting and ending your speech

Many people believe that you have to open with a joke, but you can get the audience involved better by asking a rhetorical question or by using a quotation for the opening — or the conclusion. In Chapters 6 and 7, I discuss cool ways to open and close your speech, and I give you great ideas to make sure you and your audience reach your conclusion at the same time.

Polishing It Off

Anyone can throw a speech together, but you do need to make it memorable. If you need to find just that right turn of phrase, develop the winning argument, come up with the perfect example or anecdote that an audience will never forget, or get ideas on how to deliver your speech flawlessly even if you're nervous, Chapters 8 through 10 make polishing your speech and delivery much easier.

Making sure your speech makes sense

Sure, your speech makes perfect sense to you, but the test is whether it makes sense to your audience. If you'd rather not find that out as you deliver your speech, visit Chapter 8 and find out how to put a little spit shine on your speech to make it stand out from the crowd.

Adding some style

You don't have to be a poet or literary type to give a little zip to your speech. Just remember that certain words and phrases can make more powerful statements than others — you just have to pick the right ones. Chapter 9 shows you how to use rhetorical techniques to create some colorful lines and phrases to spice up your speech.

Using visual aids

If you need eye candy to dress up your next speech, find out everything you need to know to make your graphics look good and to avoid common mistakes in Chapter 10. From PowerPoint to overheads to good old-fashioned flip charts, you can find several great choices for displaying information during your speech.

Delivering a Speech

After you've written a brilliant, witty speech that captures your message exactly, you still have to perform it in front of an audience. So, if your goal is to receive a standing ovation, Chapters 11 to 14 may give you a chance for one.

Overcoming stage fright

If you've gone to all the trouble to create a brilliant speech, you don't want to ruin it by fainting at the podium. If you need to squelch anxiety at the outset or find some stress-busting techniques used by professional speakers, check out Chapter 11.

Talking with your body

The way you move and make eye contact affects how your audience receives your message. To ensure that your verbal and non-verbal messages match, check out Chapter 12 and find out all the details on how to move, dress, make eye contact, deal with your hands and habits, and get your other body-language questions answered.

Taking questions

Answering audience questions is an art unto itself. What do you do if you don't know the answer? How do you respond to hostile questions? What if the questioners have no idea what they're talking about? Chapter 13 addresses all these issues and shows you how to anticipate questions, design perfect answers, and get an audience to ask questions.

Handling the audience

Your speech is fantastic but your audience is not: They're heckling you; they're falling asleep; they're leaving! Understanding how to read an audience is an essential skill for anyone who has to give a speech. You have to adapt quickly and know what you're adapting to. If you want to discover how to deal with tough audiences, keep their attention, and get them involved, then Chapter 14 is for you.

Preparing for Special Speaking Situations

Speaking in front of public bodies, informal speeches, introductions, panels, debates, international meetings, and virtual meetings are all common speaking situations, but they don't fit into the normal speech you may give at a convention or meeting. Special meetings require special preparation, and Chapters 15 through 20 tell you how to handle all these situations.

Talking to public bodies

Concerned citizens have lots of opportunities to give speeches: city council meetings, school board meetings, board of supervisor meetings, planning commission meetings, and the list goes on. But these types of forums have special rules, such as speaker sign-up procedures, time limits, requirements regarding handouts, and basic rules of courtesy that are strictly enforced. Chapter 15 provides the inside scoop on all these rules and describes effective strategies for persuading public officials.

Speaking on the fly

One of the most common, yet feared, speaking situations is when someone asks you to get up and say a few words about something off-the-cuff. The good news is that you didn't have to spend a lot of time preparing your speech. Of course, that's also the bad news. Chapter 16 tells you how to anticipate those situations, plan for them, and give fabulous impromptu speeches.

Introducing other speakers

If you have to introduce a speaker at a meeting, conference, or convention, you probably wonder how big a deal you should make of it: should the introduction be long and flowery, should you just recite the speaker's resume, or should you do a lot of research and find some "inside" stories about the speaker. Find out how to handle your next introduction in Chapter 16.

Speaking on panels or roundtables

Some people figure it's easy to serve on a panel or roundtable. They think they can just wing it because the other panelists can always pick up the slack. If you happen to be more of a slacker than a pick-up-the-slacker, just remember that the audience is going to *compare* you to those other panelists, so you'd better be good. Chapter 17 shows you how to stand out from the crowd when you're speaking on a panel or roundtable.

Debating

If you have to deal with kids, teachers, neighbors, parking enforcement officers, liberals, conservatives, extremists of any stripe, or the manager of a store where you want to return something, then you already know something about debate. Chapter 18 shows you some formal techniques so your next debate can be a sure bet.

Speaking at international meetings

Today's global economy has increased the number of business-people who speak before international audiences. While language differences are a big challenge, cultural differences can be even bigger. Use Chapter 19 to prepare for your next international meeting so you can avoid embarrassing gaffes.

Participating in virtual meetings

Meetings are commonly held in virtual locations, so you may be more used to attending face-to-space rather than face-to-face meetings. Before your next virtual meeting, check out the techniques in Chapter 20 to maximize the effectiveness of your participation.

The Parts of Ten

In this section, I show you how to make your speech sparkle with humor — even if you can't tell a joke. The techniques are so simple that you'll wonder why you didn't use them before. I also point out what to check just before you speak.

Chapter 2

Getting Ready to Speak

* *

In This Chapter
▶ Prepping for your speech
▶ Getting the lowdown on the audience
▶ Connecting with the audience

* *

*G*etting started is always the toughest part of any activity. And that's certainly true for writing a speech — especially if you don't want to give one in the first place. But don't worry. Speechwriting doesn't have to be torture. It can even be fun. Well, at least more fun than getting poked in the eye with a sharp object.

This chapter shows you several simple techniques for getting started with your speech.

Making Important Preparations

Giving a speech doesn't start when you step in front of an audience. Giving a speech doesn't even start when you begin writing your speech. The entire speech process begins before you even accept the invitation to speak. The sections that follow discuss items you should consider before you begin writing that speech and items you should consider even before you commit yourself to a speaking engagement.

Deciding whether you should speak

Just because you're asked to speak doesn't mean you have to. Of course, if your boss asks you to give a speech, you'd better do it, but I'm referring to voluntary situations. Unfortunately, most people give little, if any, thought to whether they want to or should speak.

Before you accept your next invitation to speak, think about the following so you can be sure to make the right decision:

✔ **Consider whether you have the time in your schedule.** Okay, most of you are rolling your eyes about now, thinking that I'm telling you something you already know. But, remember, just because you're asked to speak for 30 minutes doesn't mean that's all the time it takes out of your schedule. You have to get to the event and back, of course, but you also need to leave time to answer questions and be available after you're finished (see Chapter 13 for more information on being available after your speech). And you most certainly should give more than a nod either before or after your speech to the folks who invited you. So, a 30-minute speech can easily take up half of your day.

✔ **Consider whether you have the time to prepare.** You want to be sure that you have enough time to prepare a speech that you are proud of and that meets the expectations of your audience — you want to have a good speech. While having an exact formula to follow would be great, in reality, preparing a 30-minute speech can take hours, days, weeks, or months depending on who you're speaking to and how important the speech is. You're the only one who can decide how much time is necessary for preparing your speech.

✔ **Consider whether you have something to say.** Just because someone asks you to speak doesn't mean you have anything to say. Sometimes your best speech will be the one you don't give.

✔ **Consider whether to accept immediately.** You don't have to decide the moment someone asks you and you probably shouldn't. Take your time. Sleep on it. Get back to the person after you've had time to think about the considerations above.

Although I'm sure you are a great speaker, bear in mind that some people resort to all forms of flattery just to get you to accept their invitation, especially if they're desperate to fill a speaking slot. Don't be swept away by their praise. Even if you truly are the perfect person for their engagement, it may be not be something you want or can do. It's okay to politely decline if, after you've made the above considerations, you've concluded that this speaking engagement is not for you.

Figuring out why you're speaking

There are three types of speakers in the world: those who make things happen, those who watch things happen, and those who wonder what happened.

If you want to avoid wondering what happened, you better know why you're speaking in the first place. Following are two effective ways to find out why you're speaking:

- ✔ **Look at the function of your talk.** Are you trying to inform, persuade, inspire, or entertain?

- ✔ **Examine your motivation for speaking and the audience's motivation for listening.** Have you been asked to speak? Have you been ordered to speak? Do you want to speak? Does the audience want to hear you? Have they been forced to hear you? Will they listen to you?

However you slice the analysis, the purpose remains the same — you want to know why you're speaking. You don't want to end up wondering what happened.

Setting specific goals

Most people either set no goals when they decide to give a speech or their goals are vague, such as wanting to be a hit, wanting to impress a co-worker or management, or wanting to get the speech over with. However, deciding what you hope to accomplish through speaking — your goals — makes developing your speech easier.

Some examples of goals you may have are

- ✔ **Wanting to build your credibility**
- ✔ **Wanting to get the audience to agree with your position**
- ✔ **Wanting to make the audience understand something**
- ✔ **Wanting to make the audience laugh**

Write out your goals before you write your speech. Then you can easily decide what material to include and exclude. Anything that doesn't further your goals is excluded.

Getting the essential information

No matter what type of speech you've been invited to deliver, certain information is basic and essential. You must first know the name of your contact person. Armed with that knowledge, you can ask your contact to provide the rest of the information that you need. The following lists show some of the questions you want answered.

Ask these questions about the event so you'll know the tone of the meeting and what will be expected from you:

- ✔ What's the purpose of the meeting?
- ✔ Is it a regularly scheduled meeting or a special event?
- ✔ Is it a formal or informal event?
- ✔ What's the atmosphere — very serious or light?
- ✔ Is your talk the main attraction?

Ask these questions about the format to make sure your speech content is the right length, style and fits properly into the meeting:

- ✔ What's the agenda for the day?
- ✔ What's the format for your speech:
    - A general session?
    - A breakout session?
    - A panel discussion?
    - Before, during, or after a meal?
- ✔ What time do you begin speaking?
- ✔ How long are you expected to speak?
- ✔ Will there be other speakers?
- ✔ When will they be speaking?
- ✔ What will they be speaking about?
- ✔ Will any of them be speaking in opposition to your views?
- ✔ What occurs before your speech?
- ✔ What occurs after your speech?

Ask these questions about the location to make sure that everything you need is available and arranged the way you prefer:

- ✔ Where will you speak?
    - Inside or outside?
    - What type of room: banquet, meeting, auditorium, and so on?
- ✔ How will the room be set up?
- ✔ What audio/visual and sound equipment is available for you?
- ✔ Will there be a podium/table/platform?

Ask these questions about the audience to get an idea of the mood they'll be in when you speak and how they'll react to you:

- ✔ What's the size of the audience?

- ✔ Is the audience required to attend?

- ✔ Are the people there to hear you or for some other reason?

- ✔ How much do they know about your topic?

- ✔ Will they be in a rush to leave?

- ✔ Will they be drinking?

- ✔ Will they be walking in and out as you speak?

- ✔ How have they responded to other speakers?

- ✔ What other speakers have they heard?

- ✔ What do they expect from you?

See the section below, "Analyzing Your Audience," for a detailed discussion of audience analysis. (See Chapter 14 as well.)

Agreeing on a topic

 You have a lot more control over your topic than you might suspect. When you're asked to speak about a certain subject, that's not the end of the discussion. It's just the beginning. If you don't like the topic, ask to change it. Many organizations will quickly accommodate your request. If you can't completely change the topic, try to slant it in a way that suits your needs.

Even when you're locked into a particular topic, you still have a lot of leeway in how to proceed. Suppose that you're a computer guru and you've been asked to speak about the latest upgrade to some software package that everyone wants to use. Will you give a broad overview? Will you give a list of specific tips for using it most effectively? Will you give a history of how it was developed? You can still essentially pick your topic because you can narrow the topic that was assigned to you.

Sometimes you may have free rein over the topic because the sponsoring organization doesn't care what you speak about. You may be given only the vaguest of guidelines — such as "speak about business." The organization may just want you to show up and talk. (For more ideas on selecting a topic, read the section on Analyzing Your Audience below.)

Analyzing Your Audience

How do you relate to an audience? You start by discovering as much about the people in the audience as possible — who they are, what they believe in, and why they are listening to you. This process is known as *audience analysis*.

The more information you possess, the more you can target your remarks to reflect an audience's interests. By targeting your audience's interests, you increase the likelihood that members of the audience will listen to you. Displaying your knowledge about an audience usually scores some points with them. It compliments the audience. It shows that you bothered to learn about them.

Audience analysis also helps you develop your message. Such analysis structures the content of your speech by shaping what types of arguments you should make; what the most effective examples will be; how complex your explanations can be made; what authorities you should quote; and so on.

Discovering demographics

The first thing I always want to know about an audience is its size. Will it be 10 people, 100 people, or 1,000 people? The size of the audience determines a lot of aspects of a speech. For example, a large audience eliminates the use of certain types of visual aids and requires the use of a microphone. A smaller audience is often less formal. Certain gimmicks that work with a large group will seem silly with a small one. (Telling the audience to, "Turn around and shake hands with the person behind you," just doesn't cut it when the entire audience is seated in one row.)

The second thing I want to know is the general nature of the audience: What's the relationship of the audience members to each other? Do they all come from the same organization? Do they share a common interest? I use this information to shape my message at a very basic level. If they have a lot in common, my speech can use terms and concepts that they all understand. I won't have to explain as much.

The next thing I want to find out is specific demographic data about audience members. Check out the following list of standard demographic items:

✔ Age

✔ Sex

✔ Education level

✔ Economic status

✔ Religion

✔ Occupation

✔ Racial/ethnic makeup

✔ Politics

✔ Cultural influences

Instead of wasting a lot of time impersonating a census taker, zero in on the audience characteristics that will make a real difference to your speech. I'm sure you were taught at some point that you should gather as much demographic information about your audience as possible. But you can collect a lot more of this stuff than you'll ever use. Yes, theoretically you may want to tailor your speech to reflect every last characteristic of your audience, but in reality, you may not have the time or inclination to do that.

For example, suppose that you work for a drug company. You've been asked to present an overview of the company to a group of prospective investors. Is their age, sex, or religion going to affect what you say? Certainly you could think of ways to take advantage of your knowledge of these characteristics, but the shape of your talk will probably be a lot more heavily influenced by your knowledge of the audience's occupations and educational background. Are some of the prospective investors doctors? (They may know more about drugs than you do.) Are they professional investment advisors? Or are they wealthy individuals without a clue about corporate finance? (How sophisticated should you make your analysis of the "numbers"?) You get the idea.

Discovering what the audience is thinking

While speakers tend to focus on audience census data, they tend to overlook audience beliefs, attitudes, and values. The reason is simple. It's difficult to develop this information. It's easy to figure out how many audience members are male or female, but it's tough to figure out what they're thinking. Yet their beliefs, attitudes, and values will color their interpretation of every aspect of your speech.

What exactly do you need to know? In essence, you want to compose a mental profile of your audience. You want to know "where they're coming from." And the person who asked you to speak should help you find out. Here are some of the questions you want that person to answer:

- ✔ What is the audience's attitude about the subject of your talk?
- ✔ What is the audience's attitude toward you as the speaker?
- ✔ What stereotypes will the audience apply to you?
- ✔ Will anyone have a hidden agenda?
- ✔ What values does the audience find important?
- ✔ Does the audience share a common value system?
- ✔ How strongly held are its beliefs and attitudes?

The answers to these questions determine your approach to the subject.

Finding out what the audience knows

Legendary football coach Vince Lombardi was giving his team a lecture on the basics. "We're going to start from the beginning," he said. "This is a football." That's when one of his players responded, "Hold on, coach, you're going too fast."

Want to start at the beginning with your audience? Then you'd better find out how much they already know. Two of the biggest mistakes speakers make are talking over the heads of their audiences and talking at a level that's too elementary. Talk to the person who has asked you to speak and find out how sophisticated your speech should be.

Here are some questions to ponder before you make your speech:

- ✔ How sophisticated are the audience members about your topic?
- ✔ Will any experts be in the audience?
- ✔ Have the audience members heard other speakers talk about your topic?
- ✔ Why are they interested in your topic?
- ✔ Will they understand jargon related to your topic?

✔ Do they already know the basic concepts of your topic?

✔ Do they think they know a lot about your topic?

✔ How did they get the information that they already have about your topic?

✔ Are they familiar with your approach and attitude toward the topic?

Once again, the answers to these questions play a major role in how you construct your speech. What your audience knows determines how much background you need to provide, the sophistication of the language you can use, and the examples you include.

Relating to Your Audience

The major goal when relating to your audience is to establish rapport with them — a feeling of mutual warmth and a sense that you're on the same wavelength. The following sections present a few ways to achieve that goal.

Putting your audience in the picture

Putting your audience in the picture — putting their needs and interests ahead of your own, is a great way to make your audience relate to you. In the following sections, I discuss some great techniques for getting the audience into the picture.

Focusing on what interests the audience

You don't have to ignore your own needs, but your needs won't be served if no one is listening. For instance, if your audience has been sitting and listening to hours of speeches all day, give them a break and cut your 60-minute speech down to 20 minutes — they'll love you for it.

Discussing the world from the audience's point of view

Let the audience know that you can see the world or issue their way. One of my favorite examples of this comes from management communications advisor Jim Lukaszewski. He was scheduled to make a presentation to the executives of a large waste removal company. Because "the whole hierarchy of the company was run by people who had started as garbagemen," Jim explains, prior to his presentation, he arranged to spend three days working on a garbage truck. So as soon as he got up to speak, he let them know that he'd just spent three days hauling garbage. "They were eating out of my hand," he recalls. That's not quite the words I'd use to explain it, but Jim's point is well taken. His audience could relate to him because he demonstrated an understanding of their experience. He had thrown garbage into the back of the truck.

People like to hear data related to what they do. So if you don't have an experience to share, you can substitute a study. But first acknowledge that you don't have the experience — otherwise, you'll lose credibility. (Also see Chapter 3 for more on using numbers effectively.)

Making personal experiences universal

Although an audience wants to hear about a speaker's personal experience, using "I" all the time can turn them off. You can end up sounding like a raging egomaniac. So go ahead and describe that experience — just find and emphasize the universal aspects of your personal experience. The late John Cantu used to emphasize this point to prospective comedians who wanted to relate to their audience. But it applies to anyone using any kind of personal material.

- ✔ **Example 1:** "You know, I used to be a plumber. Let me tell you about the time I flushed an alligator down the toilet and it got stopped up."

- ✔ **Example 2:** "Did you ever have a job that you really hated but you couldn't quit because you needed the money? I used to be a plumber. And I couldn't quit because I needed the money. And let me tell you about what happened when an alligator got flushed down a toilet and stopped it up."

In the second example, the plumber tells the same story but the audience relates to him differently. Now he's not just a plumber talking about plumbing. He's a person who had a humorous experience with a lousy job — something everyone can understand.

Customizing your remarks

Customizing grabs the audience's attention and gets the audience involved in your speech. It makes the speaker a bit of an insider and lets the audience know that the speaker went to the trouble of learning about the audience. And the good news is, a little, and I mean very little, customization goes a long, long way. I've given speeches where I made five or six references geared specifically to a particular audience, and afterward I was showered with praise for the research I did to learn about the group. Make comments — humorous comments, praise, or just simple observations — about local businesses, the people you're speaking to, an organization's history, or local news, events, or customs.

President Ronald Reagan relates to his audience

When Ronald Reagan was president, he would connect to his audience by finding a common bond, showing his knowledge of them, or empathizing with their concerns. Here are a few examples:

The International Association of Chiefs of Police: "You and I have a few things in common. Harry Truman once said about the job I have that being President is like riding a tiger: A man has to keep on riding or he'll get swallowed. Well, that's a pretty good description of what you do for a living."

The American Medical Association: "I'm delighted to address this annual meeting of the AMA House of Delegates, and I want to congratulate Dr. Jirka and Dr. Boyle on their new positions. I can't help but think what a great place this would be and what a great moment to have a low back pain."

Presidential Awards for Excellence in Science and Mathematics Teaching: "Well, it's wonderful to have all of you here today at the White House. We want you to enjoy our little get-together today. So please lean back, relax, and stop worrying about what the students are doing to the substitute teachers back home."

Use your imagination and consider what may impress you if an outsider referred to it.

Don't be offensive! If you're going to use a name of someone in or related to the group, clear it with a high-ranking official first. It's also a good idea to make sure that if you plan on poking fun at anything else local, that you discuss it with someone first — you don't want to poke fun at the real estate firm owned by the boss.

Pushing their hot buttons

Purposely work in a reference to a buzz issue — something that's a source of minor controversy with the audience. Find an issue that cuts across the entire audience, not one that only affects key players and that no one else would understand. In addition, make sure that the issue isn't too controversial to mention — your contact will probably be reliable here.

One of my favorite examples is the time I suggested that an audience ease up on memo and report writing. "You're wasting too much Xerox paper," I explained. The room burst into laughter and applause. Why? The people in the audience, employees of a Fortune 500 company, had been ordered to reduce their use of copier paper as a cost-savings measure. They thought it was ridiculous.

One of the simplest ways to find a buzz issue is to ask your contact whether any recent or pending legislation will negatively affect the audience. When the answer is yes, you have your issue.

Acknowledging what the audience is feeling

If you're speaking under any special circumstances, acknowledge those circumstances. Is the audience sweltering in a hot, stuffy room? Would the audience prefer to be anywhere but listening to you? Has the audience made certain assumptions about you? Get it out in the open. Otherwise, it will remain a barrier between you and your audience.

Identifying and addressing audience subgroups

Keep in mind that an audience may be made up of numerous subgroups — each with its own special needs and agendas. You need to include something for each of them if you want to create rapport with your entire audience.

A common example of this situation is the convention dinner attended by spouses. Half the audience is made up of people with the same occupation — engineers, doctors, whatever. The other half — the spouses — fall into two major categories: those who have careers outside the home and those who are homemakers. So you immediately have three subgroups. The spouses with careers can probably be even further subdivided.

Highlighting the benefits

Make sure that the audience knows what they are going to get out of your speech. Identify and emphasize the benefits early in your talk and issue frequent reminders.

All audience members subconsciously ask themselves how a speech benefits them. They wonder if they will hear anything to help them save or make money; save time; or reduce stress, anxiety, ambiguity, and confusion. Sex and health are also topics of   universal interest. They span age, gender, culture, and geographic boundaries.

Chapter 3

Making the Most of Research

In This Chapter

▶ Getting great information from a variety of sources

▶ Getting your research done by someone else — and for free

▶ Finding great material and ideas on the Web

An executive put up a sign in his office that said, "Do It Now." The next day his top salesman quit, his secretary asked for a raise, and his partner made a deal for immunity with the IRS. Despite these risks, I'm going to advise you to "do it now." If you have a speech to make, get started on it. Open a quote book. Go to the library. Tap into the Internet. Call a museum. Do something. Do anything. Just get started.

Of course, you need to know *where* to get started — where to find the information to create your speech. Whether you're looking for a topic idea, major points to include or material such as jokes, quotes, statistics, and stories, you're going to do some research. In this chapter, I give you some starting points and techniques for basic research. (You can also find these techniques useful for finding the speech material described in Chapter 5.)

Gathering Sources

An old philosopher once said that it's more interesting to hear a speaker who met an old philosopher than a speaker who read about one. That's true. People like to hear firsthand accounts of events and experiences when possible. And when it's not possible, research usually turns up someone who did talk to him.

When you speak with the philosopher, you've got a primary source. When you read about someone who spoke with him, you've got a secondary source. Both types of sources are valuable. In this section I show you how to find sources that provide the information you need to create an effective speech. Some are primary. Some are secondary. All of them are worth exploring.

Mining yourself for material

If you're old enough to give a speech, you're old enough to have life experiences that you can use in your speech — personal anecdotes, war stories, insights, and observations. These are often the most interesting parts of your speech; the parts that the audience listens to closely and remembers. But how do you find these stories? Even though they're in your own head, many people have trouble getting them out. In the next two sections, I tell you how to identify personal stories that can work in your speech.

Creating new personal material

No matter what you discuss, you can always find an easy way to develop personal material. If you don't have any personal anecdotes that directly relate to your topic, simply go out and get some. Just check out these examples:

- **If you plan on mentioning new housing starts as an economic trend indicator,** just drive around and count the number of housing developments you see under construction. Now you've got a personal experience that you can fit to your data. You can say, "One of the most important indicators of our economic future is housing starts. As I drove to work the other day, I counted 15 houses under construction. Each one was swarming with workers sawing, hammering, and nailing; piles of wood and bags of cement covered each site; dump trucks pulled in and out, hauling earth away; architects studied plans; little sandwich trucks stopped by to sell lunch to the construction workers. It's amazing how much economic activity building a house can generate. So it's good news that housing starts nationally have increased x percent during the past year."

- **If you plan on speaking about television,** just watch some. You can say, "The other day I was turned off the moment my TV was turned on. It's not just the commercials, which were endless, or the cable shows, which were mindless, it's the networks' new emphasis on reality shows. If that's reality, I'm ready for fantasyland."

- **If you plan on discussing politics,** just attend a city council meeting. You can say, "A famous senator once said 'All politics is local.' I saw what he meant when I went to a city council meeting. It doesn't get more local than that. Every pothole, crack in the sidewalk and overgrown tree seemed to come up in their discussions. And the politics behind these issues was fascinating; and just as complex as national political issues. Because when you get to the heart of it, politics is really about problem solving."

Using what you already have

Of course, everyone knows that the easiest and most accessible material is the material you already possess. For example, if you're a teacher and you have an anecdote about the dumb excuses your students make when they're late for school, you can use the story to illustrate your point about the need to take responsibility and not make excuses. This technique works especially well if your audience is filled with teachers or people that have to manage others and oversee team projects.

You can add even more power and punch to the anecdote and reach a wider audience if you unleash the anecdote's emotions. You can emphasize the *frustration* you felt when the students made their excuses. Then, even if your audience members aren't teachers, they'll understand what you mean because everyone can relate to frustration.

To find your best material with emotion that the audience can connect with, the late John Cantu suggested that after you've picked a topic, take a sheet of paper and list some basic emotions — love, anger, fear, hate, embarrassment, and so on. Then think of experiences that you've had that caused each emotion. Mechanically go through a variety of situations. For example, think about experiences that made you angry. If you get stuck, narrow it down to specific situations. Try to remember situations about your work that made you angry; situations about your family that made you angry; situations about your school that made you angry; situations about your softball team that made you angry. After you find a good anecdote based on anger, write it down and edit it into its best form.

Interviewing people

One of the best, and most neglected, sources of primary material is other people. They have stories. They have experiences. They have insights. You just have to interview people to get hold of this vast source of information. Writers and journalists do it. Police do it. Even game show hosts do it. Speakers, however, tend to ignore interviews as a source of information, and that's a mistake.

It's really no big deal to arrange and conduct an interview. People love to talk about their work and hobbies. If you have to speak about cars, you can call an auto dealer, tell them that you'll be giving a speech about cars, and ask if they could spend five minutes talking with you. Most people won't refuse that request. They'll be delighted to give you information. Whatever your topic happens to be, interview a few people in that profession or industry.

Now let's talk about the interview. Usually, people end their interviews by asking the following two questions: "Is there anything you thought I should have asked that I didn't ask?" and "Do you want to add anything?" While this may give you some additional details about your subject, such common questions won't often yield much useful information.

Fortunately, there's another approach — questions that make a person dig deep and reveal fresh information that common questions can't produce. The late comedy coach John Cantu suggested preparing yourself with the single best question you can ask: What do you know now about (the topic) that you wish you knew when you were starting out? This question becomes especially useful in situations when you may have less than a minute to conduct the interview — talking to someone in an elevator, buttonholing someone at a business function, meeting a celebrity on a plane, and so on. If you can ask only one question, ask this one.

Utilizing the library

Everyone knows that the library is packed full of research and reference tools. But while everyone else hits the reference shelf, follow some more advice from the late comedy coach John Cantu: Make the *children's section* your first stop at the library. A children's book about your topic can be the best way to begin an outline because it will probably cover most of the key points of your topic clearly.

For example, let's say you have to give a speech about minerals. A kid's book might have chapters discussing how minerals form, minerals from the ocean, minerals from the earth, precious minerals and gemstones, minerals used in construction, and so on. Each chapter could potentially be a major point in your speech. Or you could use the chapter titles to help you narrow down the scope of your topic.

Reading The Wall Street Journal

I like *The Wall Street Journal* as a source of statistics, anecdotes, and examples because the front page stories follow a specific formula: Each article uses a specific anecdote to lead into a general discussion. For instance, a front-page article may describe a child who suffered injuries while in daycare and use it to springboard into a general discussion of the conditions in child-care facilities. So, if you're talking about the percentage of parents using daycare, injuries occurring in daycare facilities, the interview process for daycare workers or any other number of related topics, you can use that opening anecdote somewhere in your speech. You may even find some relevant statistics elsewhere in the article. So, *The Wall Street Journal* can become a goldmine of research for your topic.

Personal anecdote checklist

Personal anecdotes are among your most valuable assets as a speaker. They gain a lot of attention because they're real. So you should stockpile as many as you can remember. Need some help recalling an anecdote based on a real-life experience? The following list will help jog your memory:

- Your most embarrassing experience
- The angriest you've ever been
- The most inappropriate letter you've ever received
- Your first date
- The strangest habit of a friend, relative, or coworker
- The dumbest thing you've ever heard
- Your first day on the job
- The worst boss you've ever had
- The saddest thing that ever happened to a friend
- The biggest mistake you ever made
- A strange dream
- The most bizarre thing you've ever seen or heard
- Your wildest vacation story
- The weirdest thing that ever happened at a business meeting
- Eating out: strange restaurants, waiters, food, poor service
- Relatives
- Learning to drive
- High school: prom, teachers, classes
- College: dorm, professors, exams
- Anecdotes your parents told you
- Your first job interview
- Something that seems funny now but didn't when it happened
- The strangest gift you've ever received

Pulling info from the Day and Date Book

The *Day and Date Book* can also be a great research tool. Because you can find out what was occurring on a particular date, the *Day and Date Book* often provides interesting information that easily sets the mood or provides a context for your topic.

Let's say you're giving a speech about why people should donate money to a certain charity. You can look in the *Day and Date Book* and find out about past trends in the economy; when volunteerism became a national issue; and why some charities have thrived or declined. All of this information can be very useful for your speech.

Perusing Chase's Calendar of Events

Chase's Calendar of Events is a book published annually that provides an easy way to write the opening to a speech. Just look up the events from past years for the date on which you're speaking. Then pick one or more events and use them to lead into your speech. "Today is the Fourth of July — the birthday of the United States, but also the birthday of Abigail Van Buren, who you know as Dear Abby. So in honor of the occasion, I'm going to spend our time together today by giving you some advice."

The introduction is only the most obvious place to refer to an event of the day. You can drop this type of reference into any section of a speech. The line about advice could be used as a transition to a major point or to lead into the conclusion. In addition to the standard birthdays and events, *Chase's* includes lots of local and regional listings as well as bizarre ones, which is a great feature. For example, the Big Whoppers Liar's Contest is held in New Harmony, Indiana, on September 19. So, you can use this not only to add content to your speech but also to add a touch of light-hearted humor.

Dialing up databases

Hopefully you're not still living in the Dark Ages of research by avoiding computers. Computers can dramatically speed up your research for a speech. In almost any public or school library, you can find computers equipped with electronic databases that provide an enormous source of easy-to-locate information. You just type a word or phrase into the computer, and the computer searches through hundreds or thousands of journals. Then it spits out a list of relevant citations. Okay, maybe you need five minutes to learn the computer commands, but that's still easier than searching through a thousand journals by hand. Besides, if you go to the library, you can usually find librarians who are happy to show you how. Or just go to the children's section and ask the nearest seven-year-old — she can probably work it better than you can anyway. If you want to know more about computerized researching of all kinds, get a copy of *Researching Online For Dummies* by Reva Basch (Wiley Publishing, Inc.).

 How much does searching electronic databases cost? Not necessarily anything. A recent trip to my local university library revealed that dozens of electronic databases are available to anyone free of charge. These include the SOCIOFILE (a database of sociology-related articles from more than 1,600 journals), PSYCHINFO (a database of more than a million citations from 1,300 journals in psychology and related subjects), and the ERIC Database (more than 700,000 citations indexed by the Office of Educational Research and Improvement of the U.S. Department of Education). Other databases cover areas such as business, government, medicine, science, and engineering. If you're not sure how to use them, just ask a reference librarian for help.

If you want to pay for information, you can use commercial electronic databases such as nexis.com (extensive collection of newspapers, periodicals, financial info and related materials) and lexis.com (same info, plus law-related resources), both from LexisNexis, a division of Reed Elsevier, Inc.

Getting Someone Else to Do Your Research — For Free

Yes, you really can get other people to do some of your research free of charge. No, you don't have to trick them, you don't have to beg them, and you don't have to know any secret passwords. You can easily find people who get paid by others to do research for you.

Checking out reference librarians

The most valuable resource at any library isn't found in a collection of books or periodicals. It's found behind a desk answering questions. It's called the *reference librarian*. This person doesn't know everything, but a good one knows how to find anything.

Don't be shy. Tell the reference librarian what you're working on and what you're looking for. She can provide invaluable assistance in directing you to the appropriate resources and can save you a tremendous amount of time when you're beginning to prepare your speech.

Find out whether the reference librarian will answer your questions over the telephone. Many libraries provide this service. It's a great convenience, so you should take advantage of it. If you want to speak with someone at a library that's out of town, all it costs is the price of a long-distance telephone call. Yes, it's obvious, but most people don't think of it.

All kinds of libraries employ reference librarians — everything from college and university libraries to corporate and association libraries.

Talking to museum research staff

Major museums have large research staffs devoted to pursuing knowledge about their specialized areas of interest. These staffers are an incredible resource for speech material. Call them up — they enjoy sharing their knowledge.

Using government public information officers

If you need information from an agency, department, board, or commission at the local, state, or federal level, contact the public information officer. Almost every governmental entity has one, and she gets paid to give you information. If you're a taxpayer, these people are *your* employees. Ask them to obtain the facts and figures that you need for your speech. Just remember to treat them politely and with respect — they're public servants, not public slaves. An inch of kindness and respect on your part may make them go the extra mile for you.

Researching on the Web

The Web is like the Wild West of knowledge and information. It's an untamed frontier that keeps expanding faster than anyone can rein it in. And while it's full of gold mines and oil wells, you don't see a lot of street signs. So, in this section, I point you to some useful Web sites so you can research topics, find visual aids, and even improve the delivery of your speech.

Rustling up the three best Web sites

 If I had to give a speech on a desert island and I could only bring three Web sites with me, these are the three I'd bring: the Virtual Reference Desk, the Online Speech Bank, and the Museum of Humor.com. (Yes, this is totally subjective. So what?)

- **Virtual Reference Desk** (www.refdesk.com): You have to see the Virtual Reference Desk to believe it. It contains links to anything that may conceivably pertain to any speech that you might write or deliver. (And just in case the site missed anything, it contains links to numerous search engines.)

- **Online Speech Bank** (www.americanrhetoric.com/speechbank.htm): You guessed it; this site contains transcripts of speeches, everything from business leaders to government officials to clergy from around the world. Use it as a resource for getting ideas, quoting other speakers, learning about particular topics, and seeing how others organize their ideas.

- **Museum of Humor.com** (www.museumofhumor.com): Here you've hit the goldmine of humor for speakers and speechwriters — especially ones who can't tell a joke. It divides humor into types — quotes, anecdotes, definitions, one-liners, and so on — and offers hundreds of links to each kind. If you want to use humor but have no joke-telling ability, you can find plenty of material on this site. You can also find a large list of links to offbeat news items as well as additional amusing material that applies to a wide variety of subjects.

    The Museum of Humor.com also has indispensable writing tools such as rhyme generators, simile generators, cliché lists, phrase finders, "Today in History," Guinness World Records, and new word generators. A special section for clergy has hundreds of sermons about humor, as well as searchable databases of sermon-appropriate humor. There is also a special section for educators.

    And if you have to use statistics in a speech, check out "Calculated Humor" in the Exhibits section of the museum. It provides tools for making statistics less boring and more entertaining. (Just to see the Penguin-O-MaticConvertor is worth the visit. It converts weights and distances into numbers of penguins.)

Getting the most out of Web researching

The Web can be a bit overwhelming, even if you know what you're looking for. So, I've added some tips to make your electronic research a little easier and more productive. To avoid following Alice down an electronic rabbit hole try the following:

✔ **Search engines:** An entire book could be devoted to search engines now available on the Web, but I'll just mention one — www.google.com. Now the most popular search tool in cyberspace, Google is easy to use and comprehensive. Simply type a search term into the search box, and Google brings up enough links related to the topic that you could research from this search engine alone for days.

Usually, Google lists the most relevant links first. So, rather than clicking onto each link provided on each, glance through the summaries of each link on the first couple of pages. Once you've found the ones most relevant to what you're looking for, then you can begin clicking away.

If you want to check out additional search engines, go to www.searchenginewatch.com/links. You can find enough to keep you busy for life. (Or look at the selection at the Virtual Reference Desk discussed earlier.)

For best results, make your search terms as specific as possible to filter out thousands of useless links and to increase the chances that you find what you want. For example, a search for "eulogy" produces better results than a search for "public speaking" if you're looking for information about eulogies.

✔ **Web rings:** One of the best-kept secrets about conducting research on the Internet is the Web ring. A Web ring is a group of linked Web sites devoted to a similar topic. If you can find a Web ring related to your interests, you have an instant goldmine of relevant information. For example, say I'm giving a speech about smoking and cancer. I type smoking and cancer into the search form at www.webring.org. It finds two Web rings. One is called Stop Smoking Ring and it contains 60 Web sites — all of which are relevant to the topic of smoking and cancer.

✔ **News Archives:** Many traditional sources of information — newspapers, magazines, newsletters, and so on — are represented on the Web. Even better, many of them have online archives that let you search through old editions. Use these sites to get started:

- NewsDirectory.com (`http://newsdirectory.com/archive/press/`): This is where you will find a long list of links to searchable newspaper archives.

- FindArticles.com (`www.findarticles.com/PI/index.jhtml`): This index claims to have more than 3.5 million articles from 700 publications. You can search it by topic or keyword.

Finding visual aids

Need a picture for a slide, overhead, or PowerPoint presentation? The Web has almost anything you may want. You can find the best material at the following sites:

✔ **ImageFinder** (`http://sunsite.berkeley.edu/ImageFinder`): A large collection of images (and the rules for using them) is available at the Berkeley Digital Image SunSite ImageFinder. It provides search forms for 11 databases of specialized images including photographs and images from the Library of Congress, Smithsonian Institution, and the National Library of Australia.

✔ **Clipart.com** (`www.clipart.com`): This site includes easy-to-search databases of 1,200,071 clipart images and 148,711 photos. The bad news is you have to pay for access. The good news is you don't have to pay much.

✔ **PowerPoint templates:** Thousands of professionally designed PowerPoint templates are available on the Web. And they're free! Find them by typing "free PowerPoint templates" into any search engine. Get started by checking out the following sites (also check out Chapter 10 for more on PowerPoint presentations):

- `www.soniacoleman.com/templates.htm`

- `www.websiteestates.com/ppoint.html`

- `www.presentersuniversity.com/downloads.php`

Picking up performing tips

The Web not only has great sites for researching and writing a speech, but it also has great sites that can show you how to *deliver* your speech.

On the Web, you have access to thousands of hours of speeches; you can review which delivery techniques work and which don't; you can listen to timing and pacing; and in many cases, you can hear the audience response.

You can use any search engine and find a large assortment of speeches. Or you can get ideas for gestures, movements, and other delivery techniques by watching and listening to speeches on the following sites:

✔ **History Channel Archive of Speeches** (`www.historychannel.com/speeches/index.html`): This collection of historic speeches (surprise!) includes speeches by everyone from Mahatma Gandhi and Anwar Sadat to Richard Nixon and Queen Elizabeth.

✔ **FedNet** (`www.fednet.net`): FedNet provides live broadcasts of select U.S. House and Senate committee hearings, as well as floor debates, free of charge. Archives of past broadcasts are available for a fee.

Chapter 4

Organizing Your Speech

. . . .

In This Chapter

▶ Choosing material for your speech

▶ Selecting the best organizational pattern

▶ Making an outline that works for you

▶ Dealing with the limitations of time

▶ Figuring out how to organize your speech

. . . .

*H*ere's the standard advice for organizing a speech: Tell the audience what you're going to say, then tell them, and tell them what you've told them. I've heard many consultants offer this bromide to their clients, look meaningfully into their eyes like they've just delivered some great insight, and then wait to be hailed as geniuses. But the problem with the tell-tell-tell formula is that it doesn't really tell you anything. (How's that for irony?) It's like telling someone that you build a ship by assembling a bunch of material so that it will float while you're in it. Okay, great. But how do you do that?

This chapter provides a detailed look at how to organize a speech. You find everything from how to decide what to tell an audience, to how to arrange what you tell an audience, to how much to tell an audience. It's a tell-all chapter. (Hey, at least it's not a kiss-and-tell.)

Selecting Material to Include

Before you can organize your speech, you must first choose the material for your speech (see Chapters 3 and 5 for more on researching and finding material). But your real task is deciding what *not* to use. No matter what your topic, you'll always be able to find a lot more material than you'll have time to discuss. And, more importantly, audiences have a limit to how much material they can absorb. Here are a few guidelines to keep in mind when choosing what material to include:

- ✔ **Select a variety of material.** You know the expression "different strokes for different folks"? Applied to speeches, it means using different types of material — anecdotes, statistics, examples, quotes, and so on. A variety of material makes your speech more interesting. It also increases the chance that each member of your audience will find something appealing in your speech.

- ✔ **Keep your audience in mind.** Choose material that your audience will understand and find interesting. The question isn't what you know about the topic. It's what does the audience need to know in order to make your speech a success.

- ✔ **Carry a spare — always.** Keep some material in reserve — an extra example, statistic, or anecdote. You never know when you'll need it, especially in a Q&A session following the talk.

Following Patterns of Organization

Imagine that someone hands you a piece of paper that says "m," "d," "u," "y," "m." It doesn't seem to mean much. (Unless it's supposed to be an eye test.) Now assume that the person hands you the paper with the letters arranged as "d," "u," "m," "m," "y." Is your reaction a little different? Congratulations, you've recognized a pattern.

Patterns play a critical role in how we assign meaning and how we interpret messages. You could read a lot of perceptual psychology theory to figure out this stuff, but I'll give you a break and skip it. Suffice it to say that human beings have a natural tendency to organize phenomena into patterns. The way we shape those patterns determines much of the outcome of our communications with each other. So, the patterns you put into your speeches play a vital role in how well your audience understands what you're communicating.

Following two key rules

If you want the pattern to strengthen your speech as much as possible, abide by the following two rules.

Make the pattern obvious

Have you ever seen those pictures that are all little dots? You know, the ones that you can't tell what the picture is supposed to be until you hold it close to your face? And then you're supposed to be able to see an image? Yes, the dots form a pattern because some people see the image, but the pattern sure isn't obvious — at least to me and many other people who have never perceived the image. (I've flattened my nose trying to see the image, but it still looks like dots.)

Keep this in mind when you put together a speech. You don't want
a "little dot" pattern that won't be recognized by everybody. You
want a pattern that your whole audience can perceive. Your speech
isn't an intelligence test. You don't want to find out whether your
audience is smart enough to discover your hidden structure.
You want to make sure that your pattern is obvious so that your
audience can perceive it — easily. Your pattern can never be too
obvious.

Choose an appropriate pattern

Consider your topic and audience when choosing a pattern. What
pattern will best help get your message across? For example, if
you're talking about the history of a land-use dispute in your neighborhood, a chronological pattern probably makes more sense than
a theory/practice pattern. (See "Checking out commonly used
patterns," below for more information on types of patterns you
can use.)

Checking out commonly used patterns

Although patterns are infinite in variety, certain ones appear over
and over again. Here are a few of the most common patterns for
speeches:

- ✓ **Problem/solution:** State a problem and offer a solution. For
  example, your speech to the school board criticizes the poor
  physical condition of local schools. You then talk about a prop-
  erty tax measure that could increase school funding. What you
  emphasize depends on what the audience members already
  know. Do you need to make them aware of the problem or do
  they already know about it? Are there competing solutions?
  And so on.

- ✓ **Chronological:** If you plan to speak about a series of events
  (the history of accidents at that corner where you want a stop
  sign), organizing your speech in a past/present/future pattern
  makes it easy to follow.

- ✓ **Physical location:** You may want to use this pattern if you're
  talking about things that occur at various locations. If you plan
  on giving the company orientation speech to new employees,
  you can divide the talk by floors (first floor, second floor, third
  floor), buildings (Building A, B, and C), or other physical areas
  (North American operations, European operations, Asian
  operations).

✔ **Extended metaphor or analogy:** This pattern uses a comparison of two items as a way of organizing the entire speech. It's commonly used in speeches given by teachers or trainers. "Today I'll talk about how giving a speech is like the flight of an airplane. We'll talk about the takeoff, the landing, the flight, the passengers, and the control tower. The takeoff is the introduction. . . ."

✔ **Cause/effect:** You state a cause and then identify its effect. This pattern is common in scientific speeches but it also works great for assigning blame. "The southern region decided to listen to some management guru this quarter. So it instituted new procedures, bought new expense-reporting software, and made a commitment to innovative sales methods. As a result, its gross sales declined by 50 percent, and its margins shrank 10 percent." (But the guru had record profits.)

✔ **Divide a quote:** Each word of a quote becomes a section of the speech. Clergy often use this technique in sermons. "The Bible says, 'Wisdom is better than rubies.' What does this really mean? Let's start with wisdom. Is it just your IQ? No. Most of us know people who have a high IQ who aren't very wise." This technique is also frequently used by motivational speakers and sales trainers.

✔ **Divide a word:** Pick a word and build your speech around each letter of the word. "Today, I'm going to talk about 'LOVE.' 'L' stands for laughter. Laughter is very important in our lives because. . . ." This pattern is popular with clergy and other inspirational speakers.

✔ **Theory/practice:** Start by explaining what you though would happen — the theory. Then describe the actions taken and what actually happened — the practice. You can use this pattern when talking about something that didn't turn out as planned by explaining the big gap between theory and practice.

✔ **Topic pattern:** This is a free-form pattern that can be used for any type of speech. You divide your topic into logical segments based on your own instinct, judgment, and common sense. I often use this pattern in my speeches about humor. The segments are: why humor is a powerful communication tool, how to make a point with humor, and simple types of non-joke humor anyone can use. It's an easy-to-follow pattern that makes sense for the material.

Packaging and bundling

According to management communication advisor Jim Lukaszewski, one of the most powerful ways to organize information is in the form of a numerical list. For example, you can say, "I have some good ideas." Or you can say, "I have four good ideas." The number makes the statement much stronger. Because the audience tends to keep track of numbers, using numbers grabs their attention, keeps their attention, and helps them follow along and understand what you say.

You can use this technique to organize your entire speech, such as "Ten Ways to Stop Crime". Or you can use it for individual segments, such as, "We've talked about the importance of humor, how to write a joke, and how to tell a joke. Now let's talk about six simple types of humor that don't require comic delivery."

But don't go overboard — keep your lists short. If you make the list too long, you can actually lose the audience. Suppose your boss walked into a meeting and said, "I've found 50 ways to raise revenue." How would you feel after you realized he was going to discuss every one of them?

Creating Your Outline

An outline is a blueprint for your talk. It lets you see what points you're making, how they're related to each other, and whether they're arranged in a proper order. A good outline shows you how to construct a good speech. And like a blueprint for a building, an outline for a talk can take many shapes and forms.

Most people associate outlines with the traditional method emphasized in high school — the Roman numeral outline. (Each Roman numeral represents a major point. Each uppercase letter represents a subpoint, and each Arabic numeral represents a support for the subpoints.) But you can create outlines in many different ways. The key is to choose or make up a method that works for you. As long as you can tell which points are main points, sub points, and so on, how you outline your speech is not important. What's important is that the method is functional and useful for you.

Figuring out when to start your outline

You have two basic choices regarding when to make an outline: Make the outline before you've written your speech or after you've written it. The experts disagree on which way is best. But I can resolve that issue. The best way is the one that works for you. Consider the differences between writing the outline before or after you write the text of your speech, and then decide which approach works best for you:

- ✔ **Before you write the speech:** With this approach, you focus on your purpose and identify the ideas that will achieve that purpose. Then you turn the ideas into major and minor points and fit them into an outline structure. Only then, when you can see exactly what you'll say, do you begin to flesh it out. This is an absolutely logical way to proceed. If the outline makes sense, it helps ensure that the speech will make sense. In fact, I was taught to answer exam questions this way in law school — always outline first.

- ✔ **After you write the speech:** Alternatively, you may just plunge right into developing the speech word for word. Allatia Harris, District Director, Faculty Development and Core Curriculum Evaluation Dallas County Community College District, prefers this method. She advises that you think about the order in which you'd tell it to your friend, as well as what examples you'd use. Then write the outline after the speech is written. That will enable you to discover any flaws in your speech's structure so that you can rewrite where appropriate.

Deciding the number of points to include

The number of points in an outline should reflect the number of points in your speech. So you need to decide how many points you should have in your speech. To make the best decision, follow these guidelines:

- ✔ **Decide what the audience needs to know.** Determine which points are absolutely essential for you to include in your message. And I mean *absolutely* essential, as in, if one of these points were omitted, your speech couldn't succeed.

✔ **Avoid putting in too much information.** Many people try to pack too much information into a single speech. But there's a limit to how much an audience member can absorb. Figuring out how much is too much may sound tricky but the following two guidelines can make it easier on you:

- **Use no more than seven main points.** Experts disagree over the maximum number of points that you should have in a talk, but the highest number I've come across is seven. Less is usually better. The amount of time you have to speak is also a critical factor. Many experts suggest three major points for a half-hour talk.

- **Reorganize to reduce the number of points.** You've gone through your material and found 15 main points that are absolutely essential. Don't even think about doing your speech that way. First, make sure that you really can't lose a few of them. Second, reorganize the points so that they're included under fewer headings. Think of 5 to 7 major points under which your 15 points can be subcategorized.

Timing

Most people associate *timing* with how to tell a joke. But by *timing,* I mean how much time it takes to deliver the speech you've written in the time slot you've been given. Check out the following sections to find out the important concepts of *timing.*

Setting the length of your speech

William Gladstone once observed that a speech need not be eternal to be immortal. His point is well taken. The tendency to speak longer than necessary is a stereotypical trait long associated with public speaking. But longer does not mean better or more meaningful in the world of public speaking. Follow these guidelines to make sure you set an appropriate length of time for your speech:

✔ **Don't feel obligated to fill your entire time slot.** Use your common sense. You shouldn't stretch your speech to fill an hour-long time slot if you can get the job done in just 45 or 50 minutes. Your speech can end up sounding disorganized, and your points can get hard to follow when you throw in extra information just to cover another 15 minutes. On the other hand, I recently spoke at a conference where another speaker, who was slotted for a one-hour speech, completed his talk in ten minutes. The conference organizers were less than thrilled.

Although concluding early can thrill your audience, concluding late can have the opposite effect. Even tacking on just an extra five minutes can make the audience impatient and possibly angry. Your audience members are busy, and they don't appreciate a speaker putting them behind schedule. They expect you to be done on time, so don't disappoint them.

✔ **Twenty minutes is a good length.** If you can choose how long you'll speak, pick 20 minutes. It's long enough to cover a lot of information thoroughly, let the audience get to know you, and make a good impression. And it's short enough to do all that before the audience's attention span reaches its outer limit.

Polishing your timing

Einstein's theory of relativity may say that time and distance are identical, but many public speakers apparently disagree. They just can't go the distance in the time they've been allotted. You certainly don't want to join that group. So check out the following tips to ensure that you and your audience finish at the same time:

✔ **Estimate the time from the length of the script.** Here's the late John Cantu's script-to-speech ratio: one double-spaced page of 10-point type equals two minutes of speaking time. So preparing a standard 20-minute talk is like writing a 10-page essay. (Keep that in mind when the person inviting you to speak says it will be easy to do.)

✔ **Convert practice time into a realistic estimate:** Many speakers practice their speech aloud to get an idea of how long it will take to deliver. Here's a warning from the late John Cantu: For every minute that you practice your speech alone, you'll have a time increase of about 33 percent when you speak in front of people. "There's an automatic slowing down when you talk to an audience because you're waiting for feedback," explained John. "So a 5-minute talk to yourself at home might run 6½ or 7 minutes in front of an audience. A 10-minute talk could run 13 or 14 minutes." The time increase may range as high as 50 percent when you speak to an audience of several hundred people. Of course, this is just a general rule of thumb. And if you're frightened when you face an audience, you may speak faster than you did while practicing. (See Chapter 11 for help eliminating stage fright.)

✔ **Make an adjustment for humor:** If you use humor in your talk and it's effective, part of your speaking time will be consumed by audience laughter and applause. Don't forget to account for that time especially for audiences of more than 300 people. "Large groups laugh in three waves," observed the late John Cantu. "The first group gets the joke right away. The second group gets it a little later. And the third group laughs after they hear everyone else laughing. His rule of thumb: 10 to 15 seconds per wave of laughter in a large crowd. "So figure 45 seconds per joke," he said.

✔ **Be prepared to cut:** You were told that you'd have 30 minutes to speak. But the meeting doesn't go as planned and the organizer says you have only 15 minutes. What do you do? "The biggest mistake you can make is trying to give your 30-minute talk in 15 minutes," said the late John Cantu. "Speakers think that if they talk louder and faster, then some of what they're saying will sink in." Wrong! Here's what really happens. The speaker comes across as hyperactive and the audience comes away with nothing — except a bad impression of the speaker.

✔ **Don't cut the conclusion:** When you need to cut part of your speech, don't cut the conclusion. Your speech is like the flight of a plane, and the passengers are your audience. When you forgo the conclusion, you're attempting a crash landing. If you've been told in advance that your time will be shortened, cut from the body of your talk. Eliminate some examples or even a main point if necessary. What if you need to cut while you're speaking and you're rapidly running out of time? Find a logical place to stop and sum up what you've already said. Even better, have a conclusion that you can go into from any point in your talk.

Organizing Your Speech Effectively

There are as many ways to organize speeches as there are people giving them. One of the simplest and most effective that I've come across was used by the late San Francisco comedy coach John Cantu. He made sure the deck was stacked in his favor when he gave a speech. He prepared the cards himself.

1. **Write ideas on cards.** John began by writing down each idea he gets on a separate 3 x 5 card. He wrote on only one side of the card and left lots of room for editing. "Let's say I'm giving a talk on memory," he explained. "One card might say Trudeau's book — there's something good on page 57. Another card will have a quote about memory from JFK. By the time I'm done, I might have 50 cards."

2. **Pile the cards into patterns.** So now John has 50 cards full of ideas. What next? "I spread them out on the floor and try to group them," he said. "I look for patterns." Then he sorts them into piles. "I'll get maybe eight piles," he said. "A history of memory pile. A famous people involved with memory pile. A pile for specific tips for improving memory. Things like that."

3. **Sequence the cards in each pile.** "Let's say a pile has seven cards," said John. "I'll keep rearranging them until there's a good flow." During this process he sometimes finds a gap in the sequence. "I might find that cards one through four and six through seven go together well," explained John. "But card five doesn't fit in. I'll write a note to myself that I need something else on card five. Then I'll put that pile aside and sequence the cards in the next one." And here's an important tip: Number the cards. It helps you keep track of them much more easily. "I'll label the piles A, B, C, and so on, and then number the cards within each pile," explained John. "So they'll be A1, A2, A3, B1, B2, B3. That doesn't mean A goes first. It just means that all the cards in that pile go together."

4. **Sequence the piles of cards.** "I look at what I've got and see which pile is logical for starting my talk," he said. "Then I look for the second, third, and so forth, until all are in the best order."

Short takes on long speeches

The long-winded speaker has inspired a plethora of folk wit regarding the subject of public speaking. Here's a small sample:

✔ Many a public speaker who rises to the occasion stands too long.

✔ No speech is all bad if it's short.

✔ The longest word in the English language is "And now a word from our guest of honor."

✔ If the speaker won't boil it down, the audience must sweat it out.

✔ An after-dinner speech is like a headache — always too long, never too short.

✔ It's all right to have a train of thought if you also have a terminal.

✔ Second wind: what a speaker acquires when he says, "In conclusion."

✔ A speech is like a love affair — any fool can start one, but it takes a lot of skill to end one.

Part II
Preparing Your Speech

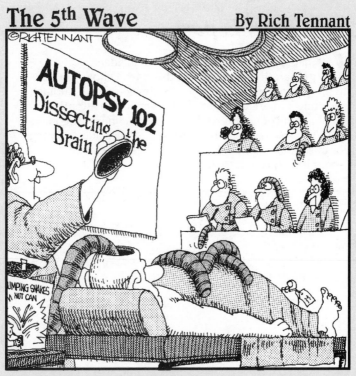

The 5th Wave   By Rich Tennant

"NOW THAT I'VE LIGHTENED UP THE ROOM...."

In this part . . .

Great speeches don't happen by accident. Careful preparation is the key. In this part, I show you how to prepare a great speech. I cover developing an outline, selecting and organizing material, writing an attention-grabbing introduction, and creating a memorable conclusion. You also discover how to use statistics and quotations for maximum impact, as well as how to develop stories, examples, and analogies.

Chapter 5

Body Building: Strengthening the Content of Your Speech

. . . .

In This Chapter

▶ Using logical and emotional appeals

▶ Muscling up with stories, quotes, and statistics

▶ Supporting your ideas with definitions, analogies, and examples

. . . .

After you have a topic and an outline (see Chapter 4), you only have the skeleton of your speech figured out. You still have to create the body of your speech by adding support to the outline you've created. Although searching for various forms of support for every point you plan to make sounds like a lot of sweat, you can consider this chapter the protein shake for speech writing. I show you the proper techniques to ensure that you define the muscle behind your points so you can build the speech body of your dreams.

Making Appeals to Your Audience

While speaking to your audience, making appeals can connect them to your topic as well as sway them to your line of thinking. Thus, making appeals can be very important to your speech. You can use logical appeals, emotional appeals, or both to bolster the effectiveness of your speech.

Using logical appeals

You base a logical appeal on rational evidence and arguments, appealing to the "heads" of your audience. Think of Mr. Spock from *Star Trek* or Sherlock Holmes. They are the ultimate practitioners of the logical appeal.

For example, say you're giving a talk about the need for a traffic light at a busy intersection. You could point out that a large number of accidents have occurred at the intersection, that the city has spent a lot of money defending the resulting lawsuits, and that the city's insurance premiums would decrease if a traffic light were erected. These are all logical reasons that will appeal to the common sense of the audience.

A logical appeal works best when you're trying to influence an audience of "left brain" thinkers — engineers, scientists, and anyone else who won't be easily swayed by emotion.

Making emotional appeals

You base an emotional appeal on feelings and passions. Unlike the logical appeal, which appeals to the "heads" of your audience (see "Using logical appeals," earlier), an emotional appeal speaks to the "hearts" of your audience. Politicians use this appeal every time they talk about patriotism, the American way, and the American dream. An emotional appeal is supposed to tug at your heartstrings.

Again, say you're giving a talk about the need for a traffic light at a busy intersection. You could point out that helpless toddlers have been among the accident victims there or that recovery time for an injured adult caused his family great financial hardship. Describing such loss or hardship can appeal to the emotions of your audience.

An emotional appeal works best when your audience consists of people who like to take feelings, not just facts, into consideration when forming their opinions.

Finding Solid Forms of Support

This section isn't about hosiery. Support refers to the items you use to prove and illustrate your points — the basic material that makes up your speech — stories, quotes, and statistics.

Because your support is the basic material for your speech, what kind of support you use, as well as how you use it is very important. Three basic rules regarding forms of support are:

1. **Make sure that your support really supports something.** Don't throw in quotes, statistics, and stories just to show off or to beef up the length of your speech. Use them only to prove, clarify, or illustrate a point.

2. **Use a variety of support.** Different people respond to different types of information. Some people like statistics; others like quotes and stories.

3. **Remember that less is more.** Using one dramatic statistic gets more attention than three boring statistics. One great example makes more of an impact than two so-so examples.

Mastering the art of storytelling

A famous rhetoric professor, Walter Fisher, has suggested that a major difference between people and animals is our ability to tell stories. And he's right. Throughout history, people have passed down customs, ideas, and information by telling stories. We seem to be hardwired to recognize and respond to this type of communication. That's what makes them so powerful when used in a speech.

Anyone can use a story, but using a *good* story and using it effectively sets you apart from the average speaker. Management-communications advisor Jim Lukaszewski provided some of the following guidelines to give you some ways to use stories effectively in your speeches:

✓ **Tell stories for a purpose:** You should have a reason for telling a story. And the reason — a lesson, moral, or objective — should be obvious to the audience. One of the fastest ways to turn off an audience is by telling pointless stories. (Just think of how you feel when Uncle John corners you at Christmas after hitting the eggnog a little too hard.)

✓ **Tell personal stories:** You know how much you like to hear stories about yourself or people you know. So just think of all the attention your speech can receive if you use stories about yourself or people familiar to your audience. Personal stories interest an audience much more than just plain facts.

If you don't have many personal stories or many stories about real individuals to tell, you can still add personal stories to your speech. You can either use hypothetical stories or interview other people and tell their stories. Other people's stories are so simple to find and are such a great source of material that you shouldn't overlook them, although many speakers do. Audience members will also tell you stories after your speech. Collect the more relevant and interesting of these — don't forget to ask permission to use them, of course.

✔ **Tell success stories:** Nothing succeeds like success, and that includes success stories. Think of the stories that you liked as a child. Most of them ended with the words "happily ever after." Those words are the sign of a success story. People like to hear stories about how an idea or action worked out successfully.

✔ **Try out stories first:** The first time you tell a particular story shouldn't be when you're standing at a podium addressing your audience. You need to know how the story works — what kind of response it gets from others. So, try stories out first on your friends, neighbors, colleagues, and anyone willing to listen. Their responses — body language, facial expressions, laughter, and other verbal and nonverbal responses — give you an idea of how to tweak the content, delivery, or timing of your story. The story should get better every time you tell it, and by the time you use the story in a speech, you should have a polished gem.

✔ **Develop more powerful stories:** You can make your stories more effective if you understand exactly how and why they affect an audience. To accomplish this task, ask yourself (and answer) the following questions:

- What's the communications objective, moral, lesson, punch line, or purpose of the story?

- What's the plain-language synopsis of what you're trying to get across?

- What are the beginning, the middle, and the end?

- Does the story have a people focus? Who are the main characters in the story? Why are they interesting?

- What is the sequence of events that makes the story work? Are there some facts or data that should be put into the story? Does the story as you currently tell it have too many facts and too much data? Do they really help the story or hurt the story?

- What are the human factors in the story that make it interesting?

Making an impact with quotations

Quotes get immediate attention — especially when they're attached to a famous name. In today's sound-bite society, quotes provide a great way to make a strong impression in the minds of audience members, if you know how to use a quote effectively. Improve the quality of your speech by following these guidelines the next time you include a quote in your speech:

✔ **Relate the quote to a point:** A quote should be used to make a point. Otherwise the quote is irrelevant — no matter how funny or insightful it is. Sometimes you may find a great quote that just doesn't fit, and you can't make it fit without reworking a great deal of your talk. Just accept the fact that the quote doesn't fit, and save the quote for your next speech.

Using quotes that have nothing to do with your topic can make you sound like a namedropper. The audience can tell when you're trying to appear smart by dropping names in your speech. Throwing around phrases, such as "As Albert Einstein once said. . . ." or "According to Socrates. . . ." sounds forced. While you're trying to sound smart, using such quotes often has the opposite effect.

✔ **Use a variety of sources:** Unless you're doing a tribute to a particular celebrity, no one wants to hear endless quotes from a single source. That type of repetition gets boring fast. If you're only going to quote Yogi Berra, then why didn't you just get Yogi to give your speech? Mix it up a bit. Go ahead and quote Yogi, but quote Aristotle, Confucius, and Captain Kangaroo, too.

✔ **Keep it brief:** You don't want to lose the conversational quality of your speech, and a long quote starts to sound like you're reading it, even if you're not. Shorten lengthy quotes and tell the audience that you're paraphrasing. Just say "To paraphrase Mr. Whoever," then say the shortened quote.

✔ **Use a simple attribution:** Just say, "Mr. So-And-So once said . . ." and give the quote, or give the quote and then say who said it. You can sound a bit ridiculous if you say "quote . . . unquote" unless you're doing a dramatic reading from a trial transcript.

✔ **Cite a surprising source:** You can bolster support for your argument in a powerful way by using quotes from an unlikely source. It's so unexpected for a Republican speaker to support his position by quoting a Democrat, or a union leader to advance her cause by quoting management, or a Sunday morning televangelist to prove his point by quoting Snoop Dogg. Such startling contrasts always get attention and can be very effective.

✔ **Hedge your bets whenever you're in doubt:** If you're not sure who said the line that you're quoting, you don't have to delete the quote from your speech — you just have to know how to cover yourself. Simply say, "I believe it was Mr. Famous Name who once said. . . ." or use the great cover phrase, "As an old philosopher once said. . . ." After all, everyone is a philosopher of one sort or another. So if you find out that the line came from Donald Duck, you can still argue that he was being philosophical.

Doing it by the numbers

Benjamin Disraeli, the famous British Prime Minister, once said, "There are three kinds of lies: lies, damned lies, and statistics." He may have overstated the case, but not by much. Statistics enable you to slice up reality in a way that suits your perspective.

Statistics and numerical data can provide some of the most influential support in your entire speech, but they commonly lose their impact because speakers use them ineffectively. Get your numbers to register on your audience's bottom line by checking out my suggestions in the following bulleted list:

✔ **Give your audience time to digest:** Most people can't process numbers as rapidly as they can process other types of information, so don't drown your audience in numerical data. Give your listeners time to digest each statistic; don't just spew numbers at them. If you don't space statistics out, the audience will — space out, that is. (An exception to this rule involves *startling* statistics. See the bullet "Use startling statistics" later in this list for a discussion of this exception.)

✔ **Round off numbers:** If you're telling aerospace engineers how to build a more efficient jet engine, then by all means, use exact numbers. But if exact numbers aren't critical to your subject matter or to your audience, give everyone a break — round them off. Your listeners don't need to know that the candidate you backed won with 59.8 percent of the vote. Just say 60 percent.

✔ **Use a credible source:** A statistic is only as impressive as its source. Did you get your numbers from *The Wall Street Journal* or *The National Enquirer?* A big difference lies between the two.

What many people don't realize is that *The Wall Street Journal* may not always be the more credible source. Credibility all depends on your audience. You may be speaking to people who read *The National Enquirer* religiously and distrust *The Wall Street Journal,* categorizing it as a tool of the rich. Only your audience can bestow credibility upon a source. Keep that point in mind when you select your statistics.

✔ **Repeat key numbers:** If you want people to hear and remember an important statistic, say it more than once. Just think of the audience as a person you've wanted to date and who has just asked for your number. You wouldn't just say it once, would you?

✔ **Use startling statistics:** The big exception to the general rule that statistics are boring is the *startling* statistic. This term refers to numerical data that's so surprising that it just grabs your attention. A startling statistic is inherently interesting.

For example, if you were giving a speech about the need for more recycling, you might start by using this statistic from the GreenFund Network Web page: Every 2 seconds a printer cartridge is thrown away in the United States alone. That's 1,800 cartridges per minute, 108,000 per hour, almost 3 million per day!

✔ **Relate the numbers to your audience:** Numbers are abstract concepts, and if you want to make an impact with your numbers, you have to make the audience relate to the numbers you plan to discuss. To make numerical data more concrete, try the following techniques:

- **Put statistics into familiar terms:** Discuss numbers in a way that people can understand. Explain numbers in terms that have real meaning for your audience.

  Here's how Richard Stegemeier, former Chairman, President, and CEO of Unocal Corporation, did it in a speech about global competitiveness: Economist Thomas Hopkins estimates that federal regulations are costing American consumers $400 billion every year. How much is $400 billion? It's about ten times the size of our trade deficit with Japan. It is about double the annual cost of public education in America, from kindergarten through the 12th grade. It's about 33 percent larger than our entire defense budget. It's enough to give every household in America $4,000 every year.

- **Create a picture:** Transform your numbers into a concrete image so your audience can see the statistic. Paint a picture for them.

Here's an example from a speech about evolution given by William Johnson, when he was Associate Dean of Academic Affairs at Ambassador University: Brontosaurus, "thunder lizard," was 70 feet long and weighed 30 tons. It was longer than a tennis court and equaled the weight of six elephants.

- **Use analogies:** Analogize your abstract statistics into easy-to-visualize images.

Here's an example from a speech given by Dr. Lonnie Bristow when he was President-Elect of the American Medical Association: Right now it requires four workers to pay for each Medicare beneficiary. But in a few years, as the whole population gets older and older, there'll be only two workers available to pick up the tab. And all the while that bill keeps swelling up just like a balloon. That means by the time most of the baby boomers are ready for Medicare, the balloon may have burst.

- **Create visual aids:** If you have a great deal of numerical data in your presentation, consider putting it into a visual format — using computer technology, slides, or overheads of charts or graphs. If your audience members can see the data, it will be much easier for them to digest it. (See Chapter 10 for an extended discussion of this topic.)

Clearing the air with definitions

A famous legal case involving a contract worth thousands of dollars turned on the definition of the word *chicken.* One side said that *chicken* referred to a fryer. The other side said that the same word referred to a roaster. If you don't want to be fried or roasted by *your* audience, make sure that you're all speaking the same language. The following list shows you a few ways to use definitions in a speech to prevent misunderstandings:

✔ **Use the dictionary definition:** The simplest way to define a term is to look it up in a dictionary and use the definition in your speech. Here's an example from a speech about ethics given by Dexter Baker, retired Chairman, Executive Committee, Board of Directors, Air Products and Chemicals, Inc.:

"*Webster* says ethics is about dealing with good and bad, with moral duty and obligation. A system of moral values. Principles of conduct that help mold our judgments and guide our decisions."

✔ **Use your personal definition:** If you don't like the dictionary definition, then give the meaning of the term as you define it.

Here's an example from a speech given by Brent Baker as Rear Admiral, United States Navy, Chief of Information:

How do I define *quality* in a news report or analysis? My measure is summed up in three words: *accuracy, objectivity,* and *responsibility.*

When a word is emotionally charged, some members of your audience may misinterpret your remarks unless you clearly explain *your* use of the term. The following is an example from a speech that George Marotta, a Research Fellow at Stanford's Hoover Institution, gave to a local chapter of the National Association of Retired Federal Employees:

Thank you for inviting me to speak to you today about two subjects which I believe are very much positively correlated: bureaucracy and the national debt.

Bureaucracy is a pejorative term used to refer to organizations which are large and hierarchically structured. Today I am using it to refer to the bureaucracy of the federal government. In all of this, please understand that we all were federal bureaucrats and were proud to serve our government.

✔ **Use the derivation of a word to define it:** Explaining the history of a word's meaning reinforces its definition with your audience. (Doing so also makes you sound smart.)

Here's an example from a speech about the crisis in solid waste management given by William Ruckelshaus when he was Chairman and CEO of Browning-Ferris Industries:

Many of you have seen the famous old painting of a Victorian doctor at the bedside of a sick child. The doctor is sitting with his head bowed, not performing any medical miracles, just waiting. The title of this painting is *The Crisis,* and it refers to the period in an illness when all that can be done has been done; the patient will either get better, or she will die.

This was the original meaning; but a word like "crisis," so exciting and laden with emotion, could not long be confined to medicine alone. It became our general term for any situation in which disaster is somewhere in the offing, however remote. We don't have squabbles, or problems, or difficulties; in everything from international affairs, to government budgets, to education we have crises.

And naturally, we have a crisis in solid waste disposal, too. I mentioned the original derivation of this term, and its true meaning, because I think it's important in understanding where we really are regarding solid waste in this country. . . .

. . . In the past few years we've been able to diagnose the "disease," as it were, and we've been able to apply some basic cures. Is the crisis over?

Unlocking concepts with analogies

An analogy is a comparison that highlights similarities (and differences) between two objects or concepts. An analogy provides one of the fundamental ways that we gain new knowledge. An analogy allows us to explain the unknown in terms of the known. When a toddler asks, "What's heaven?" and you answer, "It's like school, but there's only recess and no homework," that's an analogy.

Analogies are particularly well-suited for speeches that teach, train, or educate an audience — any speech in which you're explaining something. They also provide an opportunity to add a touch of humor. Let's say you're giving a speech about the lack of leadership. You might say, "Leadership is like the Loch Ness Monster. You hear about it a lot, but no one sees it very often."

Getting heard with examples

Two of the most frequently used words in the world are "for example." We use these words to illustrate what we're talking about, and that's why examples are probably the most common devices for supporting ideas and assertions.

You can use two types of examples in your speech: real and hypothetical. You base a real example on fact. You base a hypothetical example on imagination — it's made up.

Real examples tend to be more powerful than hypothetical examples because they're, well, real. It's something that actually exists that you can point to. Hypothetical examples are always subject to the criticism that they're not real. However, they can be very effective in speeches that involve philosophy, law, or theoretical concepts.

Mark Twain said what?

One of the biggest media brouhahas during Dan Quayle's tenure as Vice President involved his misspelling of the word *potato*. While visiting a school in New Jersey, Mr. Quayle told a sixth grader that the word was spelled "potatoe." He made the mistake because he read from a flash card that had the word misspelled that way. Two days later, the national press was still hounding the Vice President about the incident, and he responded by saying that he should've realized the word was misspelled on the card. Then he continued by quoting Mark Twain as saying, "You should never trust a man who has only one way to spell a word."

That should have been the end of the incident. But a new controversy ignited when reporters checked the quote with Twain scholars around the country. The scholars claimed that Twain had never said it. And then the whole thing hit home — Mr. Quayle's staffers defended him by saying the quote came right out of a book that I had written.

It was true. I had written a book called *The Light Touch: How to Use Humor for Business Success (Simon & Schuster)*, and in it, I had advised using the Twain line to defend yourself if you were ever accused of making a spelling mistake. The Vice President used it perfectly. The defense should have worked. (And it would have worked for anyone else. The fact that reporters bothered to call Twain scholars around the country to check the quote shows how much they had it in for the Vice President.)

But this is a cautionary tale, and I bring it up now to show you the dangers involved in quote attribution. My source for the Twain quote was a book called *The Dictionary of Humorous Quotations*. Published by Doubleday in 1949, it was a reference book from a major publisher, and it was written by Evan Esar, one of the major American humor scholars for the first half of the twentieth century. If you can't rely on that type of source, what can you rely on? And that's my point: Use good sources when you do your research and be ready to identify them if necessary. You can quote me on that.

Regardless of whether you use a real or hypothetical example, if you want to get maximum mileage from your examples, don't ignore positive examples. Too often, speakers tell you what you shouldn't do, but they never say what you should do. That's a pet peeve of communication expert Jim Lukaszewski, and I agree with him. So Jim suggests using wrong way—right way examples, and make sure that you're prepared to show the right way. "You can take a specific situation and talk about how it might have been handled differently," notes Jim. "But if you're going to give just one side, talk about the right behavior and allude to the wrong one — not the other way around. You don't want to leave the audience hanging."

Chapter 6

Getting Off on the Right Foot: Introductions

. . . .

In This Chapter
▶ Setting audience expectations
▶ Figuring out what to include in your introduction
▶ Discovering several different ways to get off to a great start

. . . .

My model of making a speech is like the flight of an airplane (which you'll hear about ad nauseam throughout this book). In this model, the introduction is equivalent to the plane's takeoff. You're the pilot. Your audience (the passengers) wants your introduction to lead smoothly into the body of your talk (the flight). How you perform the introduction affects your credibility and determines the audience's mind-set for the rest of your speech.

Making the best introduction depends on several factors. In this chapter, I discuss important concepts to consider before you write your next introduction. So check out the sections below to ensure your next introduction sets your audience up for a great flight.

Discovering What the Introduction Must Do

Since ancient times, speech teachers have taught that an introduction has three basic functions. It must gain the attention of the audience. It must create rapport between the speaker and the audience. And it must provide reasons for the audience to listen to the speaker.

But the real purpose of the introduction is to *set the expectations of the audience*. Basic psychology tells us that the way we perceive things is highly affected by what we've been led to expect. So the introduction is critical — it determines how the audience interprets and reacts to everything else you say. And it's your best chance to shape the audience's reaction in your favor.

Yes, the introduction has to gain attention, lead into the rest of your talk, and perform all those other traditional functions you always hear about. But all of those functions are encompassed in setting expectations.

Your goal is to set the audience's expectations and *surpass* them. That guarantees your speech will be a success.

Creating the Perfect Introduction

It's been said that a journey of one thousand miles begins with the first step. That also applies to speeches — a speech of any length begins with the introduction. The following sections cover the steps that you must take in making this first leg of your journey.

Answering audience questions

The audience has several questions that they want answered within the first few minutes of your talk. Think of the questions journalists ask to report a story: who, what, when, where, why, and how. Your audience wants to know those same things. So be sure to answer the following questions in your introduction:

- ✔ Who are you? (Do you have any experience or credentials?)
- ✔ What are you going to talk about?
- ✔ When will you be through?
- ✔ Where is this talk going? (Is there some sort of organization?)
- ✔ Why should I listen? (Really a "what" question — what's in it for me?)
- ✔ How are you going to make this interesting?

Including necessary background

If the audience needs certain information in order to understand what you'll be talking about, give it to them in the introduction. If your speech won't make sense unless audience members know the definition of a certain term or they're aware of a certain fact, tell them. Also, you may need to provide background about why you *won't* be covering a particular subject or subtopic — especially if the audience expects you to address it.

Tuning up your introduction

You've heard of singers introducing songs? Meet a speaker who sings introductions. Bill Zachmeier makes a lot of speeches. As a professor of school administration at San Jose State University, he speaks to students, teachers, administrators, professional associations, and countless other groups of people. And he almost always begins his speeches by singing. He uses no musical accompaniment. He just tells the audience he's going to sing a song before he gives his talk.

Initially, people tense up — until he starts to sing. They relax after a few seconds, smile, and even give him a round of applause after he's done. He always promises to sing another song at the end, although he always jokes with them, threatening to sing two more songs if they don't behave themselves.

Not until after his song does Bill tell them what he'll talk about. But by then he's built rapport, and the audience stays with him. And he keeps his promise: He sings another song at the end.

Using greetings and acknowledgments

Many speakers open talks with endless greetings and acknowledgments to the sponsoring organization and key members of the audience. Boring! No one wants to hear you list the names of every dignitary on the dais. All right, sometimes you have to name names, but you don't have to do it as your opening line. If you have to acknowledge a bunch of people, do it as the second item in your introduction — not the first.

Making your introduction the right length

The introduction should usually be about 10 to 15 percent of your speech. Don't take forever.

Writing out your introduction

Write out your entire introduction word for word. Don't worry that you're just supposed to use key words or sentence fragments when writing your speech, and don't worry that a fully scripted speech might sound strained. The introduction is an exception, and writing out the introduction actually provides the following benefits to your speech:

✔ **You can edit it into its best form.** If you just make a note that you're going to tell a certain story in the introduction, you don't write out or practice the story. You figure you already know it. Then when you tell it, you end up rambling; you don't economize words; and the story doesn't achieve its maximum impact.

✔ **You can deliver a successful intro even if you're anxious.** The introduction is the most anxiety-producing section of your speech in terms of delivery. This is when stage fright is at its peak. If you get really nervous and your introduction is just a few key words, you may not even remember what they represent. Writing out the introduction word for word helps ensure that you'll carry it off successfully even if you suffer from a case of the jitters.

The introduction is the first part of your talk, but you should write it last. Why? It's an introduction. You need to know what you're introducing. After you write the body of your speech and your conclusion, then you've got something to introduce. That's when you write the introduction.

Using the show biz formula

In planning your introduction, it never hurts to recall the show biz formula: strong opening, strong close, weak stuff in the middle. Your introduction is the strong opening. Your conclusion is the strong close. Those are the two parts of your speech that have the most impact on how the audience remembers your performance. So make sure your introduction *is* strong.

Avoiding common mistakes

Sometimes what you don't say in your introduction is even more important than what you do say. You don't want to get started on the wrong foot — especially if it's in your mouth. Here are some common mistakes to avoid:

✔ **Avoid saying "Before I begin. . . ."** This is a patently absurd phrase. It's like airline personnel who ask if anyone needs to preboard the plane. You *can't* preboard. After you start going on the plane, you *are* boarding. And as soon as you say, "Before I begin," you've begun.

✔ **Avoid getting the names wrong.** If you're acknowledging people, organizations, or geographic entities, such as towns or cities, make sure that you know their names and pronounce them correctly. No one likes to be called by the wrong name.

Messing up names makes you look very unprepared, lowers your credibility, and makes the audience wonder what else you're going to goof up.

✔ **Avoid admitting that you'd rather be anywhere else.** If I'm in your audience, my response is "So get out of here." Yes, you may be in a position where you're giving a speech that you don't want to give, but don't whine to the audience. No one wants to hear it, and it doesn't help. You still have to give the speech, and you just seem like a big baby.

✔ **Avoid admitting that you're not prepared.** It's insulting. If you're not prepared, why are you speaking? No one wants to waste time listening to someone who isn't prepared. Although this is common sense, a lot of speakers make this mistake. Why? They're really making excuses in advance. They know they're not prepared. They know their speech will stink, and they want the audience to know that they're really not a terrible speaker — they're just not prepared. The logic seems to be that if you alert the audience in advance that you know your speech is lousy, somehow that improves your image. Wrong. You just seem like a jerk for being unprepared. If you're not prepared and you're going to speak anyway, just do it.

✔ **Avoid admitting that you've given the identical speech a million times for other audiences.** Even if your audience knows it, don't rub their faces in it. Every group likes to feel unique. Let your audience operate under the illusion that you prepared the talk especially for it. And if you're smart, you'll throw in a couple of customized references to promote this illusion.

✔ **Avoid using offensive humor.** A lot of speakers still labor under the myth that you've got to open with a joke. You don't. But if you do, it better not be a racist, ethnic, sexist, or off-color joke. There's no faster way to turn off an audience.

✔ **Avoid announcing that you had a ghostwriter.** It's like a magician showing how the tricks are done. Your audience likes to think they are hearing from you. Let them think so. Remember, a "ghostwriter" is supposed to be invisible — you know, like a ghost.

✔ **Don't apologize.** Unless you accidentally activated the emergency sprinkler system, shut off the power for the room, or knocked the podium off the stage, *never begin by apologizing*. Apologizing sets a horrible tone for audience expectations. When you start by apologizing, the audience expects something bad. Why else would you be apologizing? Plus, an apology draws attention to something the audience might not otherwise notice. If you don't start by apologizing for your speech, the audience may actually think it's good. And if they don't think it's good? You can always apologize later.

Getting Started in Fifteen Fabulous Ways

No matter how the introduction begins, the effect that every speaker desires is identical — you want to knock the socks off the audience. You want it to focus its full attention on you and hang on your every word. The big question is how do you do this? Well, there's no magic formula.

But there *are* lots of ways to begin. On the next several pages is a list of ideas just to get you started. It's not exhaustive — it may even inspire you to create your own unique introduction.

Using a Quotation

Quotations make good openings for several reasons: They're easy to find; they're easy to tie into your topic; and they make you sound smart. Whether funny or serious, they get the audience's attention.

Here's how Warren Manshell, as an investment banker with Dreyfus Corporation and a former ambassador to Denmark, opened a speech about the Constitution:

> "The Constitution is an invitation to struggle for the privilege of directing foreign policy." That is Edwin Corwin's famous description of the Constitution, and the history of executive-congressional interplay in the area is replete with examples to prove his point.

Using rhetorical questions

Asking questions is an effective way of introducing a topic. A rhetorical question involves the audience as they mentally answer.

Here's how John Lewis, a managing partner with Squire, Sanders & Dempsey, used rhetorical questions to begin a speech:

> Why are 300 people with a deep interest in education gathered in Southern California to debate "school choice"? What is "school choice"? Why do some believe it is a solution to the problems that confront public education today? What are those problems?

Using a story or anecdote

Everyone loves stories — especially if they're real, personal, and relevant. Here's how Alexandra York, founder and President of the American Renaissance for the Twenty-First Century, used a personal anecdote to begin a speech about American culture:

> What is the *current* state of our culture? By way of a short answer, let me relate a true, personal experience.
>
> A few years ago, while recovering from a tennis injury, I worked out regularly with a personal trainer. At that time, the new Broadway musical casually named *Les Miz* had reawakened interest in Victor Hugo's immortal book, *Les Miserables,* on which the play was based. New Yorkers were reading or rereading the book with fervor — on subways and buses, on bank lines, in doctors' offices, and even on exercise bikes. One day at my "very upscale" gym, the woman next to me warmed up on her bike reading a paperback of that great, classic novel which she had propped up on the handlebars while she cycled. A trainer wandered by — a male in his mid-30s with a B.S. degree — and noted the reading material with visible surprise. He stopped short and asked in wonderment, "They made a book of it already?" So may we ask in wonderment, "What is the state of a culture where such a question can be asked by a college graduate?"

Using a startling statistic

There's some good news and some bad news about statistics. The bad news is they tend to put people to sleep. The good news is that dramatic, carefully chosen statistics keep people *from* going to sleep. They serve as a wake-up call. A startling statistic is particularly effective in an introduction. (See the section on statistics in Chapter 8.)

Here's an example used by C.E. Ritchie, former Chairman and CEO of The Bank of Nova Scotia, in a speech about Canada's competitive position:

> In the current issue of the *Harvard Business Review,* there is an article entitled "The New Labour Market" that speaks volumes about globalization and competitiveness, two ideas that will be the subject of my remarks today.

The article contains some striking figures showing the number of college graduates in science and engineering in 13 countries. By now, it will surprise no one that Japanese engineering graduates — 75,000 strong in 1986 — outnumbered our class of 8,400 by a ratio of almost 9 to 1. But who would have guessed that Mexico graduated more than 25,000 engineers in that same year — *four times* Canada's production. Or that the Philippines graduated 23,000 engineers, again almost four times Canada's output.

Using a startling fact

An interesting or startling fact always provides a good way to start a speech. If you find the fact fascinating, chances are your audience will too. Douglas E. Olesen, President and Chief Executive Officer of Battelle, used an intriguing fact to begin a speech about waste minimization:

> In just a few years, the most widely viewed artwork in the world may not be the Mona Lisa, or the Statue of Liberty, or even the Mapplethorpe exhibit. No, it just might be a landfill in Kearny, New Jersey. The state recently closed the landfill, and now it's considering one artist's idea to beautify this 100-foot high mountain of buried garbage. The artist wants to turn the dump into an enormous celestial calendar and call it "Sky Mound." Really. It will have steel posts, earthen mounds, a plume of burning methane, and radiating gravel paths aligned with the seasonal movements of the sun, the moon, and the stars. Why might that be the most widely viewed artwork in the world? Well, I'm not sure how many people will go out of their way to visit, but it just so happens that the site is bordered by the New Jersey Turnpike and an Amtrak commuter line. Also, Newark Airport is nearby. So we're going to have millions of commuters driving, riding, and flying by wondering if they're looking at art or at trash, or both.

 Good sources for unusual facts include Paul Harvey's radio program *The Rest of the Story.* (Many episodes of *The Rest of the Story* have also been collected in book form.)

Using a historic event

A historic event that relates to your topic is always a good way to begin. Historical references make you look smart and put your topic in perspective.

Julia Hughes Jones, former Auditor of Arkansas, used this device in a speech about women and equality:

> Why is a vote important? Many times, a single vote has changed the course of history. More than a 1,000 years ago in Greece, an entire meeting of the Church Synod was devoted to one question: Is a woman a human being or an animal? It was finally settled by one vote, and the consensus was that we do indeed belong to the human race. It passed, however, by just one vote. Other situations where one vote has made a difference:
>
> In 1776, *one vote* gave America the English language instead of German.
>
> In 1845, *one vote* brought Texas and California into the Union.
>
> In 1868, *one vote* saved President Andrew Johnson from impeachment.
>
> In 1923, *one vote* determined the leader of a new political party in Munich. His name was Adolf Hitler.
>
> In 1960, *one vote* change in each precinct in Illinois would have defeated John F. Kennedy.

Using something that happened today

Any fact about the date you're speaking can be used to open your speech. Is it a holiday? Is it a famous person's birthday? Is it the day the light bulb was invented? This device is closely related to the historical event opening, but it's not identical. You're not looking for an historic event related to your topic. You're looking for an event that occurred on this date. (When you find it, then you relate it to your topic.)

John V.R. Bull, as Assistant to the Editor, *The Philadelphia Inquirer,* used this device in a talk called "Freedom of Speech: Can It Survive?"

> Today is marked on my calendar as "Traditional Columbus Day," which seems a particularly good time to take stock of our legacy from that adventure of 500 years ago. A consequence of that journey was the creation of the United States of America, a nation that *Time* magazine last week called "a daring experiment in democracy that in turn became a symbol and a haven of individual liberty for people throughout the world." But today as we survey — and presumably celebrate — that "daring experiment," there are strong indications that we may have

failed to create a lasting monument to freedom, for those very blessings of liberty that we thought were enshrined forever as inviolate constitutional guarantees — freedom of speech, press, and assembly — are under attack as seldom before in our nation's 215-year history.

A good source for devising this type of introduction is *Chase's Annual Events*. It lists significant birthdays and events — both current and historical — for every day of the year.

Using the title of your speech

Many speakers use the title of their speech as part of their introduction. Here's how Harry Freeman, President of The Freeman Company, began a speech entitled "Corporate Strategic Philanthropy":

Corporate strategic philanthropy — hardly a striking phrase. In fact, it's quite a mouthful. And yet this wordy phrase describes one of the fastest-changing, most exciting, and challenging, and most often overlooked facets and opportunities of the modern business world.

Provoking your audience

Want to get your audience's attention? Get them riled up about something as soon as you start speaking.

Here's how James P. Grant, the late Executive Director of the United Nations Children's Fund (UNICEF), used a provoking opening at an international development conference: "Permit me to begin with a few friendly provocations: First, I would suggest that nobody — not the West, not the United States, nobody — 'won the Cold War.'"

Showing your knowledge of your audience

An audience is always complimented if you know something about them. This shows that you made an effort to learn about the audience members. The perfect place to display this knowledge is in the introduction.

Here's how C.J. Silas, former Chairman and CEO of Phillips Petroleum Company, did this at a speech to the Alabama Business Hall of Fame:

Thank you for honoring me as your guest this evening and for inviting me to take part in the induction of four outstanding leaders into the Alabama Business Hall of Fame. Tom Moore tells me that when the Board of Visitors organized the Hall of Fame in 1973, it was the first of its kind in the nation.

Since then, you've been the standard by which other such halls of fame have sprung up nationwide.

In the process, you've honored dozens of Alabama business leaders — not just for their accomplishments, but for their character.

Developing a common bond

Anytime you can show how you have something in common with the audience, that's good. John Rindlaub, CEO of the Pacific Northwest Region for Wells Fargo Bank, used this type of opening in a speech to an insurance industry conference:

I appreciate the invitation to be here . . . since I've always had a warm spot in my heart for the insurance industry. I know that's hard to believe. But there's a reason.

My father was Controller of American Re-Insurance . . . and one of the founders, and an Executive Vice President of the Municipal Bonds Insurance Association.

For 20 years, around the dinner table, I heard stories about the insurance industry. So it's a pleasure to be here today with insurance professionals.

Emphasizing the subject's importance

Saying that something is important gets immediate attention. Here's how Kevin J. Price, as Executive Director of the Free Enterprise Education Center, used this device to begin a talk to the Rotary Club in Warsaw, Poland:

I am pleased to be here with you today and to share with you the free market discussion. This topic is important because many of the activities that are part of the free market — marketing, capitalization, etc. — cannot be done without a free enterprise system.

Referring to the occasion

Want an easy way to begin? Just remind the audience of why you're speaking — the occasion that has brought you all together.

Here's how former U.S. Surgeon General Antonia C. Novello referred to the occasion in the opening of a speech at the regional meeting for Universal Salt Iodization Toward the Elimination of Iodine Deficiency Disorders in the Americas, held in Quito, Ecuador:

> It is a pleasure to be here. More than a pleasure, it is a thrill. If that sounds dramatic, I need remind you of why we are here. This is evolution, human history in the making. There is a palpable sense of progress in this room, at this conference, in many of the rooms and buildings I have visited while traveling throughout Latin America over the past several months. There is the power of knowledge in this room, the excitement of knowing that a momentous decision about the future of humankind is ready for the taking. We have made the slow ascent up the learning curve of Iodine Deficiency Disorders, and now we are nearing its peak: There is no more pressing need for research or investigation into the problem, and it is no longer necessary to search for solutions. We are ready to act.

Relating your talk to previous talks

If you're not the first speaker of the day, you can begin by telling the audience how your speech relates to what they've already heard. This helps them to see the big picture.

Here's how Shaun O'Malley did it in a speech about international accounting standards when he was Chairman and Senior Partner of Price Waterhouse:

> I've been listening with great interest to the preceding sessions and to what Messrs. Damant, Tweedie, and Wyatt have said this afternoon. Much of what I've heard has been remarkably similar to the comments we at Price Waterhouse hear regularly from our clients and to the kind of feedback we here at the Financial Accounting Federation, or FAF in the U.S., hear routinely from local companies and securities analysts.

Chapter 7

All's Well That Ends Well: Conclusions

*W*hen I was a kid in New York, a popular battle cry on the playground was, "Don't start what you can't finish." This advice was inevitably directed at a bespectacled young scholar who, after receiving an endless dose of harassment, had finally mustered enough courage to mumble a negative remark to the source of his ill fortune — the school bully. But the advice always arrived too late. Even as it was shouted, the bully was preparing to thrash him into tomorrow. Although my young colleagues' advice referred to the fisticuffs of the moment, they could have been talking about speeches. Too many people who start speeches don't know how to finish them.

The conclusion is one of the most important parts of your speech. If the introduction is your first impression, the conclusion is your last one — *and your last chance to make one.* It plays a key role in determining how your audience will remember you and your message.

In my model of a speech as the smooth flight of an airplane, the conclusion is the landing. The passengers — your audience — don't want the landing to be sudden or bumpy. They don't want to land in the wrong place. And most importantly, they *do* want you to land.

Making Your Conclusion Work

A cynic may say the conclusion's job is to let the audience know when to wake up. For non-cynics the conclusion must accomplish each of the following three major functions in order to be successful:

- ✔ **Summarize your speech.** The conclusion must provide a summary of your major points. This quick review should also remind the audience of your attitudes toward the ideas you've expressed. It should also show how the points relate to each other and your topic.

- ✔ **Provide closure.** The conclusion must give the audience a feeling that your talk is complete. People have a psychological need for closure. They want a speech to have a beginning, a middle, and an end — especially an end. They don't want to be left hanging. Your conclusion must address this need.

- ✔ **Make a great final impression.** The conclusion is your last chance to influence audience expectations. You want to end on a high note. Go out with a bang. Leave them stamping in the aisles. (Pick your own cliché.) The conclusion should grab their attention and score a direct hit on the gut level. It should possess an emotional appeal (see Chapter 5 for more on emotional appeals) that illuminates the compelling nature of your entire speech.

Creating the Perfect Conclusion

Remember the ending to every fairy tale you've ever heard? "And then they lived happily ever after." Your speech may not have much in common with a fairy tale, but you can create a similarly perfect ending for it. The following sections give you the simple rules.

Cueing the audience in advance

The audience likes for you to let them know in advance that you plan on concluding. Tell them when you're getting *close* to your conclusion. "Turning now to my final point" and "I'll give two more examples before I wrap up" are types of statements that give the audience confidence that you'll reach your final destination — soon. It also helps the audience formulate an estimated time of arrival.

Making it sound like a conclusion

People expect a conclusion to sound a certain way — like a conclusion. Audiences tend to become upset if you think you're finished but they don't. So make the wrap-up obvious. Use phrases such as "in conclusion," "to conclude," or "in closing." They're always good starting points — for ending.

Finding the right length

The conclusion should usually be about 5 percent to 10 percent of your speech. It can be too short, but a much more common mistake is making it too long. Don't go on forever. Sum up and sit down.

Writing it out

You should write out your conclusion for two reasons. First, writing out your conclusion combats stage fright. The period when you're concluding is the second most jittery time for speakers. (The most likely time for stage fright to strike is when you begin; see Chapter 6 for more on introductions.) If you write out the conclusion, you don't have to worry about forgetting it. Second, and more important, if you write out the conclusion, you'll know when to conclude. It's insurance against rambling.

Making the last words memorable

The last few lines of your conclusion are the most important. So make them memorable. Go for an emotional connection with the audience members. Make them laugh. Make them think. Make them stand up and applaud.

Here's a simple formula for setting up your final line: Just say, "I have one final thought that I want to leave you with." (An alternative is "If you remember just one thing I've said today, remember this . . .") Then give them a heck of a thought. Word it strongly and make it relevant — to your talk and your audience.

Announcing your availability

No matter what the circumstances of your speaking engagement, always make time to answer questions after you're finished. Announce your availability during the conclusion.

Let's say you're in the audience. You hear a speech that you think is absolutely terrific. When it's finished, you go to talk with the speaker, and he gives you the brush off. Bummer. First, you feel stupid. Then you get angry. And then you change your opinion of the speaker and the speech, right? Now you think the speaker is a jerk, and the speech wasn't so great after all. So don't be a jerk. Be kind to your fans. And don't forget — the fact that you're finished speaking doesn't mean that you're done.

Avoiding common mistakes

Sometimes what you don't say in your conclusion is even more important than what you do say. What follows are some common mistakes to avoid.

- ✔ **Avoid going over your time limit.** Make the conclusion coincide with the end of your allotted time. If you want to be perceived as a genius, finish five minutes early, but don't go longer than expected. An old joke on the lecture circuit defines a "second wind" as what a speaker gets after he or she says, "In conclusion." Don't let that happen to you. It's not pretty. (The classic example is Bill Clinton's nominating speech at the 1988 Democratic convention. It clocked in at 32 minutes and became a source of national amusement.)

- ✔ **Avoid rambling.** Reviewing the points you've already made should be done in a brief and orderly manner — preferably in the order you discussed them. Make the conclusion easy to follow. Stick to your plan.

- ✔ **Avoid adding new points at the end.** The conclusion is a time to review what you've already said — not make another speech. Introducing new ideas in the conclusion means that you haven't properly fit them into the overall framework of your talk, which in turn means that these ideas will have less impact. The audience will have to figure out where they belong. And you know what? The audience wants to go home.

> ✔ **Avoid saying you forgot to mention something.** It makes you look disorganized, and the audience worries that you'll make another speech. Here's one solution: If the point is really important, boil it down to a very succinct statement. Then, after you've summarized the points you've already made, say you want to leave the audience members with one final thought. Then give them the point you forgot to mention. If you had already planned to leave them with a different final thought, don't worry. Just say you want to leave them with two final thoughts. First give the point you forgot and then give the final thought you had planned. (Yes, this is an exception to the rule against adding new points at the end.)

Wrapping It Up in Style

It's been said that a speech is like a love affair: Anyone can start one, but it takes a lot of skill to end one well. This section contains some ways to end *your* speech that will keep the audience loving you.

Referring back to the opening

If one of the functions of the conclusion is to provide closure, then referring back to the opening is a great way to do it. You use the conclusion to return to remarks you made in your introduction. If you asked a question in the opening, you answer it in the conclusion. If you told a story, you refer to it again. This technique gives a wonderful sense of completeness to your speech.

Using a quotation

You can never go wrong ending with an inspirational quotation related to your message. Just make sure it's inspired and related.

Asking a question

Asking the right question can be a powerful way to end a speech. Presumably the question implies an answer — the one you want the audience to reach.

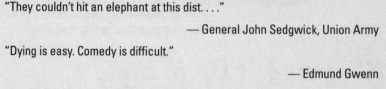

Famous last words

Every speech must have a conclusion, including the big speech we call life. And that's when our words take on a special significance. Even condemned murderers are given an opportunity to make a statement before they're executed. In fact, their final interaction with another human being is when the warden asks, "Do you have any last words?" The following are some famous "closing" remarks.

"They couldn't hit an elephant at this dist. . . ."

— General John Sedgwick, Union Army

"Dying is easy. Comedy is difficult."

— Edmund Gwenn

"Don't let it end like this. Tell them I said something."

— Pancho Villa

"Give me a match and I'll see if there's any gas in the tank."

— Anonymous

As Governor of Michigan, John Engler used a powerful question to close an address to his state legislature about a school reform plan: "My friends, the eyes of the nation are upon us. This is Michigan's moment — a moment that will tell future generations here and across America what kind of leaders we were. Will we put our kids first? That is the question before every single person in this chamber. *Our* answer is *their* future."

Telling a story

You can choose from several types of stories: funny, shocking, moving, dramatic, educational, personal, fictional, biblical, or allegorical. Any one of them can be effective.

Reciting a poem

If you recite a poem, it should be short. It can be inspirational or funny, but it must tie into your talk. Here's a verse used to conclude a speech by Albert Casey, former President and CEO of the

Resolution Trust Corporation (and it ties into any talk), "I should like to close with the immortal words of Richard Goodwin: 'I love a finished speaker. I really truly do. I don't mean one who's polished. I just mean one who's through.' Thank you."

Telling the audience what to do

This type of ending is very specific. You conclude by telling the audience *exactly* what to do. Here's what the late J. Peter Grace, Chairman of W. R. Grace & Co, told his audience to do as he concluded a speech on government waste: "Get behind Citizens Against Government Waste and join the 535,000 Americans who care about the future of their country and are willing to stand up and be counted. Call 1-800-BE-ANGRY and find out how you can get involved."

Asking for help

Just ask for help. It's a simple but overlooked conclusion. Most people really do respond. My favorite example is a speech I gave to a local Rotary Club. The speech was about a joke-writing contest I was sponsoring at a local high school. I explained why it was good for kids and why prizes were critical to the success of the contest. The conclusion was a plea for help with prizes. Guess what? They helped.

Part III
Making Your Speech Sparkle

In this part . . .

What's the difference between an average speech and a truly engaging one? Exciting words and eye-catching visual aids. Coincidentally, these are the areas that I cover in this part. In these chapters, you discover how to choose and order words into their most powerful combinations and make stunning visual aids.

Chapter 8

Making Sense of Your Speech

In This Chapter
▶ Editing your speech painlessly
▶ Tacking on plenty of transitions

*L*ife would be a lot simpler if we could dictate a perfect speech on the first try. Unfortunately, most people can't — except one professor I had in law school, but that's another story. So we must face the inevitable: editing our speeches and adding effective transitions. But don't worry. I've put together some techniques that minimize the time you spend on these chores and make them relatively pain-free. And while a shot of whiskey may have the same painless effect, my techniques for editing and adding transitions leaves you with a solid speech — instead of a hangover. (You can turn it into a great speech by reading Chapters 9 and 10.)

Editing Your Speech — Pain-free

Just thinking of the word "edit" can give some people a headache. But just as you would never think of giving a speech without practicing it, don't think of even practicing your speech until you've edited it. Just check out the guidelines in the sections that follow. You'll find that the time you spend editing your speech is not only painless, but also worth it.

Using conversational language

One of the most common mistakes speakers make is the failure to distinguish between oral and written language. They write a speech as though it's a memo or a report, which is a big mistake — because a speech must be read orally, not visually. It must be designed for the ear, not the eye.

When you write a speech, some of your writing vocabulary will inevitably creep into your talk. When you edit the speech, you must find those instances and eliminate them. Keep your language conversational.

Reading your speech out loud

Reading your speech aloud is not just for practicing your speech. If you write for the ear, you need to hear what you're writing so you can edit out text that just doesn't sound right. While reading your speech out loud, check for the following:

- ✔ **How does it sound?** You can't tell how a speech works by reading it. You have to hear how it sounds. Or ask someone else to listen to it. If it doesn't sound like a speech, which is a totally subjective judgment, you have more work to do.

- ✔ **Does it have a good rhythm?** No you're not writing a song, but you are creating a performance designed for the ear.

- ✔ **Can you communicate each idea without running out of breath?** Long sentences may be impressive if you're writing a dissertation but they can be tough on your lungs when you're giving a speech if you're not a swimmer or trumpet player who has mastered the art of breath control and incorporated that talent into your delivery style. Whew.

- ✔ **Have you cut out all the tongue twisters?** Words can look good on paper but be difficult to say out loud. If you find yourself stumbling over a word, change it.

- ✔ **Have you eliminated phrases that appear harmless on paper but are embarrassing when spoken?** For example: "One smart fellow, he felt smart. Two smart fellows, they both felt smart. Three smart fellows, they all felt smart." Say it aloud quickly a few times. You'll find out why it's cherished by little kids throughout the English-speaking world.

Keeping the language simple

Many speakers feel that they have to throw in a lot of big words to show how smart they are. Wrong. Smart speakers do just the opposite. Abraham Lincoln is a good example. Smart guy, right? Well, check out his "Gettysburg Address." Most of the words aren't more than five letters long. Or how about Franklin D. Roosevelt? Legend has it that one of his speechwriters wrote, "We're endeavoring to create a more inclusive society." Roosevelt changed it to: "We're going to make a country in which no one is left out." Which one sounds smarter to you?

Avoiding long sentences

Brevity is the soul of understanding. No, that's *not* a mistake. I know the expression is really "Brevity is the soul of wit," but I want *you* to know that brevity also has a big impact on comprehension. The more words a sentence contains, the more difficult it is to understand. Look through your speech. If you find a lot of sentences with more than 20 words, your audience had better be Ph.D.s. If you're talking to anyone else, start rewriting (and shorten those sentences).

Using the active voice

The active voice makes your sentences more forceful and powerful because a sentence using active voice has someone doing something. The passive voice sounds wimpy. A sentence in passive voice may read: "There's a bonus given by the boss once a year." But the same idea using active voice would read: "The boss gives a bonus once a year." The passive voice is like a weed that creeps into your writing. You must keep pruning it out.

Being specific

Writing instructors have an old saying that also applies to speeches — specific is terrific. It means that concrete words and examples are more effective than vague words and descriptions. Contrast "I went to the store" with "I went to Safeway." The word "Safeway" is more specific than "store." It creates a stronger image. Or let's say you're talking about an accident that occurred in a schoolyard. You could say, "A boy ran into the wall and got hurt." You could also say, "A boy ran into the wall and scraped his arm in three places. The school nurse had to apply gauze and bandages to stop the bleeding." Be specific — it makes a difference.

Using exciting verbs

Verbs are where the action is. So make them exciting. Let them help create a picture for your listeners. Let's say you're telling some war story from work: "I asked Smith to give me the file." Asked? Why not begged, pleaded, or implored? A good thesaurus can do wonders.

Of course a thesaurus can also be used excessively. The sentence "Run Dick run" doesn't have to become "Dash Dick gallop." The thesaurus should be used as a tool not an obsession. As discussed above, you still want to keep your language transparently unaffected — I mean simple.

Getting rid of clichés and buzzwords

"People are our most important resource." "We partner with our customers." "Think outside the box." Enough already. Give everyone a break. Instead of parroting the latest corporate clichés, come up with something fresh. It gets more attention.

And that goes double for buzzwords. "Synergy." "Re-engineering." "Excellence." "Strategic." What's your reaction when you hear a bunch of these strung together? It sounds like the speaker is a corporate robot. And your mind goes on automatic. Peppering your speech with buzzwords invites your audience to ignore what you're saying — if they even understand it.

Once in awhile a cliché or buzzword may actually fit into your message. But most of the time, they get used due to laziness. So take a few moments to think about what you're really saying. It's not that difficult.

Perfecting the pace

If all your sentences are the same length, you can end up sounding more like a lullaby and run the risk of lulling your audience to sleep. So vary the pace. Use short sentences and long sentences. Throw in a rhetorical question. Don't let the rhythm become monotonous.

Avoiding foreign words and phrases

So you were a French major in college. Good for you. But if you want to speak French, go to France. (Or to paraphrase a quote attributed to Dan Quayle — if you want to speak Latin, go to Latin America.) Here's the point: Dropping a bunch of foreign phrases into your talk doesn't impress anybody but you. It just makes you appear pompous, and can leave your audience wondering what you just said. (Besides, English was good enough for Shakespeare.)

Making Transitions

Transitions may be the most overlooked part of any speech; yet they're one of the most important. Transitions don't call a lot of attention to themselves, so it's easy to forget about them. They don't involve dramatic rhetorical devices like the introduction or conclusion. They don't offer fascinating information or anecdotes like the body of the speech, but they're still a big deal — they're the glue that holds the whole speech together.

Figuring out how to use transitions

Even if your speech has the world's greatest introduction, body, and conclusion, you still have to get from one to the other. That's where transitions come in. They connect the various parts of your speech, and they flesh out its organization. Transitions let your audience know when you're moving from one idea to another and how all your ideas fit together.

 Most people know that transitions have two traditional functions:

- ✔ To lead from one section or idea to another.

- ✔ To provide internal summaries that let the audience know where it's at, where it's been, and where it's going in regard to the speech.

But transitions can also be used to gain and hold audience attention.

Managing the transition mission

Transitions have a lot of work to do — especially for such an overlooked part of a speech. The following are three important tasks that they can perform.

Leading from one idea to another

The primary role of the transition is to lead your listeners from one idea to another.

Perhaps the most important transition is the one between the introduction and the body of your talk. In my airplane model, this is when the plane pulls out of the takeoff pattern and settles into cruising mode. Turbulence here can make the passengers very nervous. They want to know that the plane is heading in the right direction.

But the transitions between major points are also very important. This is where speakers often screw up. You know what I'm talking about. You're sitting in the audience listening to a speech. The speaker is talking about the monetary policy of Bolivia. But the next thing you know, the speaker is discussing a labor shortage in Eastern Europe. How did we get from Bolivia to Eastern Europe? Probably without a transition.

Fortunately, there's a simple way to handle the transition between the introduction and the body, as well as the transitions between main points. Here's the secret: Organize your speech around a number of points and state that number in your introduction. Then the transitions are a breeze. "Today I will be speaking about the three reasons for the coming worldwide depression. First is the monetary policy of Bolivia. . . . The second reason we are headed for a worldwide depression is the labor shortage in Eastern Europe. . . . Third. . . ." It's transitions by numbers, and it works.

By the way, this numbering technique can also be used to make transitions to and between subpoints. "First is the monetary policy of Bolivia. There are two aspects to Bolivian policy that are troubling. . . ."

There's one more important transition to discuss. It comes between the body of your speech and the conclusion. And it's very easy to handle. Sometimes you can just say "In conclusion" and it works. But remember that this transition must alert the audience that you're going into your close. "What can we learn from all this?" "Let me leave you with one final thought." "Now, in my three remaining minutes, let me remind you of what we've discussed." It has to sound like you're going to wind down and wrap up.

Summarizing

The second traditional function of transitions is to provide internal summaries — short announcements that let the audience know where it is, where it's been, and where it's going. The need for these summaries is frequently dismissed by inexperienced speakers who feel that they're too repetitive — that they're just filler. Well, yes and no. Internal summaries *are* repetitive, but they're *not* filler. They play a vital role in any speech, especially speeches longer than a few minutes.

When it comes to understanding a speech, speakers have a distinct advantage over the audience — they know what they're trying to say. (All right, so maybe you can think of a few exceptions. They're in Congress, right?) Speakers know exactly what their message is, how it's structured, and all its points and subpoints. In writing the speeches, speakers have an opportunity to read their message many times. Audiences don't have that luxury. They only hear the speech once — as it's given. They can't put it in reverse, play it again, and freeze-frame the parts they didn't catch.

Here are a few tips about using internal summaries:

> ✔ An internal summary should succinctly state what you just covered and announce where you are in the speech.

> ✔ Use an internal summary every time you move from one major point in your talk to another major point.

> ✔ Internal summaries can also be used when moving from sub-point to subpoint.

> ✔ The longer your speech, the more internal summaries you need.

Getting attention

Transitions can also be used to gain attention. Although they're not traditionally used for this purpose, there's no reason that they shouldn't be. Under the traditional view, transitions can serve as internal summaries telling your audience where it's been, where it is, and where it's going. It's this last part — *where it's going* — that raises interesting possibilities for gaining attention.

When you tell your audience where it's going, why not make it exciting? Instead of just restating the structure of your talk in a straightforward, matter-of-fact manner, employ a little pizzazz. Use a *teaser*. A teaser is the short blurb you hear on radio and television programs just before the commercial. "Coming up in the next half of our show: a man abducted by a UFO reveals recipes he learned on board." "A politician who *kept* a promise — right after these announcements." The teaser is designed specifically to get your attention and keep you from changing the channel.

You can use the teaser technique to make your internal summaries excite the audience members about what lies ahead in your speech. Give them some great coming attractions that keep them glued to their seats. How do you do that? Think about why the audience should even listen to your talk. What's in it for them? As you write your transitions about what's coming up, frame them in terms of audience benefits.

Avoiding common transition mistakes

Transitions are the glue that holds a speech together. Unfortunately, many speakers become unglued trying to insert transitions properly. Avoid the following mistakes.

Too few

The biggest mistake with transitions is not having enough of them. It never hurts to have more because you can never make your speech too clear to your audience. You've been living with your speech for quite awhile. You're intimately familiar with it; your audience isn't. The more guidance you can give the audience about how it's structured and where it's going, the better. Not sure if you need a particular transition? Apply the Kushner rule of transitions: When in doubt, *don't* leave it out.

Too brief

If the transition is too brief, it can be easily missed by your audience. That's equivalent to having no transition at all. The most common, and overused, brief transition is "and." I've heard talks that used "and" almost exclusively as a transition. The effect is almost comical. The speech sounds like it's just a bunch of disjointed ideas tacked together — the tack is the "and." And . . . And . . . And . . . A close runner-up is "in addition."

Too similar

Variety is the spice of life. It also works wonders with transitions. Don't use the same couple of transitional phrases over and over again. It gets boring. Use an assortment of transitions. "Now let's take a look at . . ." "In addition . . ." "The next point is . . ." "For example . . ." "By that I mean . . ." The possibilities for transition lines are endless.

Chapter 9

Getting the Words Right

• •

• •

*I*t's been said that there are over 10,000 useless words in the English language, but a great many of them come in handy for writing computer manuals and political speeches. Some of them may even come in handy for *your* speeches. It all depends on what you want to accomplish. Whatever your goal, there's no getting around the fact that words are the basic building blocks. If you want to be a successful public speaker, you have to get the words right, and this chapter shows you how.

Honing Your Tone and Style

A politician gave a speech denouncing the welfare nature of big government. His booming voice thundered across the room, "From federal payments for prenatal care to Social Security death benefits, the government is taking care of people from womb to tomb." The rhyming words of "womb" and "tomb" gave the line a nice ring and always got applause. But the politician got bored with the line, so he introduced a new version during a luncheon speech to a women's political club. Instead of "womb to tomb," he said he was sick of the government taking care of people from "sperm to worm." The audience silence was deafening.

What can we learn from this? Three things: Don't talk about sperm to a women's political club. Don't talk about worms while people are eating. And don't forget that tone and style are important — they have a major effect on how your ideas are received.

Polishing your word choice

Several years ago, I attended a seminar held by Ronald Carpenter, a professor in the English Department at the University of Florida at Gainesville. One of his major themes was that word choice is critical in the communication of ideas. To make the point, he posed a question. If a monument were built for John F. Kennedy, what Kennedy quote would be engraved on the monument? The seminar participants answered instantly and unanimously: "Ask not what your country can do for you, ask what you can do for your country."

That line was delivered by President Kennedy during his Inaugural Address on January 20, 1961. It's a powerful arrangement of words that is universally associated with Kennedy.

Carpenter believes that the choice of words and their order has made that line immortal. His proof? He contrasted the famous quote with a line delivered by Kennedy several months earlier. During a campaign appearance on September 6, 1960, Kennedy had said, "The New Frontier is not what I promise I am going to do for you, the New Frontier is what I am going to ask you to do for your country."

Huh? Come again. That's a clunker if there ever was one. Would that line appear on a Kennedy monument? Not a chance. In fact, it would never appear on any monument unless it was a monument to awkward phrasing. But substantively, this long-forgotten line says *exactly the same thing* as the famous line. Word choice and arrangement made the critical difference. (Need another example? Imagine the "Gettysburg Address" beginning with the words "Eighty-seven years ago. . . .")

Using power words

Management communication counselor Jim Lukaszewski also places a heavy emphasis on the power of words. He divides words into three categories: blah words, color words, and power words. *Blah words* are just what you'd expect — blah. They're colorless filler that take up space without getting notice. *Color words* exist at the other end of the spectrum. They're colorful, but they generate an emotional reaction, which can overshadow anything else you say. But *power words* such as "interesting," "unusual," "decisive," "hot," "exciting," "new," "critical," "urgent," and "compelling" should be your choice.

Power words grab attention without really saying anything. Jim's proof? "If I say 'This is an urgent matter' or 'This is really important,' I've said nothing to you, but I've got your attention," he observes. "That's what power words do. They grab attention without giving away what you want to talk about." Want to maintain an audience's attention throughout your speech? Feed them a steady diet of power words.

Figuring out how to use jargon

Real mode device drivers are fine, as long as you hook them up to a hybrid 16/32 bit OS and retain control of the configuration of the SNMP agent and log-on domains. Yeah, right. Using your own jargon in speeches is usually summed up in two words — avoid it. Jargon is often incomprehensible. It creates a barrier between you and your audience. However, if you explain your jargon — educate your audience — you shouldn't have a problem using it.

In addition, jargon can also create a bond. In order to explain why, I need to introduce an academic concept: the inclusionary and exclusionary functions of language. It sounds complicated but it's not. It simply means that one of the ways that groups of people define themselves is through the use of language. It's like knowing a secret password. If you speak the language, you're in (or *included*). If you don't speak the language, you're out (or *excluded*). Jargon is the language that's unique to each group.

Jargon is so widespread because every group creates its own jargon as a way of defining its membership. Each trade and profession has its own jargon. Many companies have their own jargon. Clubs and associations have their own jargon. Even individual families have their own jargon.

So what does this mean for speeches? Plenty. Are you an outsider in relation to the group you're addressing? You can create rapport with the audience by using some of its jargon in your talk. It is relatively easy to do, and it demonstrates that you made an effort to learn about the audience. It also suggests that you understand something about the audience. Talking to surgeons? Find out what a "lap chole" is and refer to it in your speech. Talking to real estate agents? Find out what "FSBO" means and drop it into your talk.

Creating Catch Phrases

The *catch phrase* provides a tried-and-true method for drawing attention to a key point and helping audiences remember it. Want some examples? Turn on your radio or television set. The advertisements are full of them. "When it absolutely, positively has to be there overnight." "Don't leave home without it." "Takes a licking and keeps on ticking." These phrases "catch" in your memory, and that's what they're designed to do. Every time you think about one of them, you automatically think about a product and its key sales point. Constant repetition of the phrase by advertisers augments this effect.

The catch phrase technique isn't limited to advertising. Anyone can use it in any type of speech. Howard Nations, one of the country's leading trial lawyers, advises attorneys to create catch phrases that will stick in a juror's mind. And, of course, the most famous catch phrase from legal history comes from the O.J. Simpson trial: "If it doesn't fit, you must acquit."

Business leaders are also fond of this technique. In a speech about the future of telecommunications, William Esrey, former Chairman of United Telecom/U.S. Sprint, coined a phrase to describe the marriage of the telephone and the computer — *infonics.* After defining his catch phrase, he repeated it more than 20 times throughout the rest of his speech.

You can apply this technique to emphasize points in your speech, too. Just pick an important point, build a catch phrase around it, and repeat it endlessly.

Spicing Up Your Speech with Classic Rhetorical Devices

There was some good news and some bad news if you had a dispute in ancient Greece. The good news: There were no lawyers. The bad news: You had to argue your own case. That's why the ancient Greeks developed all sorts of rhetorical devices to improve their speeches. They wanted to win.

This section presents a few of the classic devices. And don't worry, they still work today. Anyone from six-year-olds to lawyers — okay, same thing —six-year-olds to professional speakers still use these techniques, and use them effectively.

Hyperbole

Hyperbole is a fancy word for exaggeration. People use hyperbole instinctively in everyday conversation: "I was waiting a year for you to get off the phone." It's a wonderful device for emphasizing a point in a talk. Here's an example from a speech that the late San Francisco comedy coach John Cantu gave about his roots in comedy:

> One of the first clubs I performed at was a small, dark place. It was so dark I could barely see the three people in the room — the two in the front row listening to me and the guy in the back row developing film.

Allusion

An *allusion* is a reference to a person, object, or event from the Bible, mythology, or literature. Here's an example from a speech about balancing work and family given by John Adams, as Chairman and CEO of the Texas Commerce Bank:

> Opponents of work and family programs say that employers should not involve themselves more deeply in workers' lives, that to do so opens a Pandora's box of raised expectations, employer liability, invasion of privacy, and even accusations of unfairness in providing work-family programs.

Alliteration

Alliteration refers to a phrase in which the words begin with the same sound. The classic example is former Vice President Spiro Agnew's description of the media as "nattering nabobs of negativism."

You can also use alliteration to make the title of your talk more memorable. When I was in high school, an English teacher talked about a paper written by one of her college classmates. It was titled "Freshman Father of Four." She said that the alliteration had made the title stick in her mind for years. I can vouch for that because it's now stuck in my mind, too — ever since high school. (By the way Mrs. Lifshey, if you're out there, everyone loved your class. Teachers need to hear that once in awhile.)

Metaphor

A *metaphor* is a short, implied comparison that transfers the properties of one item to another. A classic example comes from Martin Luther King's "I Have a Dream" speech: ". . . the manacles of segregation and the chain of discrimination."

The metaphor can add a poetic quality to your speech while still allowing you to make a point. Here's an example from a speech about our rapidly changing world given by Max Kampelman, Attorney, formerly in charge of U.S.-U.S.S.R. Arms Control Negotiations: "Moreover, as we look ahead, we must agree that we have only the minutest glimpse of what our universe really is. Our science is indeed a drop, our ignorance a sea."

Simile

A *simile* is like a metaphor except that it's a directly stated comparison of one thing to another. (It usually uses the words "like" or "as" to make the comparison.)

Here's an example from a speech about consumer protection given by Arthur Levitt, former Chairman, United States Securities and Exchange Commission: "A massive influx of inexperienced investors, and a real potential for conflicts of interest — it's like dry underbrush and a match. As SEC Chairman, I've seen too many people's life savings go up in smoke."

Want a great source of similes? Find a copy of *The Book of Similes* by Robert Baldwin and Ruth Paris. It was published in 1982 by Routledge & Kegan Paul.

Rhetorical question

A *rhetorical question* refers to a question that the speaker asks for effect. The audience isn't expected to answer. Rhetorical questions are designed to focus attention on the subject of the question. They are often used as introductions, conclusions, or transitions.

Don't put all the egg on your face in one basket.

He'd be spinning in his grave if he could see you now.

Don't cry over spilling the beans.

Here's an example from a speech by the late Benjamin H. Alexander, President of Drew-Dawn Enterprises, Inc.:

> Are we free when we cannot leave our homes at night without fear of being assaulted, beaten, or robbed? Are we free when, as the richest nation in the world, we permit poverty, beggars, and homeless people everywhere amongst us?
>
> Are we brave or courageous when we are afraid to bring back the "Whipping Post" for hoodlums — one of whom, three months ago, in Washington, D.C., casually walked to a swimming pool crowded with youngsters; and for no reason began to shoot at children?

The rule of three

The *rule of three* refers to the technique of grouping together three words, phrases, or sentences. For some reason, a grouping of three items makes a powerful impression on the human mind. (Don't ask me why. It just does.)

Some of the most famous passages from the world's greatest oratory have used this technique.

- ✔ "I came. I saw. I conquered." (Julius Caesar)
- ✔ ". . . government of the people, by the people, for the people. . . ." (Abraham Lincoln)

Business speakers frequently use this technique. Here's an interesting example from a speech about the civil justice system given by Stephen Middlebrook when he was Senior Vice-President and Executive Counsel at Aetna Life & Casualty:

> Voltaire once said of the Holy Roman Empire that it was neither holy, nor roman, nor an empire. The same might also be said of the civil justice system in the United States: that it is neither civil, nor just, nor a system.

The beauty of the rule of three is that it can work its magic on any topic — no matter how commonplace or mundane. Just take a few minutes to think about your subject. You can always come up with three items to group together. Are you talking about a new accounting procedure that must be followed by all employees? It affects managers, hourly staff, and temps. Is your subject quality management? It starts with awareness, training, and commitment.

Repetition

Repetition refers to repeating a group of words in an identical rhythm. This device draws attention to the phrase and can even be used to pull a whole speech together. Martin Luther King's "I Have a Dream" speech is a classic example. Dr. King repeated the phrase "I have a dream" throughout the speech.

But repetition doesn't have to run throughout an entire talk. It can be used to dramatize one section, or even one sentence, of your speech. Here's how James Paul, former President and Chief Executive Officer of the Coastal Corporation, used the device in a speech about the oil and gas industry:

> It's a system with inferior public services; at the same time there are more government employees in the country than manufacturing.
>
> It's a system with intrusive government meddling increasing by the hour into every phase of your business and your private life.
>
> It's a system with entitlement programs gobbling up 49 percent of the national budget.

So repetition is a dramatic way to create a rhythm. It's a dramatic way to make a point. It's a dramatic way to show your style. It's a dramatic way to be dramatic.

Chapter 10

Making Eye Contact Count: Visual Aids

*E*veryone's heard the old saying, "One picture is worth a thousand words." If that's true, then the average 20-minute talk can be reduced to two slides or overheads, and we can spend 40 seconds looking at them and go home. But it doesn't quite work that way. One picture is worth a thousand words only under certain circumstances. This chapter explores the nature of those circumstances — when visual aids help, when visual aids hurt, and what visual aids can really do for you — get the picture?

Using Charts and Graphs

Charts and graphs are commonly used to depict numerical data. They're also useful for expressing such non-numerical relationships as organizational structure, procedures, and lines of authority. Although they appear most often on slides and overheads, they've become increasingly popular in hard copy versions that can be placed on an easel.

Choosing a type of chart or graph

The following lists some of the most common types of charts and graphs and how you may want to use them:

- **Bar graphs:** These are handy for comparing all kinds of data — sales of widgets versus gadgets, defect totals under various quality management programs, drug reactions in infants versus adults.

- **Flow charts:** These charts are good for depicting any series of steps — company procedures, how a bill becomes a law, where an emergency call gets routed.

- **Line graphs:** Line graphs are great for showing changes over a period of time. Any kind of trend data works well — stock market prices, voting patterns, productivity gains. That sort of thing.

- **Organizational charts:** Who reports to whom? What's the exact relationship between the telecommunications department and the information services department? Is the European operation an independent unit or part of the main corporation? These types of questions can be answered with organizational charts.

- **Pie charts:** Pies are good for showing percentages in relation to each other. (The western region generated 80 percent of the revenue; the east 10 percent; the south 7 percent; and the north 3 percent.)

- **Tables of numerical data:** This is your basic spreadsheet layout. It's a boring format, but sometimes the numbers are so dramatic that the format doesn't matter. ("As you can see from the numbers in column three, half of you will be laid off next week.")

Making effective charts and graphs

The following are a few pointers to keep in mind when you use a chart or graph:

- **Limit the data.** The more items included on a chart or graph, the more difficult it becomes to understand. If you have a lot of items that must be represented, rethink the graph. Maybe you can split the data into several graphs.

✔ **Size pie slices accurately.** The audience gets confused when you show a pie chart with a slice labeled "10 percent" that looks like a quarter of the pie. If you use a pie chart, make sure the slices of the pie correspond to the real numbers. (Unless you're speaking at a multilevel marketing recruitment meeting.)

✔ **Make absolutely sure that the numbers are correct.** Check the numbers. Recheck them. And check them again. It's a credibility issue. If one number is incorrect, it can undermine your entire speech.

✔ **Avoid three-dimensional bars.** Don't make bar charts with three-dimensional bars. Because it's often difficult to figure out where the bars end, the audience may not know what the numbers represent.

Making Use of Slides, Overheads, and PowerPoint

You can't attend a business presentation these days without tripping over the slides and overheads, especially PowerPoint slides. This section ensures that your audience doesn't trip over your slides and overheads.

Using slides

Well-designed slides can highlight your key points, add variety to your talk, and capture audience attention. But slides also have two big disadvantages. Projecting them requires you to darken at least part of the room. (That invites the audience to snooze.) And their order is inflexible once you place them in a carousel. (So you can't rearrange them as you're speaking.)

Another disadvantage, which can be easily avoided, is the tendency some speakers have to run through slides too rapidly. "If you're flipping slides every two seconds, that's too fast," says Rachel Brune, a professional designer based in Cupertino, California. "You've got to leave them up long enough to register with the human eye." Her general rule: Allow at least 20 seconds for your audience to view and digest each slide.

Using overheads

When I have a choice between traditional slides (not a PowerPoint presentation) and overheads, I choose overheads every time. You can project them without turning down the room lights. (So the audience isn't invited to snooze.) You can write notes to yourself on the cardboard frames around the transparencies. And most important, you can reorder them as you speak. (You're not locked into the inflexible sequence of the slide carousel.)

However, they don't work well for a large audience because not everyone can see them clearly.

Using PowerPoint

Perhaps the greatest public speaking innovation in the past 15 years, PowerPoint has grown rapidly from a novelty to a standard. Business speakers have treated it like the greatest thing since sliced bread (or the microphone). And many people now feel unable to speak without it.

That, of course, is the problem. While PowerPoint is undoubtedly a fabulous visual aid, it's often treated like an abused miracle drug. People overuse it, use it improperly, or become addicted to it. Because of this abuse, PowerPoint has spawned the following three major, negative side effects:

- ✔ **The speech is underdeveloped.** Many speakers now spend more time preparing their PowerPoint slides than their speech. They think that PowerPoint *is* their speech. It's not! You still need a compelling message with an introduction and conclusion in order to hold the attention of an audience. Throwing up a bunch of PowerPoint slides is not a speech.

- ✔ **The speaker doesn't connect with the audience.** Ever heard speakers read their speech word-for-word from their PowerPoint slides? I rest my case. It doesn't get more boring than that. The audience can read the slides, too. So, if you plan on just reading the slide, you may as well not show up and just send the PowerPoint presentation for the audience to read themselves.

- ✔ **The message is lost.** While PowerPoint can jazz up a speech, it can also overwhelm your message: animating every slide; too many graphics; lots of text popping up all over the place. Your message disappears in the gimmickry.

Fortunately, the first two problems are easily solved just by being aware of them. That means the next time you speak remember to prepare an actual speech. PowerPoint should support your speech not replace it. Remember also to talk to your audience — not read slides to them. The third problem, lost message, can also be easily avoided. Just follow the design advice in the next section.

Discovering simple design rules

Whether you're using overheads, 35mm slides, or PowerPoint slides, a few basic design rules can ensure you leave your audience dazzled not dazed. Just keep the following in mind:

- ✔ **Check for spelling errors.** Nothing is more embarrassing than a typo projected onto a large screen. So make absolutely sure that you eliminated all spelling errors from your slides and overheads.

- ✔ **Use relevant graphics.** Graphics are good, but only if they support a point. Too many speakers use graphics just to fill space or because they look pretty. Big mistakes. If the image doesn't relate to one of the points on your slide, don't use it.

- ✔ **Be consistent.** Visually, it's very important to be consistent. It shows that you're organized. What does being consistent mean? Don't mix and match slides or overheads from different presentations if they have different design styles. It's jarring, and it distracts the audience from your message.

- ✔ **Take advantage of templates.** Many software programs for creating slides and overheads include predesigned templates. You just choose a style, and the program cranks out all your slides in that design.

- ✔ **Keep the text style simple.** Many speakers feel compelled to "pretty up" their visuals with fancy text. Don't fall prey to this temptation; it makes your slides and overheads difficult to read.

- ✔ **Use builds.** A *build* is a series of slides or overheads in which each successive slide contains the bullet points from the preceding slides plus a new bullet point. Builds have become a standard part of business presentations. They provide a good way to emphasize key points, but using builds to emphasize more than just key points can result in overkill. The downside is that you need more slides. For example, say you want to make six points. You can put all six points on one slide. Or you can do them as a build, which means using six slides.)

✔ **Keep the use of your logo to a minimum.** A logo should simply be a little element that says this is a presentation from your company or organization. If you're going to put a logo on every slide, keep it small. Otherwise it may distract from your message.

✔ **Use a mixture of uppercase or lowercase text.** A mixture of uppercase and lowercase text is easier to read. All uppercase text may be okay for headings or subheadings, but don't use it for the body of the text.

✔ **Use minimal text.** A common speaker mistake is putting too much text on a slide or overhead. You don't have to include every word that you're going to say — and you shouldn't. Audience members won't read it all and it makes you appear amateurish. Instead, just use key words or phrases that outline your ideas. Some designers refer to this as the 4 x 4 rule: Don't put more than four lines on a slide or four words in a line. Other authorities place the numbers as 6 x 6.

✔ **Use only two different fonts.** Using more than two fonts gives your slides a cluttered look. But there's an exception: slides that display a logo, product name or similar item identified by a specific font. Those items don't count toward your limit of two fonts.

✔ **Emphasize major points — not everything.** Have you ever seen college students who use a yellow highlighter to mark up 95 percent of every page in a textbook? What are they trying to emphasize — the stuff that's not yellowed in? If you want to visually direct attention to certain points, go ahead. But don't dilute your message by emphasizing everything.

✔ **Use only four colors per visual.** Use one color for the background, one color for headlines, one color for body copy, and perhaps another color for emphasis. (You can make an exception for graphs and complex images because you may need more colors to make a pie chart or line graph understandable.)

✔ **The colors on your computer screen look different than the colors on your slides and overheads.** The colors you see on your computer monitor aren't going to be the exact colors that appear on your overhead, 35mm slide, or any printouts you do of your PowerPoint presentation. If you're concerned about the colors, you can run samples to check out how they look.

Flipping for Flipcharts

A flipchart is a very large pad of paper that sits on an easel. Flipcharts have become ubiquitous at business meetings — and for good reason. The flipchart is a very versatile visual aid. You can write on it as you speak or have pages prepared in advance. It's easy to use. You don't have to find any on/off switches, electrical outlets, or replacements for burned out light bulbs. It always operates properly (unless your magic marker goes dry) and is easy to transport. Plus, it's very inexpensive. However, flipcharts aren't really effective for audiences larger than 50 people. The people seated toward the back can't see what's on the chart, and many speakers misuse flipcharts so badly that people in the front row can't decipher what the chart is supposed to say. If you plan on using a flipchart in your next speech, check out the sections below so you can use this versatile tool properly.

Avoiding common flipchart mistakes

To make sure you avoid common flipchart mistakes, check out these guidelines below:

- **Use as few words as possible.** I've seen flipcharts covered with writing from top to bottom. It looks like a cave wall crammed with hieroglyphics, and it's about as easy to read. So do your audience a favor. Leave some white space.

- **Write on the top two-thirds of the sheet.** It's easier for the audience to see. More important, by not writing on the bottom you don't have to bend down and give the audience a view of *your* bottom.

- **Write with large letters and plenty of space.** Maybe some people in your audience can read the bottom line of an eye chart, but it's not your job to test them. Make your letters large enough so that they can be read easily from the back of the room, and leave a couple of inches between lines.

- **Use thick letters.** Even when the letters are large, they can be difficult to see if they're really skinny. So don't make letters that look like stick figures. Make them thick enough so that they can be read easily from the back of the room.

✔ **Use colors people can see easily.** There must be something about flipcharts that bring out the artist in speakers. Control the urge. Don't use a magenta marker to write notes on the flipchart. Yellow, pink, and orange are also bad. In fact, if you want to make sure that your audience can see what you're writing, stick with black or blue. Those two colors can always be seen from the back of the room.

✔ **Use just two colors.** A rainbow is nice to look at in the sky, but not on a flipchart. You can use a few different colors to high-light various points and add emphasis. But if you use too many colors, they lose their impact and become distracting, especially when the colors start vibrating in the audience's eyes — that's a clue that your color scheme is a tad busy.

Using flipcharts effectively

Want to turn your flipchart into a powerful presentation tool? Try the tips that separate the masters from the disasters:

✔ **Use flipcharts with paper divided into small squares.** Each page should look like a piece of graph paper. The advantage is that you can use the boxes as a guide when you write. That way you know your writing will be large enough to see. The boxes can also help you keep your writing evenly spaced.

✔ **Correct mistakes with correction fluid.** Have you ever spent a lot of time preparing a very detailed page in your flipchart presentation only to make a minor mistake when you were just about done? Don't pull out your hair and *don't* throw away the page. Put some correction fluid over the mistake just like you would on a sheet of typing paper. Then make your correction. No one in the audience will be able to see it.

✔ **Write secret notes on the flipchart pages.** If you're worried that you'll forget to discuss important points, use your flipchart pages as cheat sheets. Lightly pencil in a few key words or phrases on the appropriate page. No one in the audience will be able to see them. This technique can also improve the text and drawings that you do want the audience to view. If you need to write or draw something as you speak, draw it lightly in pencil beforehand. When you come to that point in your talk, you can just trace over it with a marker. It will look a lot better than if you start it from scratch while you're speaking.

✔ **Draw pictures from coloring books.** Drawing simple pictures can add a lot of interest to your flipcharts. Can't draw? Use children's coloring books because children's books have simple drawings that are easy to copy and modify.

✔ **Use human figures.** If you're drawing pictures on your flipcharts, use human figures whenever possible. People respond to humans. (We're a narcissistic species.)

✔ **Leave two blank sheets between each sheet you use.** If you prepare your flipchart in advance, don't use each page. The paper is so thin that the audience can see through to the next sheet. And they can often see through that sheet also. So leave two blank sheets between each page that you use. Then you know you're safe.

✔ **Save your flipchart pages.** You put a lot of work into the ones you prepare in advance. So use them again. If you've torn them off the flipchart, don't worry. You can tape the pages up on a wall when you reuse them. There's no rule that they have to be on the flipchart.

Creating Great Video (And Audio)

Video is a very powerful, yet overlooked, visual aid. Today's audiences are supposed to have a short attention span due to the influence of television. So why not capture what little attention they possess with the medium they love — video? This section also discusses how to use audio to break through the attention barrier. (While audio is not technically a visual aid, it can create pictures in your mind. Besides, this seemed like a good place to throw it in.)

Using video

Video is so powerful that it should only be used in small doses. The danger is that it will take over your speech. It makes the non-video portions (in other words — you talking) seem boring by comparison, which is exactly what you *don't* want.

Use videos in short bursts to emphasize key points and heighten audience interest. If you're speaking to a small group, just bring a VCR and TV monitor. You can work them like an overhead projector, turning them on and off when appropriate. If you're speaking to a large audience, you need to arrange for the videos to be projected onto a large screen. (That task usually requires some professional help.)

Using testimonials

No matter what you're selling — yourself, your ideas, or your products — it's hard to top the persuasive power of third-party credibility. Suppose that I'm going to give you a sales presentation.

It's much more persuasive for you to hear about the greatness of my products from some of my customers than from me. Unfortunately, they usually have better things to do and don't generally accompany me on my sales calls. (It's hard to believe but true.) That's where video comes in. I can videotape a customer singing my praises and show it to you.

Tapping into other video ideas

When commercial television first took root in the 1940s, one Hollywood executive reportedly said that TV wouldn't last more than six months — people would get tired of staring at a box. (His prediction displayed the usual amount of imagination associated with Hollywood executives.) He didn't realize that video would evolve into a wide variety of imaginative forms — all of which were designed to capture audience attention. Unless you're a Hollywood executive (or otherwise imagination-impaired), you should be able to work video into your speech in lots of clever ways. Try these options:

- **Television commercials:** I saw someone give a speech about creativity. The speaker talked about different types of creativity and various techniques for being creative, and he illustrated the techniques with TV commercials. (I assume he obtained permission to show them — see "Getting permission to use content" below.) The audience loved watching the commercials. (They were very funny.) The commercials did a good job of bringing home the points about creativity. The speaker appropriately spaced the commercials throughout his speech. The commercials helped maintain audience interest and energy till the end of the talk. Given the range of subject matter covered in TV commercials, you can probably find one or two (hundred) that can illustrate some points in your next speech.

- **Filmed vignettes:** A speaker made a speech about cross-cultural communication. He emphasized how Americans could avoid gaffes when doing business with people from other countries. He covered the usual stuff, but he made it more interesting by introducing each segment with a short video. Actors, portraying businesspeople from America and another country, acted out a brief scene of a business meeting. The actor portraying the American would make every gaffe possible. The audience responded with laughter to each gaffe. So the videos were entertaining, as well as educational.

✔ **Person-on-the-street interviews:** I've seen these used for comic relief in various types of speeches. You ask a four-year-old what he or she thinks the CEO of your company does all day and videotape the answer. Or you ask people at a trade show unrelated to your industry (gourmet coffees) what they think of your latest product (a hydraulic pump). Or you ask people in your organization to sing happy birthday to someone. You get the idea.

If you plan to use clips from television shows, movies, or commercials, you must first obtain the appropriate permissions. (See "Getting permission to use content" below.)

Utilizing audio in your speeches

Music and sound effects can greatly enhance your speech no matter what you're discussing. They can energize your audience, set a mood, and emphasize a point. Consider these ideas:

✔ **Set the mood with music.** Audience members are walking into the room where they'll hear you give a speech. You have a choice. You can arrange for them to hear the theme from *Rocky* as they enter. Or they can hear nothing. Do you think it makes any difference? You bet it does. If you play the theme from *Rocky*, they'll get pumped up and energized. And that's probably the way you want them. (No? Then play something else. Want them in a contemplative mood? Try some new age, cosmic music. Want them inflamed with patriotism? Play a Sousa march.) The point is that music can provide a wonderful warm-up act. Take advantage of it.

✔ **Add a beat to slide shows.** People love to look at themselves. That's why multiday meetings often conclude with slide shows of photos taken earlier in the meeting. (The meeting participants see themselves arriving, attending sessions, partying, and so on.) These slide shows are inevitably accompanied by loud music with a heavy bass beat. (Disco music is popular.) Why? It generates energy and enthusiasm. It makes the slide show come alive. (The slides seem to synchronize with the beat of the music.) You can adapt this technique to your own presentations. Are you giving a talk about the completion of some project? (Completion of a new building, graduation from a school or program, release of a new product, and so on.) Do you have photos documenting the project's progress? Put together a short slide show and add some music. It's simple to do and very effective.

✔ **Fill time when people are thinking or writing.** Do you have a spot in your speech when everything comes to a halt? Maybe you ask the audience members to do some exercise in which they have to think about something. Or maybe you ask them to take a few minutes to write something. In any event, you stop talking and silence fills the room. It can become oppressive after awhile, and it definitely lowers the energy level. Want a simple solution? Play some music during this interlude. (Whatever you feel is appropriate.) It helps maintain a minimal energy level. It's also appreciated by audience members who finish early. They'll have something to listen to while the slowpokes finish.

Making an Impact with Multimedia

Multimedia refers to the combination of video, text, graphics, and sound. In this section, I provide a quick overview of how you can enhance your public speaking with multimedia. And I give you a few easy-to-use techniques. But this is definitely *not* in-depth coverage. (See *Multimedia and CD-ROMs For Dummies* by Andy Rathbone or *PowerPoint For Dummies* by Doug Lowe, both from Wiley Publishing, Inc., for an extensive discussion of this topic.)

Multimedia equipment you need

Three basic types of equipment are required to stage a multimedia presentation: a computer, an input device, and a projector. You also need software, but more on that later. You also need some kind of audio set-up.

Computers

The general rule for computers is very simple — get the fastest one you can afford. The faster your hard-drive and processor, the faster screens can pop up in your presentation. You also need a sound card, video display card, CD-ROM drive, and video capture card. These items now come with most computers. But sometimes you'll need to get a video capture card — that's what allows you to record and digitize video from sources such as TVs, VCRs, and camcorders.

Input devices

Input devices allow you to get sound and images into your computer in a digitized format — everything from music and video images to photographs and business cards.

✔ **Images:** Still images, such as slides and photographs, can be input to your computer from a digital camera or scanner. Moving images can be input from a VCR or camcorder with a cable you can find at any Radio Shack.

✔ **Sound:** The cabling deal also works with any audio device — cassette player, CD player, stereo, or radio. You run a cable from the "headphone out" jack directly to the "audio in" jack on your computer's sound card. Or plug in a microphone and record interviews or voiceovers directly in digitized form.

Projectors

You also need hardware that projects the sound and images of your multimedia presentation. The sound part is easy. If the room where you're speaking has a sound system, you can just plug your computer into that system. If the room doesn't contain a sound system, you have to bring your own speakers. For image projection, you need an LCD projector. This is a special projector that allows anything displayed on your computer screen to be projected onto a large screen or wall. The latest-and-greatest models are small enough for easy portability and bright enough that room lights don't have to be turned off. (They may need to be dimmed.) Most LCD projectors also have an input for video directly from a VCR. You need to hook up audio to the audio output of the VCR separately.

Software for multimedia presentations

The basic software requirements are Windows and Video for Windows or Windows Movie Maker. Beyond that, you need software to develop the individual pieces of your presentation and authoring software to put it all together.

Creating and editing images, sound, and text

Your first task is to construct the various images, video clips, audio clips, and slides that will make up your presentation. The following list shows you the software you need.

✔ **Graphics:** Graphics software ranges from simple tools, such as Paintbrush (which comes with every copy of Windows), to high-powered packages such as CorelDRAW!. Two of the more popular programs for image creation are Persuasion and PowerPoint. Both offer lots of help for the nonprofessional designer. (In other words, your slides won't end up with words written in 12 different fonts and 8 different colors.)

✔ **Audio and video:** You also need special software for capturing and editing the audio and video clips that you want to use in your presentation. Almost any sound card or video capture card comes with recording and editing software that covers your basic needs. Adobe's Premier is among the better-known software products for editing video clips.

✔ **Text:** Most word-processing packages are capable of tagging your word-processing files for multimedia access. Your multimedia-authoring tool determines how this should be accomplished.

Authoring systems

After you assemble the various pieces of your multimedia presentation, you need a method of putting them all together and controlling them. That's the function of software known as an *authoring system*. It allows you to choreograph all the other programs — sound, video, graphics — into a coherent presentation. One of the more popular systems now on the market is Macromedia Director MX.

If using an authoring program is too much of a challenge (they do take some time and effort to learn), don't worry. Use PowerPoint or any similar program. Many people use PowerPoint to make and show slide presentations. But it's very easy to add sound and videos. (See *PowerPoint For Dummies* for more help.)

Getting permission to use content

The good news about multimedia presentations is that you *can* use text, graphics, video, and audio. The bad news is that you need the rights to use that stuff.

There's a widespread misconception that you can use anything you want in a multimedia presentation. People use VCRs to capture video clips of news items, sports events, and scenes from their favorite movies. They record audio clips of music from CDs or the radio. They digitize photos and images found in books and magazines. Technically those activities are known as copyright infringement — a federal offense punishable by fines and imprisonment.

So where can you get the materials you need for a multimedia presentation? Remember these two magic words — *public domain*. When an item is in the public domain, anyone is allowed to use it. No permission is required. Or just get a cassette recorder or camcorder and create your own audio and video.

Wowing Your Audience with Simple Multimedia Techniques

Want to get started fast? Try one of these three easy suggestions. They'll knock the socks off your audience (assuming that your audience wears socks).

✔ **Use a testimonial from someone in your audience:** Videotape or audiotape people from the organization that you'll be addressing. Then include the clip in your presentation. Nothing is more impressive to a group than suddenly seeing one of their own members talk about how great you are.

✔ **Throw in a clip or image of something that just happened:** If you're speaking at an event, get there a few hours early, record people on audio or video, and work them into your presentation.

✔ **Use a customized effect:** The speed with which you can change a multimedia presentation creates one of its biggest advantages — it's easy to customize. Put in as many images and audio and video files related to the audience as you can. Are you talking to car dealers? Scan in some pictures of cars.

Get a business card from someone in the company that you'll be addressing and scan in his company's logo. Then you can make it appear in the corner of every screen with your own logo. Customize as much as possible.

Hitting a Home Run with Handouts

In today's self-reliant times, everyone says they don't want handouts. They don't want handouts from government. They don't want handouts from corporations. They don't want handouts from nonprofits. But when *you* make a presentation, then they want handouts. Consider the following things before you prepare and distribute handouts.

Making handouts that get a hand

If you're going to make handouts, make them look good. It's not hard to do. Desktop-publishing programs give you a lot of options for jazzing up handouts and making them look professional. Reproduce them on good quality paper. If you can afford it, put them in a binder.

Everyone likes to receive handouts. But it's better to give out a few good-looking ones than a lot of hard-to-read, poorly designed ones. Remember, the handouts represent *you*.

Including the right information

Are you using slides or overheads in your presentation? Your audience would probably appreciate hard copies of them. Put some in the handouts. (If you don't, you inevitably receive requests for them.) Reprints of relevant articles, by you or others, are always popular items. Checklists are also very good. People love checklists. Your audience also wants to be able to contact you. So make sure you include your phone number or address or e-mail. (Or something.)

Rachael Brune once pointed out that the more contact information you provide, the better people like your handouts. If you recommend products or services, talk about sources of information for a particular topic, or discuss calling publicly elected officials to voice concern about some issue, include lists of contact names and numbers.

Knowing when to give them out

Never give out handouts before you speak. They distract the audience, and people read them instead of listening to you.

The appropriate time to distribute handouts depends on their function. If the handouts summarize your points and present supplemental information, then distribute them after your talk. But if your handouts include audience participation exercises or other materials that you want to reference while you're speaking, give them out *before* you begin. Handouts distributed before you speak can also encourage the audience to take notes — especially when properly designed. Here's a tip from Allatia Harris: Instead of reproducing your slides or overheads to full page size, print them so they occupy 25 to 50 percent of a page. Then the audience can use the rest of the page to take notes while you speak about each slide or overhead. (Check out the automatic printing format for handouts in PowerPoint.)

Part IV
Delivering Your Speech

In this part . . .

*I*t's show time. In this part, I show you how to deliver a speech that wows your audience — that means knowing how to carry yourself, answer questions, and handle any audience no matter how tough or wacky. You also discover how to convey messages using your voice and body, how to deal with a podium, and how to produce commanding eye contact. These chapters also cover ways to get your audience involved and engaged with your speech. And if you suffer from stage fright, I give you some great ways to overcome it and use it to make your speech even better.

Chapter 11

Overcoming Stage Fright

- -

In This Chapter

▶ Reducing mental anxiety with proven techniques

▶ Controlling the physical symptoms of stress

▶ Handling stage fright

▶ Using your nervousness

- -

*S*tage fright. The words themselves make me nervous. Maybe that's why social scientists have abandoned the term. First they changed it to "communication anxiety." Now they talk about "communication apprehension." (If you've ever heard a social scientist speak at an academic conference, you know why these people are apprehensive.) But whatever you want to call it, the symptoms are universally recognized. Your heart pounds. Your hands shake. Your forehead sweats. Your mouth goes dry. Your stomach feels like a blender on high speed. And that's just when you get asked to speak. You feel really bad when you actually have to give the speech.

If you do experience stage fright, congratulations; you're in the majority. According to a frequently cited survey, most people consider public speaking more frightening than death. And you're in good company — celebrities alleged to suffer from this affliction include Abraham Lincoln, Mark Twain, Carol Burnett, Johnny Carson, Erma Bombeck, and Laurence Olivier. Although you just have to accept that stage fright will always be with you, I discuss some great techniques in this chapter so you can figure out how to control it and use it to your advantage.

Changing Your Perceptions

Teacher to pupil: "Think positive." Pupil to teacher: "I am. I'm positive I'm going to fail." It's an old joke, but it highlights an important point — stage fright is a mental phenomenon. However, if stage fright can be caused mentally, it can be cured mentally. It's all in the way you look at things.

Realizing how your audience really feels

Stage fright is a very egocentric affliction. *I'm* scared. *I'm* nervous. *I'm* going to pass out. Me. Me. Me. It's easy to lose sight of your audience's interests, but the audience has as much at stake as you. In fact, your audience may be more scared than you. They may suffer from *seat fright* — the fear of wasting time listening to a bad speech. For you to succeed in giving a great speech and controlling your fear, you need to know the following four things about your audience:

✔ **The audience wants you to succeed.** By showing up, members of your audience give you a tremendous vote of confidence. They don't want to spend their precious time to come and hear you fail. They want your speech to be a success. Their success is linked to yours. When your speech is terrific, people in the audience feel brilliant for attending.

✔ **You have knowledge that the audience wants.** You were asked to speak for a reason; it's probably because you have information that the audience desires. You're the expert. You have the data that audience members clamor for. Even on the rare occasion that the audience knows more than you about your topic, you can still provide new information. Only *you* can provide your own unique insights. No one else knows *your* view and interpretation of the material. Think of yourself as sharing valuable knowledge and ideas with your audience.

✔ **The audience doesn't know that you're afraid.** Social science research shows that the speaker and the audience have very different perceptions about stage fright. Often, an audience can't even detect anxiety in a speaker who claims to be extremely nervous. This situation is like the acne lotion commercial you see on TV. A teenager gets a pimple on his nose.

He imagines the pimple is as big as a watermelon and that people are staring at it wherever he goes. Of course, no one even notices it. Stage fright works the same way. It's a mental pimple that seems a lot worse to you than to your audience.

✔ **You can treat audience members like individuals.** Dr. Allen Weiner says that his clients tell him all the time that "they love to answer questions, but they hate to give speeches." As president of Communication Development Associates, Allen gets paid a lot to advise these people. (And his clients include senior executives of Fortune 500 companies.) Take his advice free of charge: View your speech as the answer to an *implied* question. In other words, what question does your speech answer? Instead of "making a speech," make believe you're just "answering a question." Speeches are far less frightening when thought of this way.

Visualizing success like a pro

The concept of visualization is simple and straightforward. You just imagine yourself performing a task successfully. A number of athletes use this training technique. They imagine themselves hitting home runs, scoring touchdowns, or signing autographs for $100 apiece. They imagine these activities in vivid detail and try to remember past successes and build them into the image.

Apply visualization techniques to *your* speech. Imagine yourself giving your talk. Your voice fills the room with wisdom. People in the audience hang on your every word. (If they lean any further forward, they'll fall out of their chairs.) They give you a standing ovation and rush the stage to carry you out on their shoulders.

Talking yourself into a great speech

Your audience only has to hear you once. You have to hear yourself all the time, so the messages you send yourself are very important. I'm talking about your *internal dialogue* — the things you say to yourself in your head. When you repeat them over and over, you start to believe them. So you've got to be careful what you say. If you keep telling yourself that you'll flub your talk at a critical moment, you probably will.

Popular Cures That Don't Fight Fright

Throughout history, human maladies have inspired remedies that claimed fantastic curative powers but actually proved worthless. Snake oil for the common cold. Blood-sucking leeches for fevers. Ear plugs for political speeches. Naturally, there have been a few "cures" for stage fright. Here are two famous ones that don't work.

✔ **Imagining the audience naked:** An alleged cure for stage fright that's probably as old as human speech itself is to imagine your audience naked. (I can just see this advice being dispensed by one caveman to another. Caveman #1: "Don't be nervous; just imagine that the audience is naked." Caveman #2: "But they are naked.")

✔ **Taking booze and pills.** Another folk remedy often suggested for stage fright is to have a drink or take a tranquilizer. This is supposed to help you calm down. Here's the problem: The desired effects normally wear off just before you get in front of an audience — especially if you consume the drink or pill 30 to 60 minutes before you're scheduled to speak. Then the fear returns with a vengeance, and it makes the speaking experience much worse instead of better. In addition, you won't be at your best because you'll still be a bit groggy.

In a way, talking to yourself is the flip side of visualizing success — not talking yourself into failure. But it's more than that. Successful visualization techniques apply to a specific task — like giving a speech. Your internal dialogue has a much broader focus. It applies to *everything* you do.

So how can you keep the self-chatter positive? Follow these techniques from Dr. Steven Resnick, a prominent psychiatrist and stress management expert:

✔ **Dispute irrational thoughts.** Say that you have the irrational thought, "If I stand in front of an audience, I'll forget everything I know about the topic." A disputing thought could be "I'll have no reason to remember all that stuff if I *don't* tell it to an audience."

✔ **Use personal affirmations.** "I'm the greatest speaker in the world." "My subject is fascinating and the audience will love it." "I'm an expert." Yes, they're corny, but they build confidence. The more you talk yourself into believing them, the less stress you'll encounter with your speech.

> ✔ **Imagine the worst-case scenario.** Face your fear directly. Think about the worst possible thing that could happen and realize that it's not that awful. If you make a mistake while you're speaking, you can correct it and continue. If the audience doesn't give you a standing ovation, they may still applaud. Even if the speech is a total disaster, it's not the end of the world.

Transforming Terror to Terrific

A man went to the doctor for a physical. He said, "I look in the mirror and I'm a mess. My jowls are sagging. I have blotches all over my face. My hair is falling out. What is it?" The doctor said, "I don't know, but your eyesight is perfect."

Unfortunately, a lot of other people have perfect eyesight, too — especially when it involves examining your physical symptoms of stage fright. But it's not that hard to eliminate or disguise the sweating and shaking.

Discovering stress-busting exercises

Even though stress is technically all in your head, its effects can be quite physical. So if you can't treat your mental state, treat your physical symptoms. Following are some recommendations from prominent stress expert Dr. Steven Resnick.

Breathing

Take a deep breath. Hold it. Hold it. Now let it out slowly. Good. Do it again. Breathe deeply and slowly. Keep it up. Don't you feel better already? Dr. Resnick says breathing exercises are one of the world's oldest techniques for relieving stress. "We release carbon dioxide every time we exhale," he explains. "That decreases the acidity of our blood." It also increases the oxygen in your brain. (And gives a whole new meaning to the term "airhead.")

Stretching

Stretching is a great way to relieve muscle tension quickly, and it doesn't take long to do. Stretching for as little as 10 or 15 seconds can be beneficial. Now, you can't just do yoga in the middle of a banquet when you're the after-dinner speaker, but you can excuse yourself and do a few quick stretches in the restroom just before you speak. Use the following exercises to get you down the home stretch:

- ✔ **Head rolls.** Slowly turn your head from side to side. That's the warm-up. Now move your head clockwise in a circle (look up, right, down, and left). Do this three times and then reverse the direction. You'll feel the tension flowing out of your neck.

- ✔ **Arm lifts.** Stretch your right arm up into the air as far as it will go. Hold it a few seconds. Bring it back to your side. Now stretch your left arm up as far as it will go. Keep repeating the process. In high school, your gym teacher made you do this exercise as a form of torture. Now you're going to do it for relief. It helps stretch out your back.

- ✔ **Jaw breakers.** Open your mouth as wide as possible (as if you're going to scream). Then close your mouth. Keep opening and closing your mouth. This exercise helps relieve tension in the jaw. You can also use your fingers to massage the muscle that joins the jaw and the rest of the head.

Moving around

Some speakers like to take a quick walk or jog in place to get rid of nervous energy. Are there stairs in the building where you'll speak? A few trips up and down some flights of stairs may be helpful, but don't overdo it. You don't want to be sweaty, tired, and out of breath by the time you go on.

Discovering the real secret: Don't look nervous

A little nervousness is good and a lot of nervousness is bad. So you should control your nervousness and keep it at an acceptable level. You do that by following all the standard techniques described in this chapter.

It doesn't really matter how nervous you are — *as long as you appear calm.* As Dr. Allen Weiner puts it, "You have to *look like* you're under control, not *be* under control. As long as the audience thinks you're confident — that's what counts." Use Allen's tips and tricks for disguising some of the common signs of stage fright:

✔ **Fidgeting.** Fidgeting is an announcement that you're anxious. Touching your face with your index finger or rubbing it under your nose or scratching above your lip are all signs of nervousness. The solution: Keep your hands in front of you in the "steeple position." (See Chapter 12] for a description of this position). If you're using a lectern, place your hands on it as if you're playing the piano.

✔ **Pacing.** Pacing is another tip-off of anxiety. The solution: Move closer to the audience and then stop for a moment. Then move somewhere else and stop.

✔ **Sweating.** It's how you handle the sweating that counts. If you take a handkerchief, open it up and swipe at the sweat — you look like a nervous wreck. The solution: Never open the handkerchief. Keep it folded in a square. *Dab* at the sweat and then replace the handkerchief in your pocket.

✔ **Hands shaking.** If your hands are shaking like a leaf, that's a pretty good indication of stage fright. The solution: Use cards rather than sheets of paper for your notes. Paper, which is larger and weighs less than cards, makes your shakiness more apparent. Also, don't hold props or other items that show that your hands are shaking.

Preventing and Handling Stage Fright

Don't be worried about getting stage fright. Just keep the following tips in mind and you'll be ready for anything.

Writing out your intro and conclusion

Nervousness is most intense before you begin speaking. That's why giving special attention to your introduction is important from a stage-fright perspective. It's the most anxiety-producing part of your speech. If you write out your introduction and practice it until you have it down cold, you will reduce your anxiety.

Similar preparation should be given to the conclusion — the second most anxiety-producing part of a speech. (See Chapters 6 and 7 for tips on introductions and conclusions.)

Anticipating problems and preparing solutions

Anticipate any problem that can arise and have a plan ready to deal with it. For example, whenever you stumble over a tongue-twisting name or phrase, you can have an all-purpose recovery line ready, "Let me try that again — in English."

What if you forget what point you were going to cover next? You can buy time by asking the audience a survey question that requires a show of hands. Or you can review what you've already covered. Or you can skip ahead to a different point.

Arriving early

Fear of the unknown probably produces more anxiety than any other cause. Until you get to the site where you're speaking, you face a lot of unknowns. Is the room set up correctly? Did they remember to give you an overhead projector? Plenty of little questions can add up to big sources of stress if you don't have answers for them.

You can get the answers simply by going to the room, so do it early. The earlier you arrive, the more time you have to correct any mistakes and the more time you have to calm down. You also get a chance to meet members of the audience who arrive early, which can reduce stress by making the audience more familiar to you.

Divide and conquer

Many speakers who suffer from stage fright claim that it's a large audience that triggers their fear. A few people, no problem. A big group, forget it. Here's what to do: Look at one face in the audience at a time — especially faces that appear interested in what you're saying. Keep coming back to them. (No, normally you shouldn't stare at only a few people. That's a basic rule of eye contact that I discuss in Chapter 12. But stage fright creates an exception. If the only way you can prevent yourself from passing out is to look at only a few people, then do it.)

Don't apologize for nervousness

Many speakers feel compelled to apologize for being nervous. Don't apologize for making a mistake, flub, or goof-up. Just let it go. You don't want to draw additional attention to your nervousness.

Using your nervousness

Stage fright won't go away, so use it to *improve* your delivery. That means the next time you speak, you'll have adrenaline coursing through your body. And that's not bad. Adrenaline is what gives athletes the strength to hit the ball out of the park during the big game. It's what will give you an extra edge when you speak.

Use your adrenaline rush to give a more animated and enthusiastic performance. Channel your nervous energy into your speech. Believe me, your audience would rather hear and see an "energized" speaker than one who is falling asleep.

Practicing makes perfect — and confident

There's an old saying that familiarity breeds contempt. But when it comes to public speaking familiarity breeds confidence. That's why practicing your speech can help reduce stage fright. Here are a few tips for rehearsing away your fears:

✔ **Rehearse out loud:** The only way that you can tell how your speech will sound is to listen to it. *That means that you have to say it out loud.* Listening to the voice in your head doesn't count — that's not the voice that your audience will hear.

✔ **Simulate real conditions:** The more closely you can simulate actual speaking conditions in your rehearsals, the more confident you will be for the actual event. Use the actual notes that you'll use when you speak. Use the actual clothes that you'll wear. (At least wear them in your dress rehearsal. That's why dress rehearsals are called dress rehearsals.) Will you be using a handheld microphone for your talk? Most people don't have a sound system at home for rehearsal purposes. Don't worry. Here's a tip from the late comedy coach John Cantu: When you practice at home, use a hairbrush to simulate the microphone. The average hairbrush is about the same length as the average handheld mike.

✔ **Time it:** Time your talk. Do it while you're rehearsing in front of an audience. (Audience reactions can affect the length of your talk.) Everyone knows that you should time your entire speech. Timing your speech is the only way to determine whether your talk will fit its assigned time slot. And having that knowledge can relieve a lot of anxiety.

✔ **Rehearse questions and answers:** If you're going to have a question-and-answer period after your speech, being prepared for it is essential for reducing anxiety. Anticipate questions that you may receive. Rehearse your answers. (For more information about this process, see Chapter 13.)

Chapter 12

Body Language: What's Out, What's In, and What's International

In This Chapter

▶ Harnessing the power of body language

▶ Establishing commanding eye contact

▶ Dressing for impact

▶ Positioning yourself physically

▶ Using your voice strategically

*I*t's been said that public speakers should speak up so they can be heard, stand up so they can be seen, and shut up so they can be enjoyed. That advice may be harsh, but it does highlight a very important aspect of public speaking: Much of your talk's impact comes from how you look and sound.

Understanding Body Language

Body language refers to the messages you send through facial expression, posture, and gesture. You don't need a Berlitz course to learn this language. You already use it every day, and most of the meanings are obvious. A smile indicates happiness. A frown means disapproval. Leaning forward means active engagement in the discussion.

What's not as obvious is how *you* employ body language. It's amazing what watching a videotape of yourself reveals. Using this method is the quickest way to improve your body language — because the camera doesn't lie. It reveals movements and gestures that you may not know that you're making. Ask someone to videotape you giving a speech. Then watch the video with the sound off. Common sense tells you most of what you need to correct such as picking your nose while speaking. Other things to keep in mind are facial expressions, posture, and gestures.

Sending a message with facial expressions

If the eyes are the windows to the soul, then the face is the front of the house. Its appearance says a lot. And how you make your face appear says a lot about your message.

The single most important facial expression is the smile. Simply smiling at an audience can create instant rapport anywhere in the world. It is universally understood. Unfortunately, many speakers — particularly business speakers — feel they must wear their "game face" at all times. They're *serious* businesspeople. They have facts and figures. They have bottom-line responsibilities. If they smile, they might seem . . . human.

That's not to say that you should smile all the time. You don't need to be an advertisement for your dentist. In fact, inappropriate smiling can undermine your entire message. The classic example is former President Jimmy Carter. He used to punctuate his sentences with smiles. Every time he finished a sentence, he'd beam a big warm smile at the audience. While the smiles revealed his warm, compassionate nature, they were often disconcerting. He'd be talking about nuclear war and the need for disarmament and the threat of global annihilation. And he'd smile after each sentence. What was wrong with *that* picture?

Use your face to accentuate key points. Act out what you're saying. Are you incredulous about a statistic you've just cited? Raise your eyebrows in disbelief. Are you briefing the audience on a strategy that you disagree with? Frown. Are you telling a group of kindergarten students that they will be getting more homework in first grade? Stick your tongue out at them. (Just kidding. And sticking your tongue out is highly offensive in some cultures. More on that later.)

Punctuating your speech with posture

Your mother was right. You should always stand up straight —
especially when you're giving a speech. An audience may think a
speaker with sloppy posture is lazy, sick, or tired. On the other
hand, an audience thinks of a speaker with good posture as upright,
a straight arrow, a straight shooter, or a stand-up person. Every
speech involves a lot of posturing. Make yours the anatomical kind.

The following tips can help you maintain perfect posture:

- **Stand up straight with your feet slightly apart and your arms
  ready to gesture.** This is the basic, preferred posture for any
  speech.

- **Lean slightly toward the audience.** Leaning forward shows
  that you're actively engaged with audience members. Leaning
  back signals retreat.

- **Lean on the podium only once in a while for effect.** Planting
  yourself on the podium makes you look weak.

- **Avoid standing with your hands on your hips.** You'll come
  across as a bossy gym teacher. Besides, doing so makes you
  look like you're leading a game of Simon Says. Instead, use
  your hands to make gestures that enhance your message.

- **Avoid swaying back and forth.** Unless you're talking about
  how to use a metronome or discussing the finer points of sea-
  sickness, no one wants to watch you sway back and forth. It's
  very distracting. Keep your trunk stationary from the waist up.

- **Avoid standing with your arms folded across your chest.**
  You'll look like a goon from a gangster movie. What are you
  going to do? Beat up the audience? Besides, you should be
  using your arms to gesture and emphasize your points.

- **Avoid standing with your arms behind your back.** It's a tad
  limiting on your ability to gesture. And if you clasp your hands
  together, it makes you look like you've been handcuffed and
  arrested. Let the audience see your hands as you use them to
  emphasize points in your speech.

- **Avoid standing in the fig leaf position.** That's when a speaker
  holds both hands together over his or her crotch — like the
  fig leaves that Adam and Eve wore. It's fine if you're posing for

a Renaissance-style painting of blushing modesty, but it looks really stupid in any other circumstance. It's like you've just discovered your nakedness (or lack of anything intelligent to say), and you want to hide it from your audience. Instead, use your hands to augment your message with gestures.

✔ **Avoid burying your hands in your pockets.** People will wonder what they're doing down there. It's okay to put one hand in your pocket from time to time. But don't park it there. It prevents you from using your hands to gesture.

Giving the right message with gestures

A cynic once suggested that speakers who don't know what to do with their hands should try clamping them over their mouths. That suggestion, though mean-spirited, does highlight a common problem for speakers — what to do with your hands. You can't get around the fact that you have to do *something* with them. And your choice has important consequences for your speech.

Using gestures properly in a speech means breaking one of your mother's basic rules: You *don't* want to keep your hands to yourself. You want to share them with your audience. How do you do that? Just follow these simple guidelines and you'll do fine:

✔ **Create opportunities to use gestures.** If you're worried that gestures won't occur to you naturally, then stack the deck in your favor. Include a few items in your talk that beg for gestures. Talk about alternative courses of action — "on the one hand . . . and on the other hand." Talk about how large or small something is. Talk about how many points you'll make and hold up your fingers. (This technique works best if the number is ten or less.)

✔ **Vary your gestures.** If you make the same gestures over and over, you start to look like a robot. And the predictability lowers audience attention levels. Don't let your gestures fall into a pattern. Keep the audience guessing. It keeps them watching. Check out your gesturing habits by taking a videotape of yourself, hit play then fast forward. You can easily see where gestures are repetitive or overdone.

✓ **Put your hands in the steeple position.** Your hands really will take care of themselves as you speak. But if you insist on guidance, here's what to do — put your hands in the steeple position. Just put them together in front of you as if you're applauding. That's the steeple position. Now you don't keep them like that. It's just a rest stop. As you talk, your hands will naturally split apart from the steeple. Sometimes they split widely. Sometimes they split narrowly. The steeple position places your hands in a position where they'll move without your thinking about them. However, too many speakers keep their hands glued together in that position for much too long.

✓ **Make your gestures fit the space.** A common mistake speakers make is transferring gestures used in small, intimate settings to large, formal settings. For example, people at a cocktail party gesture by moving their arms from the elbow to the end of the hand. But if you're speaking to a large audience in a large space, you must adjust your gestures. You must open them up and make them larger. Are you going to emphasize a point? Move your arms from the *shoulders* to the ends of your hands instead of from the elbows.

✓ **Make bold gestures.** Your gestures should communicate confidence and authority. Tentative, half-hearted attempts at gesturing make you look weak and indecisive. Get your hands up. (No, I'm not about to rob you.) You'll look more assured if your hands are higher than your elbows. Be bold. Don't use a finger if a fist is more dramatic. Watch the Sunday morning evangelists on television. They know how to gesture with authority.

✓ **Think about your gestures ahead of time, but don't memorize them.** Think about the gestures you'll use. Think about where they might fit into your speech. But don't plan them out in specific detail. And don't memorize them. It's obvious if you've memorized them, and it just looks dumb.

✓ **Avoid these types of speakers:**

 • **The banker:** These speakers keep rattling coins in their pockets. They sound like a change machine. It's very distracting.

 • **The optician:** These speakers constantly adjust their glasses. They're on. They're off. They're slipping down their noses. Do everyone a favor and get some contact lenses.

- **The tailor:** These speakers fiddle with their clothing. The tie is a big object of affection for male speakers in this category. They twist it. And pinch it. And rub it. No one listens to the talk. We're all waiting to see if the speaker will choke himself.

- **The jeweler:** These speakers fiddle with their jewelry. Necklaces are a big attraction for female speakers in this category. And you'll find ring twisters from both sexes.

- **The lonely lover:** These speakers hug themselves. It looks really weird. They stand up in front of the audience and hug themselves while they speak. They lose a lot of credibility.

- **The beggar:** These speakers clasp their hands together and thrust them toward the audience as if they're begging for something. They probably are — a miracle.

- **The hygienist:** These speakers keep rubbing their hands together like they're washing them. It looks weird for a few reasons. There's no soap. No water. No sink. And a bunch of people called an audience is watching.

- **The toy maker:** These speakers love to play with their little toys — pens, markers, pointers — whatever happens to be around. They turn them in their hands. They squeeze them. And they distract the audience.

- **The bug collector:** These speakers keep pulling at the hair on the backs of their necks or their heads. Yes, the audience knows it's just a nervous habit, but they still wonder when was the last time you washed your hair.

Going international

As if public speaking wasn't already tough enough, it takes on a whole new level of difficulty when you address audiences from other nations. Cultural differences come into play. And navigating the proprieties of appropriate body language is as simple as walking through a minefield without a map.

To get through your speech without offense, start by following one basic rule: Remember that body language isn't universal, so how do you know if your body language will be offensive? To answer that question, I spoke with Allen Weiner, President of Communication Development Associates in Woodland Hills, California. He's spent the last 25 years coaching business executives around the world on how to be more effective communicators. He also runs www.essessnet.com, a Web-based service that provides executives, managers and employees with feedback about their communication abilities. "If you compare the feedback from Americans, Europeans and Asians, the differences standout immediately," says Allen.

Here are his general guidelines for using body language successfully when you speak around the globe:

- ✔ **Speaking to a European audience:** European audiences prefer a more formal style, and that's reflected in a low-key use of body language. "Europeans don't like the high-energy style with emphatic gestures and lots of walking back and forth across the stage favored by Americans," he explains. "They consider that type of delivery shallow and it lowers the speaker's credibility." He also points out that Europeans always stand while speaking. "In the U.S., it's becoming common for a speaker to speak from a sitting position at a conference table while showing PowerPoint slides," Allen says. "A European speaker would never do that."

- ✔ **Speaking to a North American audience:** North American audiences appreciate an animated style of delivery. "Think of a bell-shaped curve going from flat to carbonated to over-carbonated," explains Allen. "With a North American audience you can approach the over-carbonated zone. That means your gestures can be bigger and more passionate." A good example is moving your hands apart to emphasize a point. According to Allen, you could move your hands apart the width of a basketball if speaking to North Americans. For a European audience it would be the width of a baseball.

- ✔ **Speaking to an Asian audience:** The body language rules that apply when speaking to North American audience will generally apply to Asian audiences. "Asians like the North American style," says Allen. He also notes that Asian audiences will be attentive and respectful even if the speaker isn't good.

- ✔ **Speaking to a South American audience:** South American audiences like a speaker who is decisive says Allen. That means gestures and movement can be expansive and emphatic. "You can spread your hands apart a little more than the width of a basketball while gesturing," he observes. "On my 'carbonation curve,' you can move into slightly over-carbonated."

These general guidelines can help you plan a speech to international audiences, but the only way to be sure that specific gestures won't be offensive is to talk with people from that culture before your speech.

Making Eye Contact Count

At some point in many old tear-jerker romantic movies, the heroine tells the hero (or vice versa) that she doesn't love him anymore. (Usually the villain has forced this situation upon them.) The violins rise up strongly on the soundtrack. The camera pans in for a close-up. Shock and disbelief register across the hero's face. And inevitably he utters this immortal line: "Look me in the eye and say that." In other words, it's not true until she says it while making eye contact.

"If looks could kill." We've all been glad they can't when we've been on the receiving end of this statement, but when you give a speech, looks *can* kill. Depending on what you do or don't look at, looks can kill your entire speech. Use the following rules to prevent yourself from committing a capital offense:

- **Look at individuals.** As you gaze around the room, make eye contact with as many individuals as possible. A common myth is to pick out a friendly face and look at it. That gets weird fast. This poor person wonders why you're staring at him or her, and so does the rest of the audience. Look at a variety of individuals. Remember, you want to be a search light, not a laser beam.

- **Establish eye contact at the end of a thought.** Eye contact is most effective at the end of a thought. People will nod their heads under the pressure of your gaze, and that's a big plus. Because of the structure of English sentences, the important information is usually in the second half of the sentence; so, making eye contact at the end of a thought emphasizes the important part. In other words, you force people to nod when you make a point. That nodding doesn't automatically mean that they agree with you, but it subconsciously forces the audience in that direction.

- **Look at the audience, not everywhere else.** If you look out the window, so will your audience. This is also true for looking at the ceiling, the walls, or the floor. The audience plays follow the leader, and you're the leader. So, look at them so they'll look at you.

- **Look at more than one spot.** Make sure that you establish eye contact with all parts of your audience. Cover the entire room. If you look straight ahead and never look toward the sides or if you look only at the people toward the front, you risk losing a major portion of your audience because everyone towards the side and in the back feels left out. No, you don't want your head to look like a machine gun pivoting back and forth as it sprays eye contact at the crowd. But you do want to keep your gaze rotating from one part of the audience to another.

✔ **Spend more time looking at the audience rather than your notes.** Some speakers get so hung up looking at their notes that they don't look at their audience. Big mistake. The notes aren't going to applaud when you're done. And neither will the audience if you haven't looked at them. What can you do? First, make sure your notes are easy to read — large print, legible, only a few key words per card. Second, watch how your favorite TV news anchors read from their notes. They look down. They read the notes. They look up. They look into the camera. They tell you one thought. Then they repeat the process. Head up. Head down. Head up. Head down. (Just don't do it too fast or you'll look like one of those little statues you see in the rear window of a car.)

✔ **Look at the noses of the audience if you're nervous, not over their heads.** A big myth that originated in a lot of grade school public speaking classes is that it's okay to gaze over the heads of your audience. But people can tell if you're speaking to the clock on the back wall. And the smaller the audience, the more obvious this technique becomes. If you're too nervous to look in your audience's eyes, just look at the tips of their noses — it works.

Dressing to Impress

A single article of clothing can change your entire image and have a large effect on how an audience receives your message. When Dan Rather first became anchor of the *CBS Evening News,* his ratings weren't as high as desired. He was perceived as too stiff, especially when compared with his predecessor, the legendary Walter Cronkite. The problem was partially solved when Rather began wearing a sweater under his jacket. It softened his image and improved his ratings.

Although it may not be politically correct, people make all kinds of judgments based on clothes. It's human nature. Many studies of retail outlets have shown that well-dressed customers receive better service than poorly dressed customers. And the same goes for making speeches. Your attire is part of your message, and it should augment what you say, not detract from it.

Getting the right image across

Use the following handy tips to help you dress appropriately for any speaking engagement:

✔ **Dress conservatively (especially in Europe, Asia, and South America).** You want your audience to focus on you — not on what you're wearing. Even more important, informal attire may lower your credibility with audiences outside the United States.

✔ **Shine your shoes.** The audience will look at them — especially if you're on a stage.

✔ **Wear comfortable clothes.** That doesn't mean old clothes or informal clothes. It means that maybe the time to break in that new pair of shoes isn't the day you're giving your speech.

✔ **Keep the pencils, pens, and markers from peeking out of your shirt or jacket pockets.** It makes you look like a nerd.

✔ **Wear jewelry that won't distract the audience.** Distraction is defined as when your jewelry is louder than you are (both to the eye and ear).

✔ **Leave your purse somewhere other than the podium.** It's a distraction. Ask a trusted member of the audience to guard it.

✔ **Keep bulky stuff out of your pockets.** Remember Mae West's famous line, "Is that a pistol in your pocket or are you just happy to see me?" You don't want the audience wondering what's in your pockets, whether you're a man or a woman; you want them wondering what you're going to say next.

Dressing for informal meetings

Say that you're speaking at an event where the audience will be dressed casually — golf clothes, shorts, T-shirts, and maybe even bathing suits. Is it okay for you to dress casually? Great minds diverge, but if it's a business event, I say "No." Wear business clothes. I always do — even if the meeting planner says that it's not necessary. Even if the whole audience is wearing beach attire. (Beach attire isn't that unusual. Many companies hold management or sales retreats at oceanfront hotels where meetings are followed by recreation.)

Here's why you ought to wear business clothes: The audience takes your message more seriously if you wear business clothes. And speakers who dress casually may fall into the trap of speaking too casually. Besides, I don't look that great in a bathing suit.

The exception is when you're also a member of the audience you're addressing. Say that a group of managers is dressed in golf clothes because golf is scheduled right after the meeting. You're one of the managers in the meeting, so you'll be playing golf just like everyone else, and you're scheduled to make a speech during the meeting. In that situation, you probably want to be wearing golf clothes. *Not* wearing them would seem odd and detract from your talk.

Whatever the situation, the criterion is always identical. What attire will most enhance your message? That's what you should wear.

Mastering Physical Positioning and Movement

Although you may have your intro down cold and think you are totally prepared to give your speech, you may have forgotten that getting to and from the podium, as well as standing and moving when you are there have important consequences for your speech. So check out the tips I provide in the sections below to make sure your speech gets started on the right foot.

Managing entrances and exits

When Gerald Ford was president of the United States, he made headlines around the world by emerging from a plane, waving to the crowd and then falling down the steps to the tarmac before giving a speech. Not a good entrance. Not how you want your entrances, or exits, to be remembered.

Getting onstage with class

The beginning of a speech is its most critical part. Everyone knows that. But when does it begin? This is a question of great philosophical dispute. Does it begin when you start speaking? When you walk to the podium? When you enter the room?

Great minds disagree, but I say play it safe. I believe your speech starts when you leave your home. The next few paragraphs walk you through how you should begin your speech, starting from home.

After you leave your home, you never know when a member of your audience may see you. And if you're observed engaging in some questionable activity, your image may suffer. When you ascend the stage to speak, you want to project an aura of confidence and command. You want to be all-powerful. You don't want any audience members to recall that an hour ago they saw you picking your teeth in the parking lot or tailgating them on the freeway.

Get to the room early and make sure that the podium, microphone, and any audiovisual equipment are arranged properly. Pay particular attention to microphone cords and power cords. You don't want to open your talk by tripping and falling. If you're speaking on a stage, check where the stairs are located. Plan your route to the podium and practice it before your speech if possible.

While you're waiting to speak, listen attentively to any speakers preceding you. When you're introduced, rise confidently and walk assuredly to the podium. Shaking hands with the person who introduced you is optional. (Unless the person extends his or her hand!)

When you arrive at the podium, place your notes where you want them. Open them. Look out at the audience. Pause. Then give one heck of a speech.

Getting offstage in style

Saying the last words of your speech is only the beginning of the end. You still have a lot to do. And that doesn't mean hurriedly gathering up your notes and getting the heck out of there. First and foremost, you must bask in the thundering ovation that your audience will no doubt deliver. (If, for some unfathomable reason, they're not immediately forthcoming with applause, then you can give them a hint. At least that's what I do. On the rare occasions when a deafening roar of approval doesn't greet my closing, I make a short bowing motion. They usually get the message.)

After you've accepted your ovation (and answered any questions), you must disconnect yourself from the microphone (if you were using a lavaliere or wireless). Many speakers forget this step, and it can be quite embarrassing. Even if you don't wear the mike into the bathroom, everyone still hears you breathing, and you lose credibility.

After the microphone is detached, gather your speaking materials and depart from the podium in a confident manner. Stride purposefully back to your seat. Smile and acknowledge audience kudos along the way. If you're followed by another speaker, become a model audience member. Wait expectantly for the speaker with your full attention directed at the podium.

Act this way even if you've just given the world's worst speech. It's amazing how people will give you the reaction you ask for. If *you* act like the speech was a success (even if it wasn't), there's a better than average chance that the audience will play along. It makes *everybody* feel better.

You're never really finished until you've left the site of your speech, you no longer have contact with any audience members (such as in a hotel bar after your talk), and you're home in bed.

Moving around

American wit Franklin P. Jones once observed, "Veteran speakers usually gesture vigorously and walk around. A moving target is harder to hit." Maybe so. But a moving speaker has a better chance of *being* a hit. Movement helps maintain audience attention. Of course, speakers who move endlessly and erratically will distract from their message. Follow these tips to have all the right moves:

✔ **Use up and down movements.** Find a reason to bend over close to the floor or reach up into the air. Watch the televangelists on Sunday morning. They kneel down. They point up. This kind of movement makes you look more interesting to the audience.

✔ **Move purposefully.** Make every movement count. Whether you're gesturing, changing position, or walking from one location to another, the movement must support your message. Pacing is an example of *non*-purposeful movement that you should avoid.

✔ **Be aware of audience depth perception.** If you're speaking from a stage in a large room, moving left or right has much more impact than moving forward or back. (It has to do with depth perception. Don't ask me to explain it.) This is important to remember because it goes against instinct. You may assume that moving toward or away from the audience has the bigger effect. It doesn't. A step forward or back doesn't have half the impact of a step left or right. Keep that in mind when you want to emphasize a point.

✔ **Move in an irregular pattern.** A major value of movement is that it helps maintain audience attention. But moving in a regular pattern has an opposite effect. The predictability of any regular pattern lulls the audience into a semihypnotic state (also known as sleep). You want to keep moving. Just make sure no one else knows where you're going.

✔ **Avoid making nervous movements.** Speakers who constantly pull at their hair, shift from foot to foot, play with their notes, scratch themselves, and adjust their clothes are very distracting. So avoid those types of nervous movements —. Don't be a perpetual motion machine. You'll end up looking very nervous or like you have to go the bathroom. Either way, the audience won't focus on what you're saying.

Getting into the power position

For those of you dragging out a yoga mat now, when I say *power position* I'm talking about the *power position* when you're speaking from a stage. To find the *power position,* divide the stage into a nine-square grid: back left, back center, back right, left center, center center, right center, front right, front center, front left. The *power position* is front center.

But don't just stand there. Move into different squares as you speak. If you want a mechanical formula, find cues in your talk that suggest moves. "I was in a cattle store looking at bulls. And over on the right I saw (move to a square on the right) a beautiful set of china teacups. I took one to the proprietor (move into another square) and I said, 'Is this the famous china in a bull shop?'" (Now you better move to a rear square because with puns like that, the audience may start throwing things.)

This process of moving from square to square is called making an active stage picture. It ensures that you don't just stand in one place, and it makes you more interesting for the audience to watch. Just remember to return frequently to the power square.

Working from a podium

Many people believe that podiums act as a barrier between the speaker and the audience — as in, the speaker is "hiding" behind the podium. So, many public speaking teachers, communication coaches, and other professional presenter types give this advice: Don't use one. And if you do use a podium, get out from behind it as often as possible.

The big deal that's made out of the podium being a barrier is a lot of baloney. My advice: If you want to use a podium, go right ahead.

There are two reasons why you may want to use a podium, and the first is common sense:

- **If you're comfortable behind a podium and nervous in front of it, then stay behind it.** You'll give a better speech. There's no point getting out from behind the podium to "eliminate a barrier with your audience" if doing so creates a bigger barrier — stage fright (see Chapter 11 for more on stage fright).

- **The "barrier" argument is a myth.** Allen Weiner, President of Communication Development Associates, says that a speaker's first connection with an audience is facial expression and eye contact. "I've seen studies," he says, "where the speaker's facial expressions and eye contact were so good that two weeks later the audience didn't remember whether a podium had been used." What about the argument that stepping away from the podium every so often gets attention because it eliminates the barrier? Allen's response: "It doesn't get attention because they can now see your whole body. It gets attention because it's a change. You've been standing behind the podium for awhile. Suddenly you're not. Any change gets attention."

Here's one more thing to think about: When the president of the United States gives a speech, he always uses a podium. John F. Kennedy and Ronald Reagan gave pretty good speeches — some of the best in this century. If a podium was good enough for them, don't worry about using one if it makes you feel comfortable.

Using the podium effectively

Just like anything else you do while giving your speech, using a podium does have guidelines; check them out below:

- **Use the podium as a strategic tool.** The podium doesn't just have to be a place where you dump your notes and make your speech. It can play a much more active role in your talk. Timing is a perfect example. Comedian George Burns used a cigar as a timing device. He puffed when he needed a pause for effect. Executive communications counselor Jim Lukaszewski uses a podium. "If I walk into the audience and make a point I want them to think about, they can't unless I stop talking," he says. So what does he do? He makes his point, turns his back to the audience, walks back to the podium. The time it takes him to move around allows the audience to think about the point he made. Jim plans these moments in advance just like George Burns planned when he'd puff his cigar. You can, too.

✔ **Look at your notes while you're moving behind the podium.** Want to disguise your reliance on notes? Look at your notes whenever you move. When you make a gesture, shift position, or turn your head, take a quick peek at your notes. Like a magician's hand, the audience will focus on your movement rather than what you're actually doing — reading.

✔ **Use a podium to "hide" when appropriate.** Even if you don't like to stay behind a podium, sometimes you may need to draw audience attention to something other than yourself. Are you using slides, overheads, or a volunteer from the audience? Standing behind a podium makes perfect sense for these situations, especially if the podium is placed off to the side.

✔ **Avoid pressing or gripping the podium.** It's okay to use a podium — but not as a crutch. When I taught speech at USC, I had a student who wanted to do a reverse bench press with the podium. His hands were placed palms down on the podium, and he looked like he was trying to push it through the floor. He did this through his entire speech. It was a tad distracting.

The other common mistake is gripping the podium for dear life — like you'll float away if you let go. Again, it's disconcerting for the audience, because it's an obvious indication of stage fright. Instead of concentrating on what the speaker is saying, the audience is mentally placing bets on when he or she will pass out.

Paralanguage: What Your Voice Says about You

A popular radio commercial says that people judge you by the words you use. Well, they also judge by how you use them. Do you say the words loudly? Rapidly? Monotonously? Do you have an accent? Do you mispronounce them? All of these factors — *how* you say things, *not what* you say — are known as *paralanguage*.

My friend Loyd Auerbach is a corporate trainer for LexisNexis, as well as a professional mentalist, so he makes a lot of speeches. The following are some of his tricks and tips for using your voice.

✔ **Warm up your voice.** You're about to speak. You're opening line is a gem. People will be quoting it for years. You're introduced. You get to the podium. You open your mouth to deliver your bon mots and . . . your voice cracks. So much for the brilliant opening. That's why you need to warm up your voice. Go into the bathroom before you speak and do some vocal exercises. Hum. Talk to yourself. Get your voice going. (But make sure that no one is in there with you. You *don't* want anyone in the audience to remember you as the person talking to himself in the bathroom.) *Singing For Dummies* by Pamelia S. Phillips (John Wiley Publishing, Inc.) has several excellent exercises for warming up your voice that work just as well for speaking as they do for singing.

✔ **Pronounce your words clearly.** You know that it's not polite to speak with your mouth full. Well, it's also not polite to sound like you're speaking with your mouth full — especially if you have an audience. It's hard enough for one person to understand another even when they each know exactly what was said. Don't make it even more difficult. Pronounce your words clearly.

✔ **Get rid of filler sounds and phrases.** Filler sounds and phrases take up space for no reason, sound dumb, and distract the audience from your message. Banish these words and phrases from your vocal vocabulary: like, you know, um, okay, ugh, ah, actually, interestingly enough.

✔ **Use vocal variety.** Monotony refers to more than just tone of voice. Yes, a monotonous voice may be the result of speaking in one tone. But it may also result from speaking at one rate of speed, in one volume, or in one pitch. If you're monotonous in any of those ways, you have a problem. If you're monotonous in all of those ways, the audience will fall asleep. The cure is vocal variety.

✔ **Use your voice for emphasis.** You can completely alter the meaning of a sentence simply by changing the words you emphasize. Say the following line aloud and emphasize the word in italics. "Are you talking to *me?*" "Are *you* talking to me?" "Are you *talking* to me?" Alright, enough with the Robert DeNiro impressions. You get the idea. Use vocal emphasis to reinforce the meanings you want to communicate.

✔ **Slow down for flubs.** No, this isn't a road sign from Burma Shave. It refers to flubs you make when you speak. No one is perfect. Everyone makes mistakes. (You can quote me on that. It's a real insight, right?) Inevitably, you will mispronounce a word or stumble through a tongue-twisting phrase. The natural instinct is to speed up when you make a mistake. Don't. It highlights your error and increases your chances for making additional errors. Just slow down.

✔ **Use volume as a tool.** Volume is a powerful tool that's easy to manipulate. It may be tough to change your pitch or tone, but anyone can speak more loudly or softly. And it can have an amazing effect on an audience.

Many speakers think you should never speak softly. Wrong. Speaking softly can be incredibly effective. I've seen speakers whisper and draw in an entire audience. People lean forward in their seats. How can they hear? If you're speaking into a microphone, it doesn't matter if you speak softly. That's the whole point of using the microphone — it allows you to speak in a full range of volumes.

Speaking at a high volume can also be used dramatically. At a point in one of my speeches, I talk about a man who's engaged in a full-scale domestic squabble (furniture being thrown around and stuff like that). A police officer rings his doorbell, and he yells, "Who is it?" When I tell this story, I calmly and quietly describe the police officer ringing the doorbell. Then I scream, "Who is it?" into the microphone. The audience is always stunned. It gets their attention.

Any time you shift your volume, people will pay attention. It's an easy way to vary your speech pattern. So use it.

✔ **Use pauses.** A common mistake among inexperienced (and nervous) speakers is to speak without pausing. They just rush through their talks, one thought merging into another. The audience *listens* to a lot of words but doesn't *hear* a thing. They become clogged with information.

The pause is a vital part of the communication process. "It leaves time for the meaning of what's been said to sink in," explains speech guru Jim Lukaszewski. "And it clears the way for the importance of what comes next." He also notes that pausing before a change of subject, major point, or interesting fact creates an impression of confidence. Pausing also highlights the point. Loyd Auerbach believes a pause should always precede an important point. In fact, he suggests actively looking for opportunities to build pauses into your speech.

So don't be afraid to pause. And don't forget: Your audience members are like a bunch of McDonald's customers — they deserve a break today.

Chapter 13

Handling Questions

. . . .

In This Chapter

▶ Checking out some basic guidelines

▶ Designing a perfect answer

▶ Answering questions with six techniques

▶ Responding to common types of questions

▶ Dealing with special situations

▶ Discovering how to handle hostile questions

. . . .

A professor traveled from university to university speaking about quantum physics. One day his chauffeur said, "Professor, I've heard your lecture so many times I could give it myself." The professor said, "Fine. Give it tonight." When they got to the university, the chauffeur was introduced as the professor. The chauffeur delivered the lecture, and nobody knew the difference. Afterward, someone in the audience asked a long question about Boolean algebra and quantum mechanics. The chauffeur didn't miss a beat. He said, "I can't believe you asked that question. It's so simple, I'm going to let my chauffeur answer it."

Unfortunately, most people don't have a chauffeur who can answer tough questions. So you have to drive yourself through the maze known as the question-and-answer period. Many speakers let their guard down during this period. It's a big mistake. Even if you gave a great speech, a poor performance during the question and answer (Q&A) period can totally change the audience's perceptions of you and your topic. On the other hand, if you're speech was mediocre, a strong performance during the Q&A can leave the audience with a very positive impression. So, read the rest of this chapter to make sure you give a great performance during the Q&A (but read the rest of this book to make sure the rest of your speech is a hit, too!)

Discovering the Basics

If you want to give a sparkling performance during a question and answer session, you can stack the odds in your favor by following a few basic rules.

Anticipating questions

As any high school student can tell you, the secret to giving brilliant answers is knowing the questions in advance. In some circles, this is called clairvoyance. (In high school, it's called cheating.) In my system, it's called anticipation. You anticipate the questions that you'll be asked.

Just use your common sense to anticipate questions. Think about your speech and your audience. Then generate a list of every possible question that the audience may ask. Don't pull any punches. Think of the toughest questions that may come up. Then ask your friends and colleagues to think of the toughest questions they can devise.

After you've compiled a comprehensive list of questions, prepare an answer for each one. Practice until you've got them down cold. With a little on-the-spot tweaking, they may also help you answer questions that you didn't anticipate.

Answering questions at the end

It's generally better to take questions *after* you've made your speech than while you're giving it. If you take questions during your speech, it distracts both you and the audience, it makes your speech harder to follow, and it ruins your rhythm. (It's always a thrill when someone asks a question just as you're building to the climax of your most dramatic story.) Tell the audience in the beginning that you will take questions at the end.

Avoiding letting a few people dominate

Every so often, you get an audience from which one or two people ask questions — endlessly. The moment you finish answering their first questions, they're asking others. Whatever their motivation, it's not your job to play 20 questions with them. You want to have a conversation with the *entire* audience, not just one or two members of it.

You want to take questions from as many different audience members as time permits. Don't let a couple of people ask all the questions, unless they're the only ones with questions. It just frustrates everyone else whose hand is raised, wanting to ask you something. Eventually such audience members just give up.

And be fair. Don't favor one section of the room over another. The best approach is to try to call on people in the order in which they raised their hands. Don't give in to bullies who don't wait their turn and instead shout out questions. It's the oral equivalent of cutting ahead in line, and it's definitely not fair to the people who have been patiently waiting for you to call on them.

 Establish the ground rules early. When you open the session up for questions, tell the audience that everyone will initially be limited to a single question. Then if time permits, you'll take a second round of questions.

Letting the questioner ask a question, not give a speech

You just asked for questions. Despite the fact that you're standing at a podium and you've just made a lengthy speech, someone in the audience will want to give one, too. There's one in every crowd, and it's your job to make sure they don't give a speech.

You're the speaker. You opened up the session for questions — not speeches. When one of these people starts giving a speech, you must cut it off. How do you do it? Watch CNN star Larry King. Callers to his show are supposed to ask questions to his guests. If a caller launches into a speech, King immediately says, "Will you state your question, please?" If you want to be more diplomatic, say "Do you have a question?" If you want to be very diplomatic, you can gently interrupt the person and suggest a question: "So what you're really asking is. . . ." (If the reply is, "No, that's not what I'm asking," then immediately say, "Will you state your question, please?")

Listening to the question

If you want to be successful in a question and answer period, then you need to listen. I mean *really* listen. By really listening, I mean go below the surface of the words used by the questioner; read between the lines; watch the body language; and listen to the tone of voice. Doing so enables you to identify what the questioner is really asking. Yes, it's exhausting, (and you still have to look fresh and dapper — see Chapter 12 for more on appearance), but your answers will be infinitely better if you really listen to every question.

Repeating the question

One of the biggest mistakes speakers make is *not* repeating the question, and it's an enormous mistake. There's nothing more frustrating than giving a brilliant answer to a question that wasn't asked.

There are three major reasons why you should *always* repeat the question:

1. You make sure that everyone in the audience heard the question.

2. You make sure that *you* heard the question correctly.

3. You buy yourself some time to think about your answer. (If you want even more time, rephrase the question slightly and say, "Is that the essence of what you're asking?")

If a question is lengthy or confusing, don't repeat it word for word. Rephrase it so that it's concise and understandable.

Guessing isn't the answer

If you don't know the answer to a question, never guess. *Never.* It's a one-way ticket to zero credibility. Once in awhile you may get lucky, beat the odds, and bluff the audience. But most of the time, someone will call your bluff. Then you have a big problem. First, you'll be exposed as not knowing the answer you claim to know. More important, the audience members wonder if you bluffed about anything else.

If you don't know, admit it. Then take one, some, or all of the following actions:

- ✔ Ask if anyone in the audience can answer the question.

- ✔ Suggest a resource where the questioner can find the answer.

- ✔ Offer to discover the answer yourself and get it to the questioner.

Remember, nobody knows everything (except my grandmother).

Ending the Q&A strongly

The Q&A session is your last chance to influence audience opinion —
of your topic, your ideas, and you. So you want a strong ending.
Keep these two things in mind:

> ✔ **End the session on a high note.** Don't wait for audience ques-
> tions to peter out and say, "Well, I guess that's it." You'll look
> weak and not in control.

> ✔ **Make sure the last question you get is one that you can
> answer.** Don't say, "We only have time for one more question."
> It may be a question you can't answer or handle well. Again, it
> will make you look weak.

After you've answered a reasonable number of questions, start
looking for an opportunity to end the session. Wait till you get a
question that you answer brilliantly. Then announce that time has
run out. Of course, you'll be happy to stick around and speak with
anyone who still has a question.

What if you don't get any questions that you can answer brilliantly?
Don't worry. Just make the last question one that you ask yourself.
"Thank you. We've run out of time. Well, actually you're probably
still wondering about [fill in your question]." Then give your brilliant answer. It works every time.

One more word (actually four more words) about ending the Q&A
session: End it on time. Some audience members come solely for
your speech. They don't care about the Q&A. (Or they don't care
about the questions being asked.) So stick to the schedule. You can
make yourself available afterward for anyone who wants to keep
the discussion going.

Coming Up with a Perfect Answer

It's been said that experts are people who know all the right
answers — if they're asked the right questions. Unfortunately, your
audience may not always ask the right questions. This section presents some ways to make sure your answers will be expert, no matter
what you're asked.

Treating the questioner properly

Questioners may be rude, obnoxious, opinionated, egomaniacal, inane, obtuse, antagonistic, befuddled, illiterate, or incomprehensible. You still have to treat them nicely. Why? Because they're members of the audience, and the audience identifies with them — at least initially. Use these suggestions for dealing with someone who asks you a question:

✔ **Assist a nervous questioner.** Some audience members who ask questions may suffer from stage fright. These people want to ask their question so much that they try to ignore their pounding hearts, sweaty palms, and stomach cramps. As they ask their questions, they try to forget that all eyes in the room are on them, but it's often difficult to ignore this situation. So it's not unusual for anxious audience members to have trouble getting out their questions. They'll stammer and stutter, they'll lose their train of thought, and they'll make the rest of the audience extremely uncomfortable. So help these people out. Finish asking their questions for them if you can. Otherwise, offer some gentle encouragement. By breaking in and speaking yourself, you give nervous questioners time to collect themselves. They'll be grateful. And so will everyone else.

✔ **Wait for the questioner to finish.** Unless the questioners are rambling or they're nervous and need help, let them finish asking their questions. Too many speakers jump in before the question is fully stated. They *think* they know what the question is, and they start giving an answer. They look very foolish when the questioner interrupts saying, "That's not what I was asking."

✔ **Recognize the questioner by name.** If you know the name of the person asking the question, use it. This has a powerful effect on the audience. It makes you seem much more knowledgeable and in control. And the people whose names you say love the recognition.

✔ **Compliment the questioner, if appropriate.** If the question is particularly interesting or intelligent, it's okay to say so. But be specific and say why. Some communication gurus advise never to say, "Good question" because it implies that the other questions weren't. If you're worried about this, then say, "That's an especially interesting question because. . . ." This statement implies that the other questions were interesting — a compliment. It also eliminates all the value judgments attached to the word "good."

✔ **Treat the questioner with dignity.** Remember your grade school teacher saying there's no such thing as a dumb question? She was wrong. There are plenty of dumb questions, and speakers get asked them all the time. But you don't want to be the one to point them out. No matter how idiotic the query, treat the questioner with dignity. If you go into a scathing riff about the stupidity of the question, you make yourself look bad, generate sympathy for the questioner, and discourage anyone else from asking a question.

✔ **Look fascinated as they ask their questions.** It can take a lot of guts to rise out of the anonymity of the audience to ask a question, so don't discourage questioners by looking bored or condescending while they're speaking. Even if you think the question is imbecilic, look fascinated. Shower each questioner with attention. Give full eye contact. Lean forward. Show that your most important priority is listening to the question. Nothing is more insulting or dispiriting than a speaker who looks around the audience for the next question while the current question is being asked. And it's not only the questioner who gets offended. The whole audience picks up on the negative nonverbal message.

✔ **Stay calm and in control.** No matter how offensive the question or questioner, don't attack him. Use diplomacy and finesse to dispose of such annoyances. If the questioner is a major jerk, the audience will recognize it. Don't become a jerk yourself by getting defensive. The questioner wants to provoke you. Don't take the bait. (See Chapter 14 for more on hecklers.)

Designing your answer

You never know exactly how to answer until you receive the question, but that's not really helpful if you're trying to prepare in advance. The following general guidelines can help you formulate your answers:

✔ **Keep it brief.** Your answer should be a simple, succinct response to the question asked. Too many speakers use their answer as an excuse to give a second speech. Give everyone a break. If the audience wanted an encore, it would have asked for one. And remember, many members of the audience may not even be interested in the question you're answering. They're waiting to hear the next question — or ask one.

✔ **Refer back to your speech.** Tying your answers back to your talk reinforces the points you made earlier. This tactic also makes you seem omniscient. (You somehow foresaw these questions and planted the seeds of their answers in your speech.)

✔ **Define the terms under discussion.** Let's say someone asks if you think the middle class deserves a tax cut. You say "yes." The questioner immediately disagrees by arguing that it's unfair to give a tax break to the middle class. After a ten-minute debate, everyone realizes that there's no real disagreement. You don't think any family making more than $100,000 deserves a tax break, and neither does the questioner, but you define such families as "rich." The questioner defines them as "middle class." Make sure that everyone is on the same wavelength. Define the terms up front.

✔ **Refer to your experience.** It's not bragging to refer to your personal and professional experience in your answer. That experience is one of the reasons you've been invited to speak. It's part of what makes you an expert. The audience *wants* to hear about your experience.

✔ **Point out misconceptions stated by the audience and firmly state your position.** Never let a questioner define your position. An alarm should go off when you hear a questioner say something like "Well, based on your speech, it's obvious that you think. . . ." Typically, what the questioner says you think, *isn't* what you think at all. Don't let anyone put words in your mouth. If this occurs, address the problem immediately — as soon as the questioner finishes asking the question.

✔ **Dispute the questioner's facts or stats if you disagree.** You don't get locked into the questioner's facts or premises. If the questioner makes assumptions with which you disagree, politely say so. If you dispute the questioner's statistics, say so. Don't build a nice answer on a faulty question. Start by dismantling the question.

✔ **Be honest.** You shouldn't make promises you won't keep. Don't say that anyone can call you at your office to ask questions if you know you won't take their calls. Don't say you'll find out the answer to a question if you know you won't. Don't offer to send information to someone if you know you'll never get around to it.

✔ **You can politely decline to answer a question.** But don't evade questions by acting like you're answering them. You're not obligated to answer every question. (You're *really not* under interrogation although it may sometimes seem that way.) But if you evade questions, you lose credibility. It looks like you're ducking the issues. If you don't want to answer a question, say so firmly and politely. State the reasons why and move on to the next question.

✔ **Raise all of your points in your speech, rather than hoping to be asked a particular question.** Leaving important points out of your speech because you want to save them for the Q&A session is dangerous. — If no one asks the right questions, you may never get a chance to make those points.

Delivering your answer

Having the perfect answer doesn't mean much if you can't deliver it effectively. But don't worry. The following simple rules ensure that your response will be — well, perfect.

✔ **Have the appropriate attitude.** Match your demeanor to the substance of the question and your answer. If someone is confused, be understanding. If someone is blatantly offensive, be forceful and disapproving (without counterattacking). If someone is seeking information, be professorial. Never lose control of yourself. Never be discourteous.

✔ **Look at the entire audience.** Don't limit eye contact to the questioner. Start off by looking at the questioner, but as you give your answer, direct your eye contact to the entire audience. You're speaking to everyone — not just the questioner.

✔ **Avoid being smug.** It doesn't win any accolades from the audience, and it just creates a barrier. It can also backfire in a big way: The audience starts rooting for you to screw up. The first time you fumble an answer — even if it's just misstating an insignificant detail — smugness comes back to haunt you.

Using Question-Handling Techniques

How do you become an expert in deftly fielding questions? Practice. Practice. Practice. Practice what? The following six basic techniques (most of which were provided by my old friend, Dr. Barbara Howard, a Denver-based corporate facilitator) can help you build your question-handling skills.

Reversing the question

Someone in your audience may ask you a question for the express purpose of putting you on the spot. No sweat. Just reverse it. For example, the questioner makes a big show of appearing bored and asks, "What time are we going to take a break?" Don't get defensive. Just respond, "What time would you like to take a break?" It's mental judo. You use the weight of the questioner's own question against him.

Redirecting the question

Someone asks a question. You don't have the vaguest idea how to answer it. What can you do? Get the audience involved. Redirect the question to the entire group. "That's an interesting question. Does anyone have any thoughts on the subject?" Or, "Does anyone have any experience with that situation?" The audience is a great resource; take advantage of it.

Rephrasing the question

"Last week's indictment of your chief lobbyist for bribing a senator has finally revealed how your parasitic company got federal approval for a drug that's already killed 200 people. Will you now issue a recall to remove it from the market?" Hmmm. Are you really supposed to repeat this question for the audience? I don't think so. In fact, you never want to repeat a question that presents a problem — doing so is embarrassing, difficult, hard to follow, whatever. So, although you shouldn't repeat the question word for word, you should rephrase it to your advantage. "The question is about how we will convert our concern for public safety into action. Here are the steps we are taking to protect the public. . . ."

Keep in mind that a question can be a problem just because it's worded in an obtuse manner. "In your opinion, will the actions of the Federal Reserve Board to control inflation through monetary policy, combined with global financial trends — particularly the devaluation of the Mexican peso — result in economic forces that validate or prove wrong the Wall Street bulls in the short term?" Huh? Rephrase the question so that the audience can understand it (assuming *you* can understand it). Such a response may be, "The question is whether the stock market will go up or down in the next few months."

Exposing a hidden agenda

Sometimes a question contains a hidden (or not so hidden) agenda. It may be a loaded question. It may be some other type of trick question. It may be a question containing an accusation. ("How could anyone in good conscience possibly suggest cutting funds for the nursing department?") No matter the method, the question has a "hook" in it. The questioner wants to provoke a certain answer so that he or she can argue with it. The question is just a setup for a fight.

Don't fall for this trap. Instead of launching into an answer, acknowledge your suspicions. With responses, such as, "Do you have some thoughts on that?" or "It sounds like you're expecting me to give you a certain answer. What is it you're trying to get me to say?" The point is to politely expose the hidden agenda and get the questioner to speak about it first.

Putting the question in context

"Isn't it true that you were in Mr. Smith's bedroom the night he was found stabbed to death in his bed?" This is known as a loaded question. It's framed in a way that makes the audience members jump to very specific conclusions that make you look bad. Your response has to broaden their frames of reference. You have to provide the missing information that "unloads" the question. "Well, yes, as a police photographer, I did take pictures of the crime scene a few hours after Mr. Smith died. That's why I was in his bedroom the night he was stabbed to death." The meaning of any words or behaviors can be distorted if they're taken out of context. It's up to you to give a context to any question that needs one.

Building a bridge

Watch a politician evade a question in the following example. "Senator Blowhard, are you going to vote against a tax increase?" "Well sir, you want to know if I'm going to vote against a tax increase. What you're really asking is how can we get more money into the pockets of more Americans. Let me tell you about my 12-step plan for reviving the economy. . . ."

The senator has built a bridge. He's constructed a phrase that allows him to move from a question he wants to ignore to a topic he wants to address. In this case, the bridge is, "What you're really asking is. . . ." You can use lots of bridges of this sort, such as the following:

✔ "It makes much more sense to talk about . . ."

✔ "The real issue is . . ."

✔ "The essential question is . . ."

✔ "What you should be asking is . . ."

✔ "If you look at the big picture, your question becomes . . ."

Use a bridge to move a short distance away from a question you dislike, rather than to evade it completely. You lose credibility when you evade a question. (Politicians don't care because they have none to lose.) You have to give the appearance of at least attempting to answer.

Dealing with Common Types of Questions

Certain types of questions are designed to put you at a disadvantage. What follows are some questions you must be ready to identify as well as some tips on how to handle them.

✔ **The yes or no question:** Don't get trapped by this type of question. ("Is your company going to form an alliance with the Okkie Corporation, yes or no?") Unless you're under oath on a witness stand, you're not required to provide a yes or no answer. If the question requires a more complex answer, don't hesitate to say what needs to be said. ("The formation of an alliance between our company and Okkie depends on a number of factors. . . .") Does this kind of response evade the question? Not really. It evades *the form of the question* that the questioner is trying to force on you, but your answer does address the question.

✔ **The forced choice question:** This is a close relative of the yes or no question. Here, the questioner wants to force you to choose between two alternatives, and like the yes or no question, you're not obligated to do so. Sometimes both alternatives offered are bad. ("Does your plan omit security guards because they're too expensive or because you forgot to include them?" "Neither. I didn't include them because they're not needed.")

Sometimes you just don't want to choose between the alternatives. ("What is the main focus of your growth strategy — developing new products or cutting costs?" "Actually, we intend to do both of those and more. We will also be acquiring new products, expanding our sales force. . . .")

✔ **The hypothetical question:** (What if the product doesn't sell up to your expectations?) Don't get sucked into the morass of hypothetical questions. You've got enough "real" things to worry about. Just say something like, "I don't anticipate that happening, so we'll cross that bridge if we come to it."

✔ **The false-assumption question:** The classic example is "Have you stopped beating your wife yet?" The question assumes that you've been beating your wife. (And you may not even be married.) False assumptions can also include incorrect facts and statistics, as well as incorrect conclusions that the questioner has drawn from your talk. The solution: Point out the false assumption and correct it immediately.

✔ **The multipart question:** "Could you tell me if we'll be receiving raises this year, and if not, why not, and if so, how big will they be?" Whoa. Slow down there, pardner. That's what's known as a multipart question. When you get one like this, divide it up and answer one part at a time.

Responding to Special Situations

Handling questions from the audience is a very delicate situation. You often need to take a firm hand, but you don't want to alienate your listeners. Use the following tips to handle common "problem" situations.

✔ **A questioner interrupts you.** Don't interrupt the interrupter. Stop talking and let this boor finish what he is saying. Then say something like, "Please wait until I've finished." Then complete your answer. If the person interrupts again, repeat the process. Don't get into a fight. If the interrupter continues, other members of the audience will eventually intercede on your behalf. (If they don't, then they don't deserve to hear your pearls of wisdom.)

✔ **Someone asks about something you covered in your speech.** Don't say, "I already covered that in my speech." Perhaps you did, but maybe you didn't cover it clearly. If the person asking the question missed the answer in your speech, then others may have missed it, too. And if it was important enough to include in your initial speech, then you can spend time going over it again. So answer the question; just try explaining it a different way this time.

✔ **Someone asks a question that was already asked.** If your answer will take more than ten seconds, politely refuse to answer. Say something like, "We've already addressed that question." This situation is completely different than getting a question about something covered in your speech. Here, the audience member simply hasn't been paying attention. If you answer the question, then you're being rude to the rest of the audience. You're wasting their time. If you want to be nice, offer to talk with the questioner individually after the Q&A session is concluded.

✔ **Someone asks a completely irrelevant question.** You can point out that it's not germane to the discussion and go on to the next questioner. You can give the questioner a chance to ask a relevant question, or you can use the question as a springboard to raise a topic you want to discuss.

✔ **Someone asks a completely disorganized question.** You have a couple of choices. You can ask the person to restate the question (not a good idea because you'll probably get a question more disorganized than the first attempt). You can respond to part of the question (a part that you liked), or you can offer to talk with the person individually after the Q&A session is concluded.

✔ **Someone asks a rathole question.** "Why did you change the bitmap for the icons on your menu screen for the financial applications in Release 3.1?" This is a rathole question. It's of interest to only one person in the audience — the questioner. It's a painful distraction for everyone else. That's why it's called a rathole question. Any time and effort you put into answering it goes down a rathole. To handle this situation, after the question is asked, answer it briefly. Then ask for a show of hands to see if anyone else is interested in the topic. If you find significant audience interest, continue your answer. If not, offer to resume the discussion after the Q&A session has concluded.

✔ **Someone asks multiple questions.** You have a few options for handling this situation. You can tell the questioner that you'll only answer one of the questions due to time constraints and fairness to other audience members. (Offer to answer the other questions later after everyone else has had a turn to ask one.) You can answer all of the questions in the order asked, or you can answer all of them in an order you choose. (Exercise these last two options when you feel that answering the questions is to your advantage.)

> ✔ **Someone asks a long, rambling question.** If you see where the
> question is going, gently interrupt (citing time considerations)
> and pose the question concisely in your own words. Confirm
> that you've understood what the questioner wants to know.
> Then answer it. If you don't see where it's going, use the Larry
> King technique. Ask "Can you state your question, please?"

Handling Hostile Questions

One of the great fears facing many speakers is the prospect of dealing with hostile questions. Stop worrying. You can use tried-and-
true techniques for handling this problem. In fact, a little advance
planning can significantly reduce your chance of receiving these
pesky questions.

Identifying hostile questions

Don't put a chip on your shoulder and assume that anyone who
disagrees with you is hostile. Even people who disagree can have a
legitimate question. They don't necessarily want to argue with you.
They may just want information.

Also, don't assume that someone who asks pointed questions disagrees with you. The exact opposite may be true. This happens at
the U.S. Supreme Court all the time. A justice who agrees with a
certain position will ask the lawyer representing that position an
incredibly tough question because the justice hopes that a good
answer will help persuade the other justices to agree with the position too. This process can occur in your audience. Someone who
agrees with you may ask a tough question, hoping that your answer
persuades others in the audience. So some of your toughest questions can come from your biggest allies. Don't assume that these
audience members are hostile.

If someone asks you a false assumption question — that's hostile.
("Do you think you'll get 10 years or 20 years for income tax eva-
sion?" and "Isn't this an amazing achievement — for a woman?")
It's safe to assume these questioners are out to get you.

Heading them off at the pass

The simplest way to handle hostile questions is to not get any. Unfortunately, I can't guarantee that you won't, but these techniques can help you minimize the number you do receive:

- ✓ **The inoculation:** Can you anticipate specific hostile questions that you'll receive? Then raise them and answer them during your speech. By beating your antagonists to the punch, you leave them with nothing to ask you.

- ✓ **The admission:** Admit at the outset of the Q&A session that you're not the world authority on everything. Set audience expectations properly regarding the extent and areas of your expertise. Tell the audience what you don't know. This technique helps defuse potential hostility and disappointment resulting from your inability to answer specific questions.

- ✓ **The revelation:** At the outset of the Q&A session, announce that the people who ask questions must begin by identifying themselves. They must reveal their name, organization, and anything else you want to require. Having to reveal this information is a major barrier to hostile questioners. They don't like losing the cloak of audience anonymity. It's much easier to act like a jerk, be hostile, and get confrontational with the speaker if no one knows who you are.

Dealing with hostile questions

Receiving a hostile question is like being tossed a bomb. You need to know how to defuse it before it blows up in your face. Use the following tactics:

- ✓ **Empathize with the questioner.** Start by recognizing that the questioner is upset and emphasize that you *understand* his or her point of view even if you don't agree with it. Make sure you communicate that you bear no personal animosity toward the questioner. Your disagreement is solely about the issue in question. "I can see that you feel strongly about this issue, and I understand where you're coming from. Let me give you a few more facts that may affect your opinion. . . ."

- ✓ **Establish common ground.** Find an area where you and the questioner can agree and build your answer from there. "Then we agree that the budget will have to be limited to 75 percent of what we spent last year. We just differ on how to allocate the money. . . ." If you're really stuck for finding common ground, here's the all-purpose (albeit somewhat lame) response that works for any hostile question: "Well, at least we agree that this is a controversial issue. . . ."

✔ **Put the question in neutral.** If you get a question loaded with emotionally charged words or phrases, rephrase the question in neutral terms. (See the "Rephrasing the question" section earlier in this chapter.)

✔ **Be very specific.** Talk about specific facts and figures. Be concrete. The more you get into theory, speculation, and opinion, the more opportunity you provide for disagreement. You want to limit the opportunities for arguments.

✔ **Ask why they're asking.** What if you're on the receiving end of a loaded question or any other blatantly hostile query? Don't even bother giving an answer. Just say, "Why did you ask that?" This can go a long way to defusing the situation. The questioner, often embarrassed that you spotted the trap, may withdraw or modify the question. (See "Exposing a hidden agenda" earlier in this chapter.)

✔ **Elude the jerks.** Don't allow continued follow-up questions from people who just want to interrogate you in a hostile manner. (Unless they've got a badge.) There's no reason for it. You should be giving everyone in the audience a chance to ask questions. Just tell them that other people would like a turn to ask questions. You can also say that you'll be happy to discuss their concerns at the conclusion of the Q&A session.

Chapter 14

Handling the Audience

● ●

In This Chapter

▶ Assessing audience reaction

▶ Making the audience comfortable

▶ Dealing with hecklers and other distractions

▶ Keeping the attention of the audience

▶ Getting the audience involved

● ●

*Y*ou can have the world's greatest speech, but that may not mean very much if you have the world's worst audience. An audience is like a thorny, long-stemmed rose. Handled properly, it's a thing of beauty that can blossom as you speak. Handled improperly, it will prick you severely.

Reading an Audience's Reaction

Many professional speakers claim they can "read" an audience like a book. I've always wondered what that means. They read a little of the audience at bedtime, drift off to sleep, and read some more the next day? They mark up the audience with a yellow highlighter? They put a bookmark down the audience's throat? In any event, it makes a lot more sense to read an audience like an audience — a group of people who have to listen to your speech. What follows are a few ways to gauge their reactions.

Checking the energy level

One of the easiest ways to read an audience is by observing its energy level. Are people talking and laughing as they wait for the event to begin? That's a high-energy audience, and that's what you hope for. This type of audience is much more receptive to your speech. A high-energy audience is basically yours to lose. If you have a high-energy audience, you don't have to be high-energy yourself. (Although it doesn't hurt.)

Here's a tip from the late San Francisco comedy coach John Cantu: A high-energy audience laughs and applauds longer than a low-energy audience. Therefore, you need to allow extra time for laughter and applause when you calculate how much you can say in the time you've been allotted.

A low-energy audience is just the opposite. No one's talking, and the mood is kind of blah. (This mood often correlates to specific times of the day and week. For example, Monday night audiences are typically low energy.) This audience is tough. You have to be high-energy. You have to ignite the audience.

Noticing body language

The nonverbal behavior of your audience can tell you an enormous amount about the effectiveness of your speech. Are people nodding at what you say? Are they looking up at you? Are they leaning forward? Are they smiling? Or are they squirming in their seats, nudging each other, looking at their watches, and staring out the windows? (You don't need a Ph.D. to interpret these signals.)

Don't judge the entire audience by the reactions of a single person. This tip sounds obvious, but speakers do it all the time. You may see one sourpuss who won't crack a smile. You'll become obsessed with this person and make all your speaking decisions based on his or her reaction. That's usually a mistake, because nothing you do will work with the sourpuss, and you'll get nervous, feel you're bombing, and screw up. If you look at the other 99 percent of the audience members, you'll see that they're enjoying your talk — at least until you screw it up by focusing on the sourpuss.

Asking questions to gauge the audience

If you don't know whether people in an audience agree with you, disagree with you, or even understand what you're saying, ask them. That's the direct method of reading audience reaction. ("How many of you are familiar with the large oil spill that I was just talking about?" "How many of you disagree with what I just said?" "How many of you have never heard any of these arguments before?")

Making the Audience Comfortable

Most people are cautious in an unfamiliar situation. If they're interacting with a stranger, they assume a conservative demeanor. They don't let their guards down and kick back until they're sure that it's a safe behavior. Audiences react in much the same way. If Robin Williams steps up to a podium, the audience knows it's okay to laugh. If someone the audience doesn't know steps up to the podium, people in the audience don't know how they're expected to behave. You have to tell them.

Management communication counselor Jim Lukaszewski calls this process *giving permission.* "Most of us are strangers in front of crowds," he explains. "So you have to give the audience permission to enjoy your speech." Jim likens this process to having a continuing side conversation with the audience. "I give them substantive information in my speeches," he explains. "But I also keep giving them permission to react in various ways."

What kind of permissions must audiences receive? It depends on what you want to accomplish and how you want the audience to react. The following list shows you three of the more important permissions you can bestow on your listeners:

- **Permission to laugh:** Do you want to use humor successfully in your talk? One of the most important permissions you can give your audience is permission to laugh. Veteran high-tech executive Joe DiNucci is famous for his humor-filled talks to customers and employees. He starts by telling them it's okay to enjoy themselves. He'll say something like, "I intend to communicate and inform and enlighten and bring insight, but it is an explicit goal that you be entertained. So loosen up your tie. Loosen up your mind. Turn off the immune system that rejects anything that's amusing. I promise you there's a lot of meat in this material, but we also put some fun in with it too."

- **Permission to learn:** Jim Lukaszewski likes to give his audiences permission to learn. He'll say, "I believe this is a really important speech. I'm going to be talking about three sensitive, important topics. I'll go into more detail later. But I think when you leave here today, the things you'll really remember about this talk are these key areas. . . ." By telling the audience what's important, Jim gives the audience insight into his interpretation of his own talk. "I've given them permission to enter my psychological being," he explains. "Now they can actively follow the outline with me — not just react to it as I dump it out there."

✔ **Permission to write:** According to Jim, one of the most important permissions that you can give your audience is the permission to take notes. He'll start by saying something like, "My
speech is packed with information you'll want to remember.
That's why there are pencils and paper at your seats. And if
you don't have some, please make friends immediately with
someone who does because you'll need them."

This permission flies in the face of the traditional wisdom that
considers writing to be a distraction. "A lot of trainers believe
you can't have people writing and paying attention to you at
the same time," says Jim. "That's dumb. What is greater than
having hundreds of people writing things down as you speak?"
How does he make sure they won't miss anything? "I shut up
and let them write," he explains. "And guess what — if I stop
talking, they start writing."

Handling a Tough Audience

Not every audience you ever address will be an absolute delight.
When you face a tough crowd, you have some choices. You can
figure out the problem and handle it, or you can wait for a standing
ovation — on your chest.

Examining types of tough audiences

Easy audiences are all alike, but every tough audience is tough in
its own way. Here are some of the varieties you may encounter and
some tips for handling each of them.

Offbeat audience

An offbeat audience responds in ways that you don't anticipate.
The audience members laugh or applaud when you don't expect it,
and they're silent when you expect applause.

That's why they're tough. They throw off your entire rhythm.
There's nothing you can do besides go with the flow. Just don't
cue the audience members that you find their responses unusual.
Pause for their applause when you get it and keep speaking when
you don't.

Captive audience

The captive audience is tough because it's not there by choice.
Attendance at your speech has been forced upon these people for
one reason or another, and they resent it. So they're in a foul mood

before you ever begin. It's not your fault. It has nothing to do with you, but you'll have to bear the brunt of their anger. What can you do? Acknowledge the situation up front and appeal to their sense of fairness. Tell them what benefits they can expect to receive if they simply take the chips off their shoulders and give you a fair chance.

More-educated- or more-experienced-than-you audience

A classic joke from the lecture circuit tells of the last living survivor of the Johnstown flood who finally came to the end of his days. Saint Peter greeted him at the Pearly Gates and said some old-timers would like to gather and hear the latest word from earth. Peter asked if he had anything interesting to talk about. The new arrival said he'd been a major attraction on the lecture circuit on earth with his tales about the Johnstown flood. So Saint Peter brought him in, introduced him, and said he had something very interesting to say. And then, just as Saint Peter turned to leave, he whispered in the fellow's ear, "That man second from the left in the front row — his name is Noah."

What can you do when your audience knows more about your subject than you do? You can reframe your entire talk as a review of the basics. As an alternative, you may decide to make the talk intensely personal. The speech becomes a description of *your* feelings, ideas, and reactions regarding the subject matter. Or you can elevate the discussion to a higher, "big picture" level. ("I'm not here to talk about floods today. Obviously Mr. Noah knows a lot more about them than I do. My comments today will examine the basic relationship between man and nature and how mankind responds to adverse circumstances. Into each life a little rain must fall. . . .")

Hostile-to-your-position audience

You're speaking pro or con about a controversial issue — gun control, abortion, Burt Reynolds's hairpiece, whatever. Your audience holds an opinion that's the opposite of yours. So you know the audience will be hostile to what you have to say. This will be a tough crowd.

The best approach is to try to disarm the audience members immediately. Begin by acknowledging that you have a difference of opinion. (And don't apologize for your opinion; you're entitled to it.) Then appeal to the traditional values of fairness, free speech, and dialogue. Let them know that they'll have a chance to air their views after you're finished speaking. ("We are going to disagree on some fundamental issues. But that's why I'm here today — to have a dialogue about the effects of the hole in the ozone layer. If we all believed the same thing, we couldn't have much of a dialogue. And we will have one, because after I'm done speaking, anyone who wishes to express an opinion will have an opportunity to do so. I only ask that you give me a fair chance to make my case without interrupting me. You don't need to let me know how much you disagree with me. I already know.")

Didn't-come-to-see-you audience

The keynote speaker may be the latest business babble guru who has written a best-selling book on leadership, the latest politician with his own personality cult, or the latest celebrity in the limelight. That's who the audience has come to see. Unfortunately, the audience has to sit through a few other speakers before it gets to hear the guru. Even more unfortunate, *you* are one of the speakers that must precede the guru.

These audiences are tough because they want you to be finished before you've even started. You can't do very much about it, but you may find some relief by referring to the guru in your remarks as often as possible. That may be the only thing you can say to get a positive response from the audience. ("I'm honored to be here today, speaking in the same program as Mr. Guru. In fact, many of my ideas have been influenced directly by Mr. Guru's work. How many of you would agree with me that Mr. Guru's book *Babble Your Way to Leadership* is the most important business book of the century? Later on today, you'll hear Mr. Guru speak about leadership. But right now I'd like to discuss a few concepts that will give you a deeper insight into Mr. Guru's ideas.") Is this pandering to the audience? You bet it is. Do you have any other choice? Yes. You can give your speech as planned to the accompaniment of audience hoots and jeers. ("Hey, shut up and sit down." "Get off the stage." "We want the Guru.") It's up to you.

The-current-event-distracted-them audience

You're speaking to a group of fundraisers about new techniques to increase donations, and you're an expert on the topic. It's a perfect match between speaker, topic, and audience. Your audience members should pay undivided attention and take notes, but they aren't. They seem distracted; they're definitely not listening. What's the problem? Two hours before you started speaking, the space shuttle Challenger exploded, or the Oklahoma City Federal Building was bombed, or the President was shot. Some major event has usurped the consciousness of the audience, and everything else — especially your speech — seems unimportant by comparison.

The distracting event need not be national in scope. It may be very local. In fact, it may be specific to your audience. (You're scheduled to give a brown-bag lunch speech about investment opportunities to a group of employees from Thud-Tech, Inc. That morning, Thud-Tech's CEO projects a record quarterly loss and indicates that massive layoffs will be forthcoming. Thud-Tech employees will *not* be focusing on your talk.)

What if you're scheduled to speak on the day that a distracting event has occurred? Try to get your speech canceled or changed to another time. If neither is possible, be prepared to talk about the distracting event because that may be the only subject that interests your audience.

Reverse-image audience

You're the only male at a female event or vice versa. You're the only African-American at a Caucasian event or vice versa. You're the only Jew at a Christian event or vice versa.

You get the idea. You're the reverse image of your audience. Audience members are tough if they assume that you can't possibly understand their point of view. After all, you're different from them.

Start by breaking the tension. Acknowledge your difference. If appropriate, poke fun at it. Then establish your common ground. You're speaking to this audience for a reason. Members of the audience can receive some benefit from listening to you. Let them know what it is — fast.

Angry-at-previous-speaker audience

The speaker before you has really riled up the audience members. In fact, they're downright mad. Maybe the speaker was controversial. Maybe he was insulting. Maybe he was offensive. Whatever the case, the audience members are in a vile mood, and they want to take it out on you. The most important thing you can do in this situation is *be aware of it*. You need to know that the audience is angry at the prior speaker, not you.

Failure to recognize this situation can jeopardize your entire speech. You'll assume that *you* are the problem and adjust your performance accordingly. That doesn't work because you're *not* the problem. It's imperative to know what any previous speakers said to your audience. Attend their talks if possible. If not, find out what happened. If a problem occurred, you can address it immediately in the opening of your talk.

Already-heard-it audience

The speakers before you have made acceptable speeches. They left the audience in decent shape for your talk. The audience isn't angry or upset about anything. But that can change rapidly if you get up and repeat what the previous speakers have already said.

Why would anyone do that? It happens all the time, and there are two major causes. You may be unaware of what the previous speakers said. Or despite the fact that you know they've already said what you planned to say, you plow ahead with your prepared remarks anyway. Audiences absolutely hate this. (That's why so many people try to avoid all-day business conferences. When the fifth speaker in a row gets up and talks about the importance of synergy, commitment to change, and the globalization of business, you just want to puke.)

If you find yourself in this situation, don't just do your speech as if the audience members haven't already heard the same thing. You'll lose them instantly. You have to adapt. At a minimum, you have to acknowledge that you'll be saying things that they've already heard. A much more effective strategy is to abandon your prepared remarks entirely. Just wing it. Think of a different angle and speak about it on an impromptu basis. Comment on what the previous speakers have already said. Or solicit participation from the audience.

Sick audience

The sick audience is literally ill. Numerous members of this audience cough and sneeze loudly throughout your speech. It's quite a distraction, but there's not much you can do about it. You can try using humor to deal with the situation. ("Please hold your applause and coughing till the end.") If that doesn't work, you're out of luck. (Anyway, that's what you get for volunteering to speak at a meeting of AA — Allergics Anonymous.)

Haggling with hecklers

The traditional notion of a heckler is someone who interrupts a speaker by shouting out hostile remarks or questions. (Of course, that definition could also apply to the White House press corps.) I'm going to define heckling a little more broadly. My definition of heckling is anything that someone does to purposely distract you or the audience from your talk. You may encounter some of the following hecklers:

> ✔ **The one-upper:** The one-upper is a heckler who wants attention. If you ask the audience for questions, the one-upper will jump in with some sarcastic comment or tough question

designed to embarrass you. It's not that the one-upper dislikes you personally or even disagrees with your positions. You're just a prop for the one-upper to manipulate in an unending quest for attention.

✔ **The under-the-influence heckler:** If you speak at enough dinner meetings, you'll eventually run into an under-the-influence heckler. These people have had a few too many, and they exhibit the typical effects of alcohol (or drugs) — they get very angry, sad, or happy. Whichever mood it is, they display it to an exaggerated degree. They shout or cry or laugh in a way that completely disrupts your speech.

✔ **The attack dog:** The attack dog is the traditional heckler. This person doesn't like you or your opinions and is determined to stop you from speaking. He or she will try to shout you down, insult you, and do whatever it takes to cause a commotion. These people want to fight — with you.

Although technically not a heckler, you may run into the "dweeb" at some time. The dweeb is someone who unintentionally engages in distracting behavior related to your discussion, such as answering rhetorical questions. Just be prepared: They don't know any better.

Just because someone causes a distraction doesn't mean they're heckling you. Although hecklers consciously choose to cause a distraction, sometimes distracting behavior is innocent. For example, a person might be asking a neighbor for a pen to take notes. Don't become offended by such unintended distractions. If someone runs out of the room to go to the toilet, you haven't been heckled. If they come back and throw toilet paper at you, that's another story.

Now that you know what types of hecklers you may be facing, following are some pointers on how to deal with them:

✔ **Identify the type of heckler.** You need to know why the heckling started so you can determine how you'll end it. See above for more information on the types of hecklers and their motives.

✔ **Be empathic.** Sometimes you can defuse hecklers just by acknowledging their point of view. Let them know that you understand their position, even though you don't agree with it.

✔ **Suggest that the heckler speak with you after your speech.** I like to handle this by saying, "Listen, my friend, this is my speech. If you want to argue with me afterwards, you're more than welcome. I'll be glad to talk to you later, but right now, you're insulting the rest of the audience."

✔ **Look for help.** You shouldn't have to deal with audience members who are out of control. Seek help from the person running the meeting or the person who invited you to speak. You can also appeal to the audience members for assistance. (Let them tell the heckler to shut up.)

✔ **Avoid arguing.** It just gives legitimacy to the heckler and makes you look bad. And that's exactly what the heckler wants you to do.

✔ **Stay calm.** Hecklers want control. If you get angry, you give them exactly what they want — a negative reaction (and confirmation that you've lost control). So stay calm at all times. If nothing else, it will drive the heckler nuts.

✔ **Discontinue the rest of your speech.** If the heckler won't stop and no one will help you, then end your speech. Tell the audience that you can't proceed due to the disruption. Then exit gracefully.

Dealing with other distractions

Hecklers will probably remain a rare occurrence at your speeches; other distractions are far more common. If you're speaking at a lunch or dinner, a waiter will inevitably drop some dishes during your talk. If there are children present, a baby will cry. The audience member with the loudest ringing cellular phone will receive a call while you're speaking. The list goes on.

When these types of distractions occur, an audience often reacts with laughter. If that happens, you have to laugh right along with the audience. It's a control issue. You have to show the audience that you're handling the problem and that you remain in control. (It's analogous to skidding while driving a car. If you steer into the skid, you regain control.) If you get upset about the distraction, the audience becomes uncomfortable, and you lose momentum.

Anticipate things that can go wrong and have some quips ready to deal with them. For example, assume the room lights go out because of a power failure. You might say, "Now I'm really going to have to shed some light on the subject." (No it's not hilarious, but it doesn't have to be. It communicates that you're not upset and that you're still in control.)

Heckling the hecklers

The greatest nightmare for many speakers is the prospect of being interrupted by a heckler. But don't overlook the fact that being heckled provides a great opportunity for the speaker to respond with wit and acumen. In fact, a good retort is usually remembered long after the actual speech is forgotten. What follows are some examples.

Al Smith was a popular governor of New York and a presidential candidate. During a campaign speech, he was interrupted by a heckler who yelled, "Tell 'em what's on your mind, Al. It shouldn't take long." Smith didn't miss a beat. He replied, "I'll tell 'em what's on both of our minds. It won't take any longer."

William Gladstone and Benjamin Disraeli were archrivals in the British Parliament. During one of their many debates, Gladstone yelled at Disraeli, "You, sir, will die either on the gallows or of some loathsome disease." Disraeli responded, "That, sir, depends upon whether I embrace your principles or your mistress."

President William Howard Taft received the ultimate heckle during a campaign appearance. Someone threw a cabbage at him. Taft evaded the projectile and said, "One of my opponents has apparently lost his head."

Nancy Astor, the first woman to sit in the British House of Commons, was an outspoken proponent of women's rights. During one of her speeches on the subject, a heckler interrupted with comments about Lady Astor's numerous bracelets and necklace. The heckler said, "You have enough brass on you, Lady Astor, to make a kettle." Astor's reply was quick and devastating: "And you have enough water in your head to fill it."

During a campaign speech, Al Smith was repeatedly interrupted by a heckler who shouted, "Liar!" After ignoring the heckler proved fruitless, Smith replied, "If the gentleman would be so kind as to give us his name as well as his calling, we should be happy to hear from him."

Handling a Nonresponsive Audience

You can pick up subtle clues that tell you when you're not clicking with an audience. (People don't nod in agreement, but they do nod off.) If you want to save your speech, then you have to take charge. Your speaking engagement is like working in an emergency room. You need to figure out what's wrong with the patients, but first you have to revive them — before it's too late. So let's look at some resuscitation techniques for nonresponsive audiences.

Stocking your first-aid kit

An audience first-aid kit includes a variety of devices for reviving interest in your talk. Like the contents of a real first-aid kit, these devices range in strength from bandages to adrenaline shots. You have to know how to use the appropriate device for the audience in front of you. I find it convenient to diagnose a dying audience by sorting it into one of three categories, which I'll refer to as levels.

Level one: You still have audience members' attention, but they look bored or puzzled

The people in the audience are still watching you speak, but you can sense that you're not connecting. They're fidgeting. They're not responding. What can you do? You must break out of the pattern you're in. Talk directly to the audience like it's a real conversation. Ask them if they understand what you're talking about. Ask if they'd like you to give another example. Or tell them that what you're about to say is very important. Emphasize a key benefit that really puts them in the picture. ("Now I'd like to tell you the only guaranteed way to prevent yourself from being laid off in the next two years.")

Or you can say something that you feel is guaranteed to get applause. (The energy of their hands clapping helps prevent the onset of lethargy.) What if you're waiting for applause and you don't get it? Say something like, "Oh, I guess you didn't think that was as important as I did." If they laugh, you've connected with them. If they don't, you're not any worse off.

 The late John Cantu said that if you want to maximize your chances of getting applause, you should ask the audience some questions and tell them to respond with applause instead of a show of hands. ("How many of you can't wait until my speech is finished?" Thundering ovation.)

Level two: Audience attention is waning

The audience is starting to drift off. People are staring at the ceiling, out the windows, and at their watches. The only thing they're not looking at is you. One of the simplest things you can do to revive this audience is also one of the most effective — just ask the audience members to stand up. Say something like, "You've been sitting down for awhile now. And I think we could all use a short stretch. Everyone stand up. . . . Okay, sit back down. Feel better?" It's amazing how a stretch can transform the energy level in the room. (That's why they have a seventh inning stretch at baseball games.) But let me add a word of caution. The effect is temporary. When the audience members retake their seats, they pay attention for a minute or two. That's your opening. It's your chance to get your talk back on track with some exciting, dynamic stuff. If you don't, you'll lose the audience again.

Level three: Code blue — they're about to become comatose

The audience is falling asleep or in a trancelike state or just plain dazed. You don't have time to ask them to stand up or applaud. You need to do something immediately that will jar audience members out of their stupor. It must be loud or dramatic or both. Consider these tips:

- ✔ Pound your fist on the podium

- ✔ Beat your chest like a gorilla

- ✔ Move the mike toward a sound-system speaker to cause loud feedback

- ✔ Wave a $20 bill in the air and then rip it up

- ✔ Throw your notes on the floor

- ✔ Light the podium on fire

Any of these should wake up the audience. But you need to tie these actions into your speech so that they make a point. Otherwise, it looks like you were just trying to wake up the audience members. (You can't admit that your goal was to wake them up. They would resent that. It has to appear that you were just giving your talk and part of it happened to revive them.)

For example, you pound your fist on the podium. (Do it near the mike so it really makes a loud noise.) Then you tie it into whatever you're talking about. "That's the sound of people beating their head against a wall because they're frustrated with government regulations." "That's the sound of your heart beating when you go on a job interview." "That's the sound your car makes after you try to save $150 by going to the lowball mechanic."

Getting a volunteer from the audience

One of the best ways to coax a response out of an audience is to put people in the audience into your act. It's an ego thing. They identify with the audience member who stands before them. Suddenly your talk becomes a lot more personal.

Meeting members of your audience before you speak helps you get a volunteer. Whenever I've had to beg for a volunteer, the person who volunteered has always been someone I'd spoken with earlier. Why does this happen? Your guess is as good as mine. Maybe some kind of bonding takes place. The person now feels like we're friends and feels obligated to help out. Who knows? I can only tell you that it happens consistently.

Part V
Common Speaking Situations

The 5th Wave   By Rich Tennant

"I had a little trouble with the automatic video tracking camera, so during the video conference, before speaking, say, 'Here Rollo!' and wait for Rollo to get his paws up on your knees before beginning to speak."

In this part . . .

*H*ey, we live in the information age. Public speaking is one of the ways that information is communicated. So, whether or not you speak on a regular basis, most people can expect to be called on to give a speech now and then — sometimes even at the last minute. In this part of the book, I describe common speaking situations and how to handle them, situations including everything from the city council in your community to international audiences in the global workplace. I also cover debating, impromptu speaking, serving on a panel, introducing other speakers, and participating in virtual meetings.

Chapter 15

Speaking to the City Council and School Board

In This Chapter

▶ Getting the rules down

▶ Speaking effectively and persuasively

▶ Making sure you don't turn off your audience

*T*here's an old saying that you can't fight city hall. That may be true. But no one ever said you couldn't talk it into submission. And it seems like more people than ever before are trying. That's because there's more opportunity than ever before to have your views heard by public officials. Government rules now allow just about anyone to voice an opinion at a public meeting. Whether you're speaking before a city council, school board, planning commission, or any other public body, this chapter will show you how to state your position in a way that maximizes your effectiveness, or at least in a way that avoids getting a gavel thrown at you.

Remembering Some Rules

While they may not always be followed, there are rules for speaking at public meetings. You can usually find the specific rules for speaking at your city council or school board meetings by browsing a Web site or making a phone call. Although you should always follow the specific rules of the meeting, the sections that follow discuss some general rules that can make planning your statements or speeches easier.

Getting to speak

Although every board, council, and commission has its own rules, most of them require you to sign up before the meeting if you wish to speak. Signing up allows the board to identify you in the official minutes of its meeting, schedule speakers fairly (in the order they signed up), and plan an efficient meeting.

The process of signing up typically involves filling out a speaker's card or similar form that requests your name and address. Sometimes you just sign a list. And how far in advance you have to sign up depends on the specific rules of that meeting. Requirements can range from two days to five minutes before the meeting begins.

Beating the clock

The Rolling Stones may have had time on their side, but speakers at a public meeting don't. A quick survey of city and county Web sites reveals that most boards and councils limit speaker comments to two to five minutes. The most common time limit is three minutes. Some boards enforce their limits with a timer that buzzes when your time is up. Others just turn off your microphone.

Don't even assume you'll get a full allotment of time. If a lot of speakers turn out for a meeting, the board or council may limit you to one minute — or less. This makes sense from the perspective of the board. It wants to give as many citizens as possible a chance to speak. (Even if it means cutting your brilliant insights down to 60 seconds.)

While your time may be short, many boards will grant additional speaking time if you represent a group. For example the Fort Worth, Texas City Council lets you speak up to 10 minutes if you represent 10 or more people at the meeting.

Using visual aids

Visual aids such as photos, maps, and diagrams are almost always welcome if they help clarify your comments. Patty White, who has served as both mayor of Piedmont, California and chairman of its planning commission, suggests displaying photos on a board on an easel. "I always found photographs very helpful," she notes, "Especially in disputes over neighborhood conditions or whether a home addition would change the character of a street." But she advises you to have your props ready the moment it's your turn to speak. Time is precious and fumbling with props loses you points before you even open your mouth.

What about high-tech audiovisual aids? PowerPoint? Videos? Slides? Overheads? If it enhances your argument, go for it. But remember to arrange for the equipment well in advance of the meeting. Not all boards and councils are created equal. Some have state-of-the-art audiovisual equipment that can be used just by asking for it. Others have no more than a flashlight for doing hand shadows on the wall.

If equipment is available, find out if they have special rules for reserving it; who will run the equipment; and if you have to coordinate your remarks with people sitting in a control room. All these issues must be resolved before you begin to speak.

Maximizing Your Effectiveness

Speaking to a board, council, or commission involves some effort on your part. You've got to find out when the meeting will occur. You've got to go to the meeting. You've got to sign up to speak. And you've got to say something. As long as you're already putting in all that effort, you may as well make your comments as persuasive as possible. You have to come prepared, and then you have to deliver — the following sections tell you how to do just that.

Getting prepared

Like it or not, you must be prepared when you speak at public meetings. But getting prepared takes less time than you probably think. Following are some tips so you can make the most of your time:

- **Do your research:** Whatever problem or project has motivated your trip to a council or board meeting, the council or board members have probably dealt with a similar situation in the past. Really, you're not the first person to oppose budget cuts to your kid's school. Find out the history of your issue. Go to your local library and review archived copies of your local paper. Or find information on the Web. You need to know the history so you don't propose old ideas and arguments that have already been rejected.

  Once you've got the history in perspective, double check the current status of your issue. Has the situation changed since you did your research? Get your facts straight. Make sure you know what you're talking about before you start talking. Just because your neighbor down the street told you something doesn't make it true.

✔ **Write out your key points:** There's a magical process that occurs when you take stuff out of your head and put it in writing: All of a sudden you can see where your arguments don't make sense, or where they need more support, or how rearranging their order can make them more compelling. In other words, writing out your key points helps you think through your comments. It also helps you remember exactly what you want to say when it's your turn to speak.

✔ **Practice and time your speech:** Even if you're a great extemporaneous speaker, practice your speech anyway. Practicing lets you hear how you sound. Then you can make adjustments and improvements *before* you speak to the board or council. More important, practicing your speech allows you to time it. This is critical when you're limited to three minutes. Remember, strict time limits mean you're cut off when your time is up. So you'd better make sure all your points and arguments fit into the time allowed.

✔ **Pack the house:** Worried about getting a cold reaction from a bunch of strangers? Take control of your audience. Invite people you know to attend the meeting, friends, neighbors, whoever. There's nothing like having familiar faces around to give you courage and confidence when addressing a board or council.

✔ **Be creative with time rules:** Three minutes is not a long time when an issue is complex and confounding, such as school closings, location of garbage dumps, and permitting big box chain stores to open in town. These are not easy issues, and three minutes doesn't begin to provide enough time to make all the arguments for or against. So get creative. Divide your arguments among your supporters. If five people each speak 3 minutes about different aspects of your issue, the board or council will hear 15 minutes about your position instead of 3 minutes. Just make sure the speakers don't repeat each other's points.

Making your point

You will only have a short time to speak. That means you must make your points quickly and succinctly. It also means you should keep your comments focused on one main issue. If you have multiple problems or projects to discuss, choose one. Go to additional meetings of the board or council to speak about the others.

Making your point is the reason you're at the meeting, and it's the most important thing you plan to do. So, if you've come prepared, making your point can be smooth sailing as long as you follow these guidelines:

✔ **Talk into the microphone:** Does it sound obvious? It is. But lots of speakers don't do it, especially people who are emotionally charged up about the issue they've come to speak about. Or they'll start by talking into the microphone and then forget as they get worked up. In areas where public meetings are broadcast over cable television, any time you don't speak into the microphone no one in the home audience knows what you're saying. And the home audience may be bigger and more influential than the audience in the meeting room.

✔ **Identify yourself and your position:** Start by telling the board or council who you are and where you live. Aside from the fact that they want to know this information, it's needed for the public record of the meeting. Then tell them why you've come to speak and your position on the issue.

✔ **Present new information:** Boards or councils who refuse to see things your way commonly use the phrase, "We've been over this a million times." If you've ever encountered this problem, you're just repeating the same old arguments, and that won't work. The board or council has already evaluated them and rejected them. You need to offer *new* information. Present a new study, new data, or a new statistic that supports your view — that's what will be of interest to board and council members.

✔ **Start with something positive:** If you want to talk people into your point of view, start by showing where you agree with them. By showing that you have some points of agreement, you establish a positive relationship with the board or council members. "Don't go right into your complaint," says Rich Johnson, member of a school board in Sierra Madre, California. "If you start with something positive, it tells the board that you want to be constructive. You don't want to destroy the school. You just want to make it better." That makes them much more receptive to your arguments.

✔ **Tell them what you want:** Are you trying to persuade a board or council to do something? Provide funding for your project? Agree with your position? Endorse your idea? Well, tell them. This advice sounds obvious, but you'd be amazed at how often this crucial step is omitted. In sales, it's called asking for the order. Ask the board or council members for the order. Don't assume that they know what you want them to do. Tell them clearly and precisely. And remind them of what you want them to do when you conclude your remarks with a statement, such as, "And that's why I suggest you vote no/yes."

✔ **Provide a clear alternative:** Simply arguing against something is not persuasive. If you want the city council not to raise a sales tax, tell them about another source of revenue. Always provide a clear alternative.

✔ **Keep your issue in perspective:** There's a big difference between a pothole in your street and a pot farm in your community. Yes, you have the right to speak about whatever concerns you. But recognize that some issues are more important than others. And here's a clue. Something that affects everyone is probably more important than something that affects just you.

✔ **Provide handouts:** Most boards and councils appreciate handouts that contain relevant information. Remember to bring enough to give to each board or council member. And if there's an opposing side to your issue, bring a copy for that person or group.

Avoiding the Five Biggest Turnoffs for Public Officials

Whatever project, problem, or issue has brought you before a board or council, there's one outcome every speaker wants. You want them to agree with you. That's a tough enough task just arguing your position on its merits. You don't need the added burden of behaving in a way that the board and council members dislike. Although they try to be impartial, they're only human. Here are the top five things that put board and council members in a bad mood and how to avoid them.

Don't repeat yourself

Put yourself in the board or council member's shoes, or ears. Would you want to listen to the same thing over and over again? No way. And neither do they. That means they don't want to hear you repeating yourself, or previous speakers, during your three minutes. So what do you do if Mr. Smith makes your point before you get to speak? "When it's your turn, just say you agree with what Mr. Smith said and then sit down," advises school board member Rich Johnson. "Just repeating the arguments won't help your case and may turn board members against you."

Don't come unprepared

Time is in short supply at board and council meetings. Agendas are crowded. There are many tough issues to get through. And lots of people have done lots of work getting ready for the meeting. So no one wants to hear someone who is unprepared. Not only does it turn off board and council members, it makes you look bad. And it suggests that you don't really care that much about your issue — otherwise you would have prepared.

Don't get emotional

While many issues facing boards and councils are highly emotional, the most effective speakers are those who come across as rational and businesslike. "Too many speakers regard board meetings as therapy sessions," observes Rich Johnson. "If you just want to vent, do it to your family or friends." He suggests a calm and cool demeanor. "If you come in with blustery charges or emotional tirades, you get written off immediately."

Don't be rude

There's an old saying that you don't make yourself look good by making other people look bad. But lots of people try anyway — especially in board and council meetings. It doesn't work.

Don't be a professional complainer

Professional complainers are easy to recognize if you're a frequent attendee at board or council meetings. These are the people who sign up to speak at every meeting. They love to hear themselves talk. And they just complain a lot.

Use Some Kids

Kids can soften the hearts of even the toughest board and council members, especially cute kids. That's why my friend used kids to introduce her issue to the city council in Santa Cruz, California. The city had granted my friend's organization the use of city-owned land as a public garden. But a neighbor disputed this use. After lots of letters and threats, the issue came before the City Council.

My friend packed the meeting with supporters of the garden. She divided up the points they would make. (So no one would repeat arguments.) And she made the first speaker her 12-year-old daughter.

Council members smiled as the daughter went to the podium. She announced that she was there only to introduce the next speaker — my son. Also a 12-year-old, he read a statement about why he supported the garden in that adult yet childlike way that only a 12-year-old can. The Council loved it. The ice was broken and council members remained receptive as the adults took their turns speaking in favor of the garden.

Most boards and councils have to deal with professional complainers. And you don't want to be one if you want to be taken seriously. "If you're at every meeting and you're always complaining, your credibility disappears," observes Rich Johnson. "The board will metaphorically pat you on the head, compartmentalize you, and ignore you."

Chapter 16

Small Talk: Impromptu Speaking and Introducing Other Speakers

*W*hen people think about public speaking, they usually picture someone standing alone in front of an audience, delivering a carefully prepared speech and covering a few major points. But public speaking includes much more than that. You may have to give a speech off the top of your head. Or you may have to introduce a speaker. In this chapter, you find out how to successfully handle both situations.

Say a Few Words: Giving Impromptu Speeches

"Say a few words." This phrase can strike terror into the hearts of the bravest souls. But view it as an opportunity. Really. Everyone knows that you had no time to prepare, so no one expects you to deliver a speech on the level of Lincoln's "Gettysburg Address" or Martin Luther King's "I Have a Dream." You're held to a much lower standard. That's the opportunity. If you say anything remotely well organized and intelligent, you'll be perceived as a genius.

Of course, you can do a few things to help you succeed. The first is to realize that you're not likely to be asked to give an impromptu speech unless you know about the subject. So you really do have a good head start. The second is to be ready when you are asked. The following sections ensure you'll be as prepared as possible for your next impromptu speech.

Being prepared

Yes, the whole idea of an impromptu talk is that you don't know that you'll be asked to speak. But that doesn't mean you can't *anticipate* the possibility. Watch the Academy Awards some time. Only one person wins best actor, but five nominees have acceptance speeches sticking out of their pockets. Take a cue from the professionals: Be ready to speak.

How can you anticipate when you may be asked to vocally bestow your wisdom? Use your common sense. Are you going to an event honoring a friend, coworker, or relative? It's not a big stretch to assume that you may be asked to make a toast or utter a few words of praise.

Are you going to a business meeting? What's on the agenda? It may suggest topics you'd better be prepared to discuss — even though you're *not* a scheduled speaker. Think about the issues that may arise. Would you need to respond to any of them?

Buying time

There's an old saying that nothing makes time pass faster than vacations and short-term loans. Here's a third item for the list: being asked to give an impromptu speech. The time between when you're asked to "say a few words" and when you start talking can go by faster than a prayer at an atheists' convention. Yet this time is crucial to the success of your impromptu remarks. It's when you can plan and organize your entire speech.

Your goal is to lengthen this time period as much as possible. Do it any way you can. Use the following ideas to get you started.

Pause thoughtfully

When someone asks you to say a few words, you're not required to immediately start talking. You can pause and think. This technique actually increases your credibility. The audience assumes that your words are now carefully considered rather than the first thoughts that flew into your head. (Little do they know.) You can even use some showmanship. Tilt your head slightly to one side. Furrow your brow. Squint a bit. Let the audience members know that they're in the presence of some incredibly powerful thinking.

Repeat the question

This technique is the traditional stalling device, but there's a good reason to use it aside from gaining more time. There's no point knocking yourself out giving a fabulous impromptu talk if it turns out to be on the wrong subject. Put the question in your own words. Then get confirmation that you've stated it correctly.

Be ready with an all-purpose quote

It doesn't hurt to memorize a few all-purpose quotes — lines that you can use to begin *any* impromptu talk. Quoting someone makes you sound smart, and you get a little extra time to think about what you really want to say. Keep the following quotes in reserve:

> To paraphrase Richard Nixon, "Let's get one thing perfectly clear." In this case, I mean your question.

> To paraphrase Robert Frost, "The brain is a wonderful organ; it starts working the moment you get up in the morning and doesn't stop until you get asked to make a speech."

Organizing your thoughts

Samuel Johnson once said that "when a man knows he is to be hanged in a fortnight, it concentrates his mind wonderfully." Well, when you know you have to give a speech in 20 seconds, you may feel like you're about to be hanged, and you definitely need to concentrate your mind.

Make a quick decision

The big myth with impromptu speaking is that your mind goes blank as soon as you're asked to speak. It's really just the opposite. Most people get an overwhelming number of ideas, and almost any of them will do the job. You need to pick one idea and stick with it. That's the secret. Commit to one main point — quickly.

Pick a pattern

After you select your main point, you have to organize your speech. What are your subpoints? How will you support them? Do you have examples or anecdotes? You need to pick a pattern of organization — something that allows you to quickly sort out your information. The following are two popular approaches:

- ✔ **Organize around the conclusion.** Decide on a conclusion. Organize all your information so that it supports your conclusion. Then start speaking. Everything you say should be designed to move your message toward the conclusion you select.

- ✔ **Organize around a standard pattern.** Pick one of the standard speech patterns — past, present, future, problem, solution, cause and effect — and quickly fit its structure to your message. Many speakers find the chronological pattern easiest to use.

Find an opening

You can begin an impromptu speech in many ways. But if the audience members don't know that you're speaking impromptu, then you have only one way to begin — tell them. Make absolutely sure that they know. Otherwise, they apply a higher standard to your remarks. And when you're speaking off the cuff, you don't want to be judged as if you had months to prepare.

For example, you might say, "Because I've just been asked to speak and haven't had time to prepare, I may not cover the topic as thoroughly as I usually do. So please let me know if you have any questions when I'm done."

Usually the audience realizes that your talk is impromptu. Then how do you begin?

- ✔ **Tie into previous speakers.** This is probably the easiest opening. You just react to what's already been said.

- ✔ **Be candid.** If you really don't know much about the subject, admit that you're not an expert. Then offer whatever information you can contribute to the discussion. If you're completely clueless, offer to gather information and provide it in the future.

- ✔ **Tell a personal anecdote.** Think of a war story that's relevant to the issue at hand and makes your point. "That reminds me of the time I worked at Company X. We faced a similar issue. . . ."

- ✔ **Switch the topic.** This method is popular with politicians. They're asked for their opinion on a tax increase, and they give their opinion on something else.

One final word of advice on openings. There's one thing you should never do — apologize. What would you apologize for anyway? Not having a carefully polished talk ready? It's an impromptu speech! By definition, it's off the cuff.

Stop talking

Stop when you're finished. It sounds obvious — but most people don't. The most common mistake related to impromptu speaking is rambling. The way to avoid this problem is to know where you're going. Make sure that you think about a conclusion in the short time you have to organize your thoughts. Then stick to your plan. When you get to the conclusion — stop.

Introducing Other Presenters

A common task you may be called upon for is introducing other speakers. If you are tapped for this duty, a special set of rules applies. When you introduce speakers, you need to say who they are and what they'll talk about. But you also need to do several other things. A good introduction should warm up the audience and get them excited about the speaker. It should set a positive tone for the event, and it shouldn't discourage the speaker from speaking. (Most speakers are nervous enough without the added pressure of a lousy introduction.)

If you're asked to introduce someone, take the time to do a good job. The better you make the speaker look, the better you make yourself look.

Finding information about the speaker

Information is the key to making an appropriate introduction. The introduction you do will only be as good as the information you get. And that can be a problem, especially if all you have to work with is a speaker's official company biography.

Start by finding out if there are any other written materials about the speaker. Was she profiled in a company or association newsletter? Was he written up in the local paper? Your goal is to get *too much* information. Then you can pick and choose the best stuff.

No written materials? Don't worry. That's only a starting point. Now it's interview time. Interview the speaker. Interview people who know the speaker. (Or interview people who used to know the speaker. One of the most interesting introductions I've ever heard included quotes from one of the speaker's old girlfriends.) Talk to the speaker's friends, relatives, and coworkers. Talk to the speaker's clients and customers. You'll get good stories and quotes from these people.

Checklist of speaker interview questions

Interviewing the person you're introducing is one of the best ways to get the material you need. Use the following questions to get your interview started.

✔ Why are you making your speech?

✔ What do you want to accomplish with your speech?

✔ What is your expertise regarding the topic of your talk?

✔ How did you get interested in your topic?

✔ Whom should I contact to get some good stories about you?

✔ What are the two or three most important things for the audience to know about you? What are the two or three most important things for the audience to know about your speech?

✔ Do you belong to any interesting organizations?

✔ Do you have any hobbies?

✔ Is there anything that you specifically do or don't want me to mention?

✔ Is there anything you thought I was going to ask or that I should have asked you?

Making a speaker (and yourself) look good

The way that you introduce other speakers says as much about you as it does about them. The following tips ensure that you both come out looking good.

Make the introduction interesting

Anyone can get a speaker's résumé, stand at a podium, and read it. But it's boring, and it's a disservice to the speaker and your audience. It means that you didn't take the time to put together an introduction that sets a great tone and turns on the crowd.

Make the speaker real. Quote the speaker. Tell some anecdotes about the speaker. Let the audience see the speaker as a human being — not a résumé.

Now, that doesn't mean you should ignore the speaker's accomplishments. Pick out a few of the major ones and show how they relate to the speaker's topic. The audience members want to know what the speaker will talk about and why he or she is qualified. So tell them.

Get the speaker's name right

Nothing is more embarrassing than mispronouncing the name of the person you're introducing. (Maybe there are a few more embarrassing things, but they're too gross to mention.) The point is that you lose a lot of credibility if you get the name wrong. You look sloppy, silly, and unprepared.

Keep the introduction brief

The introduction should be short and sweet. If you're introducing a head of state or similar dignitary, maybe you can go as long as three to four minutes. (And that's really pushing the limit.) For anyone else, one to two minutes is plenty.

Coordinate with the person you're introducing

Check the information you use in the introduction with the person you're introducing. Make sure all the information is correct and find out if the speaker wants anything *omitted*.

Talk to the audience

The person doing the introduction gets to the podium, takes out some notes, and gives the introduction. But he only looks at the speaker he's introducing. It's a common mistake. Don't make it. When you introduce someone, look at the audience. Even if you're reading the introduction word for word, when you look up from your notes, look at the audience.

Announce if there will be a question-and-answer period

The audience wants to know when it can ask questions. Is there going to be a Q&A session after the speaker's speech? Or do audience members have to buttonhole the speaker on an individual basis? Either way, it's one less chore the speaker must deal with if you let the audience know when you introduce the speaker.

Avoiding introduction errors

Sometimes the easiest way to do something right is by not doing anything wrong. The following guidelines help you avoid common introduction errors.

✔ **Don't give the speaker's speech.** You're supposed to announce what the speaker will talk about, but that's all. Don't go into minute detail about what the speaker will cover — or there'll be nothing left to cover.

✔ **Don't give your own speech.** Again, you're just supposed to announce what the speaker will talk about. While your views on the subject may be fascinating, no one came to hear them. Holding a microphone is not a license to give a speech. Get on with the intro and get off.

✔ **Don't over-promise.** You want to get the audience excited about the speaker and the topic — but not overexcited. Raising the audience's expectations too much makes things tougher for the speaker. If you say that the speaker is a brilliant orator who will make the audience laugh while tugging at their heartstrings and changing their lives, you're setting the speaker up for a fall. Give a good build-up, but don't go crazy.

✔ **Don't gush.** I don't know who gets more embarrassed by a gushing introduction — the person being introduced or the audience. Either way, the person doing the introduction looks ridiculous. Yes, you're supposed to praise the speaker, but don't go overboard.

✔ **Don't wing it.** You did a lot of research. You have some great stories about the speaker. You edited the speaker's list of achievements down to the ones relevant to the audience. Don't blow it now by winging it. Write out the introduction and stick to it.

Chapter 17

Panels and Roundtables

*B*eing on a panel or taking part in a roundtable discussion — each poses its own unique challenge. Yet many people come to these types of engagements unprepared. Why? They don't consider these situations to be public speaking and they don't know how to prepare for them. This chapter not only points out the challenges you may face, but it also shows you how to overcome them.

Being on a Panel

Many people who don't enjoy making speeches say they would rather speak as part of a panel than as a sole presenter. Panelists usually don't have to speak for the same length of time as a sole presenter, and they can pass tough audience questions to other panelists. Of course, if you're ready for the unique challenges that the panel format presents, you'll shine. If you're not, you'll get shined.

Winning the inevitable comparison

Compared with a sole presenter, panelists have much less control over their message and image because the audience *compares* panelists to each other as they speak. To strategize for your panel session, ask yourself the following questions.

Who else is on the panel?

Finding out who else is on your panel sounds pretty basic, and it is. But it's amazing how many people don't bother to do it. It's essential to find out who else is on your panel. How can you influence the audience's comparison if you don't know who you'll be compared to?

Find out everything you can about the other panelists: their names, their qualifications, their jobs, their knowledge of the topic, their reputations as speakers, and so on. And don't forget to ask about the moderator. Is there one? If so, you want to know everything about this person, too.

What are the rules?

Every panel operates within some set of rules. (All right, once in a while you see a panel that doesn't, but it's not very pretty.) You need to know those rules. Does everyone on the panel make his or her remarks before the audience asks questions? Or does the audience ask questions after each panelist speaks? Are the panelists even expected to make remarks? How much time is allotted for the entire session? How much time is given to each panelist? Is there a moderator, or is it a free-for-all? What's the physical setup? Does each panelist have a microphone, or do the panelists have to pass one around? Whether you want to follow the rules, bend the rules, or break the rules, you have to know the rules.

What is the speaking order?

The order in which panelists speak is a major factor in determining how you are perceived. Think about these factors:

- ✔ **First speaker:** The advantage of going first is that you can't be compared to anyone — yet. So, if you're on a panel with several strong speakers, going first makes a lot of sense. Another advantage is that the first speaker can set the tone for the entire panel. Go first, give a well-structured talk, and you set the standard. The audience now expects the other speakers to do at least as well as you did. The disadvantage of going first is that you can't react to the other panelists. They haven't said anything yet.

- ✔ **Last speaker:** The biggest advantage of going last is that you can comment on what all of the other panelists have said. This allows you to have the final word in defining the discussion. Going last is also the best position if you're not prepared. You can formulate your remarks while the earlier panelists are speaking, and you can comment on what they just said.

- ✔ **Middle speaker:** The advantage of going in the middle is that you can comment on any panelists that spoke before you, and you can still shape the discussion of the panelists that go after you. The disadvantage is that you may get lost in the shuffle. A basic principle of psychology is that people most strongly remember things that come first or last. In a panel situation, that's the first speaker and the last speaker.

What other things should you consider?

How big is the panel? What time of day does the session occur? The answers to these questions may affect your choice of when you want to speak (if you have a choice). A large panel with many speakers increases the chance that the audience is burned out by the time the last speaker gets a turn. Similarly, a panel held in the late afternoon means that the audience won't be focused on the last speaker (except for wondering when he or she will end so that everyone can go eat dinner). With an early morning panel, the audience may still be waking up while the first panelist is speaking.

Maintaining control of your message

Panel discussions create special obstacles to getting your message across the way you want. You want to maintain as much control as possible. Paying attention to the following factors helps you achieve that goal.

Knowing why you're on the panel

Your answer to this question shapes your message strategy. Are you on the panel as a favor to the moderator? Are you there to showcase yourself and your ideas? Are you there to gain recognition for your company or organization? Who, if anyone, are you trying to impress? You need to know what you want to accomplish.

Preparing your message

Any speech requires you to decide how you'll get the audience to remember your key messages. This goal is even more challenging in a panel discussion because there's a lot of "noise in the channel." The audience is bombarded by messages from your co-panelists. And the audience itself may offer statements or questions that provide further distraction from your key ideas. Your messages have a lot of competition, so you have to make them powerful, persuasive, and to the point.

Start by finding out who the audience members are. What organizations do they represent? What are their jobs? What positions do they hold? You can involve them in your remarks by speaking directly to their interests, and then they don't have to wait for the Q&A period to get involved.

Anticipate where you'll be challenged on particular issues. You don't need co-panelists or audience members sinking your entire message by torpedoing you on one point — especially if you know it's coming. Defuse the issue by addressing it in your remarks before the Q&A period.

And listen to the other panelists. I mean really listen. Be prepared to refer back to specific things they said. This tip is especially effective if you get the panelists' names right. ("As Heather and Amy said earlier . . .")

Getting the timing right

Panelists get many opportunities to present information, such as when they make their remarks, answer questions from co-panelists, answer audience questions, and even when they tag statements onto the end of co-panelists' answers to audience questions. But not all opportunities to present information are created equal. Depending on what you want to say, certain times to say it are better than others.

If you have important information for the audience, don't convey it right away. Let them settle down first and get used to the panelists. And don't wait until the end. You may run out of time, or the audience members may be distracted by their preparations to leave. Key information is best presented after the audience has heard you for a few minutes or a few times.

Another aspect of timing has to do with whom the audience credits with an idea. It's not always the panelist who said it first. More often, it's the panelist who talks about an idea second — who takes the idea and runs with it. This second panelist expands the idea, puts it into new words, and makes it his or her own. The audience never remembers that someone else mentioned the idea first. Keep this in mind when you toss your gems into the discussion. If it's a diamond in the rough, don't wait for a fellow panelist to polish it. They'll be polishing off your credit.

Timing also applies to how much you speak. If you speak every time a question or issue is raised, you seem pompous, and your answers lose their impact. People stop listening to you. But if you never speak up, you seem weak and irrelevant — if the audience even remembers you're there. So monitor yourself. Be aware of how much time you spend speaking. Assert yourself but don't go wild.

Planning your delivery

It's easy to forget about the audience if you get into a debate with another panelist. That's a mistake. The majority of your eye contact and "face time" should be with the audience. Focus on different sections of the room as you answer different questions. Make everyone feel like you're talking to him or her.

And don't become a victim of microphone placement. If there's only one mike for all the panelists, make sure that you have access to it. And please, don't lean forward to use it. Lift it up and bring it toward your mouth. Too many speakers seem like they're bowing at the altar of the microphone. It's not a deity. You should control it — not the other way around.

Interacting with other panelists

Your interaction with other panelists has a major effect on how the audience perceives you. Everyone assumes that panelists will have disagreements. (Otherwise, the panel would be fairly boring.) It's *how* you disagree that's important. So here are two words of advice: Be diplomatic.

If you want to point out an inaccuracy stated by another panelist, say something like, "I understand how Matt's experience could lead to his conclusion. However, I have found that. . . ." Don't say that Matt is an idiot. The audience will get the idea.

You should also know where to turn for help. Which panelists are your allies? Which of them support your positions? Communications guru Barbara Howard calls this "knowing your second." In other words, who will "second" your motion? "If you're going to be the first person to take a certain position, you need to know who to turn to for confirmation," she explains. "And you've got to force them to provide it." She suggests two methods. Nonverbally, you can turn to your "second," establish eye contact, and put him or her on the spot to offer support. Verbally, you can do this by saying something like, "Matt, haven't you found what I've said to be true?" The main point: Don't leave it up to chance. Don't just make your statement and hope someone jumps in to support it. Make them jump in.

Answering questions when you don't get any

Answering questions from the audience is prime time for a panelist. It's your chance to shine. But what if the other panelists get all the questions? What if none are directed to you? Don't worry. It just means that it's time to play tag. As other panelists finish their answers, you can tag on your own statement: "I'd like to add one thing to what Sam just said. . . ." Is it aggressive? Yes. But it's better than sitting around after the session is over wishing someone had asked you something. If you want to make an impression, you need to have your say.

Dealing with a moderator

I have good news and bad news about panel moderators. The good news is that a good moderator can make the panel a pleasure. The bad news is that a lot of them are clueless. They see their function solely as introducing the panel members. When hassles occur — inappropriate questions from the audience, fistfights among the panelists — the moderator is nowhere to be found. And sometimes they even screw up the introductions.

Assume that moderators will be incompetent and celebrate if they're not. That means you must be prepared. Prepared to reintroduce yourself to the audience. Prepared to take charge if other panelists hog your time. Prepared to grab the microphone. And if you get a good moderator who runs a tight ship, be prepared to finish on time.

Having a secret weapon ready

Smart panelists carry a secret weapon in reserve — the *sound bite*. That's a short line or phrase designed to capture audience attention. The sound bite gets its name from the radio and television news business. A reporter interviews someone for an hour. That night on the news, you hear the person for 30 seconds. That's the sound bite.

As a Sony Electronics executive, James Harris III always had sound bites ready for panel discussions. If the discussion involved products and product futures, he'd mention the "*Field of Dreams* engineering vision — if we build it they will buy." Another line that stirred up the audience was "People win business, not products. Products enable you to get in the door." He also liked to toss in a tag line from a Pacific Bell ad: "You never get a second chance to make a first impression."

Participating in a Roundtable

Another speaking format that's closely related to the panel is the roundtable discussion. And no, you don't actually have to have a round table.

Figuring out the roundtable format

Like a panel, a roundtable has multiple participants and a moderator. But a roundtable discussion is less formal, encourages interaction between participants, and doesn't require an audience.

A roundtable discussion is best described as a guided conversation. Participants, selected for their expertise, discuss a particular topic or topics. And, as the term "roundtable" suggests, participants are seated so that they all face each other. (It's often a rectangular table. The point is that they can all take part in the discussion.)

Their conversation is guided by a moderator who facilitates the discussion and keeps the agenda moving. The moderator's responsibilities include beginning and ending the discussion on time; making introductions; keeping the participants on topic; and summarizing the discussion. The moderator also makes sure that each participant gets an opportunity to speak.

"The major difference between a panel and a roundtable is that participants in a roundtable are expected to ask each other questions," notes Scott Fivash, CEO of Seattle-based CEOMedia. And he should know. As the publisher of Washington CEO and California CEO magazines, Scott often sponsors roundtable discussions for business executives.

"Our format is standard," he notes. "A moderator will introduce the issue under discussion. Then we go around the table and each person introduces themselves and makes a comment." Scott gives out the agenda in advance so participants can think about it.

The other big difference between a panel and a roundtable is how they're structured. Panelists direct semi-formal remarks to an audience. Roundtable participants direct their remarks to each other and may not even have an audience. That's because the purpose of a roundtable is for experts to have a conversation that might yield insights into the topics under discussion.

Starring in a roundtable discussion

Although roundtable participants are usually chosen for their expertise, the term "expert" is relative. You don't have to be a brain surgeon or rocket scientist to be an expert. Roundtable discussions can cover everything from neighborhood improvements to school fundraising ideas. When you're asked to participate, here are some tips that Scott Fivash suggests you keep in mind:

✔ **Have a few talking points prepared.** "It's often the people who are most prepared who get to participate most in the discussion," observes Scott. That's why he suggests writing down three or four points that you want to make before the roundtable begins. Then you can make them as the opportunity arises.

✔ **Tell stories.** "Everyone likes short anecdotal data," says Scott. "But keep your stories very short and to the point."

✔ **Be prepared to ask questions.** Participants at a roundtable are expected to ask questions. In fact, that's one of the biggest advantages of participating in a roundtable. "Participants in our executive roundtables come expecting to get answers, too," notes Scott. "As they discuss various business topics, they'll ask each other 'How did your company handle that situation?'" And if you know who the other participants will be in advance, you can have specific questions ready to ask them.

✔ **Find appropriate openings for your questions.** The best time to ask a question about a particular topic is when that topic is under discussion. But what if you never get a chance or the topic doesn't come up? Scott Fivash suggests, "You can create your own opportunity to ask a specific question to a specific participant," he explains. "Just conclude one of your comments by saying 'Well I'd really like to hear from Mr. So-And-So about how his company achieved record sales revenues.'"

✔ **Recognize networking opportunities.** A roundtable provides more than an opportunity to state your ideas. It also allows you to develop valuable relationships with the other participants. "You can really get to know them just by discussing issues together," notes Scott. "And you can continue to cultivate those relationships after the roundtable has ended."

Chapter 18

Debates

• •

In This Chapter

▶ Discovering the basics

▶ Taking the affirmative position

▶ Knowing how to take the negative position

▶ Giving your rebuttal

▶ Using six techniques to win

• •

*E*ver since cavemen developed language to accompany the club, we've been able to change people's minds without changing their faces. (Except in certain parts of my old neighborhood.) In fact, talking someone into something is probably the second oldest profession. (It also has a lot to do with the oldest one.) No matter what you're speaking about or who you're speaking to, the ability to debate is critical for getting your ideas accepted.

In order to get the inside scoop on debate, I spoke extensively with Shawn Whalen. He's the Director of Speech and Debate at San Francisco State University. Together, we provide some ideas to improve your debating skills.

Checking Out the Basics

One way or another, debates involve change. Debaters want to change the opinions of their audience and their opponents about the subject under discussion. Debating provides a formal method for allowing this clash of ideas. But before you start changing anyone's mind, you need to check out the basics first.

Discovering types of debates

According to Shawn, people can debate about three things: values, policies, and facts. The value debate is about the priority of different values. The policy debate is about whether or not to take a particular action. The fact debate is "everything else." (A debate whether UFOs exist would be a fact debate.)

The most common type of debate, and the one we'll focus on in this chapter, is the policy debate. That's the type of debate you often see between politicians. (—for example, "We need to raise taxes" versus "No we don't.") Here's how it works. One side identifies a problem and argues for change. The other side argues for the status quo. The side arguing for change has the burden of proof. Why? Because people don't like change. It entails risk and effort. So if you want a policy change then you've got to prove the change is really needed.

Recognizing key debate terms

The process of debating comes with its own special vocabulary. Here are some key terms you'll need to know:

- ✔ **Affirmative:** This is the side arguing for change. It has to come up with a plan for change and show that there's an advantage for carrying out the plan.

- ✔ **Negative:** This is the side that argues against change (or for the status quo).

- ✔ **Resolution:** This is a statement that the affirmative side will argue for and the negative side will argue against. Here's an example: The government should increase spending on technology.

- ✔ **Constructive speech:** This is an initial speech in which you develop the arguments for your side.

- ✔ **Rebuttal:** This is a later speech in which you refute the arguments against your position and show why you're correct.

Supporting an argument with evidence

The key to debate success often comes down to the evidence used to support your arguments. "When both sides have good arguments," notes Shawn, "the quality of one's evidence is what elevates you above your opponent."

- ✔ **Using quotes and paraphrases:** Within the context of debate, evidence is usually presented in one of two forms: a word-for-word quotation or a paraphrase. For example, statistics are often paraphrased. (The National Post of July 25th this year says that 6 out of 10 space aliens can't find parking spaces for their UFOs in Chicago.)

"Debaters don't use word-for-word quotations as much as they could," advises Shawn. "Paraphrasing a source requires some extra mental effort to make the conversion. It puts additional pressure on the speaker. Using an exact quote is easier." (Although reading a quote word-for-word in a speech might be criticized, it's an accepted practice in a debate.)

✔ **Giving source qualifications:** If you quote a leading authority in support of your argument, that should be pretty good evidence, right? Not necessarily. If some members of your audience are unfamiliar with the authority, then just saying the name won't impress them. That's why you should give the qualifications of the source you're quoting. Is the person a Nobel Prize winner? A professor? A doctor? It's their qualifications that establish their credibility.

Arguing in the Affirmative

The affirmative side argues for the resolution. It attempts to show that staying with the status quo is unacceptable. The affirmative side also argues that its plan for change should be enacted because it will produce improvements.

Proving stock issues

The affirmative side can't win the debate without addressing *stock issues.* These are issues that reasonable people need to hear addressed before they would agree to change a policy. Following are the three stock issues that must be addressed:

✔ **Significance:** Significance refers to identifying a problem and establishing that it's so significant that we need to take action to correct it. This is where the affirmative side establishes the need for its plan. (If the plan is enacted then there will be an advantage because the problem will be corrected and things will get better.)

✔ **Inherency:** Inherency refers to the continuous nature of the problem. It won't just go away or disappear of its own accord. Absent change, the problem will continue.

✔ **Solvency:** Solvency refers to how much of the problem your plan will solve. You have to prove that your plan will actually work. What exactly will be done? Who will do it? How long will it take? You've got to get into specifics.

Your plan doesn't have to solve 100 percent of the problem. But it should solve a lot of it. (Your opponent on the negative side will argue that your plan solves so little it's not worth doing.)

Using additional tactics

Here are a few more ways to make the affirmative case more persuasive.

- ✔ **Put your arguments in order.** If you jump back and forth between arguments, it makes your case harder to follow. Put your arguments in an order that makes sense to your audience. Make it easy for them to agree with you.

- ✔ **Identify evidence problems.** If you know that you have a problem supporting some of your arguments, chances are that your opponents and the audience will notice, too. Don't ignore the problem. Hoping that no one notices is not an effective strategy. Find better evidence or adapt your argument to compensate for the problem.

- ✔ **Anticipate arguments from the negative side.** There's a reason that lawyers are trained to argue either side of a case. (And it's *not* just about getting more clients.) If you anticipate what your opponent will say, then you can make your own arguments more effective. What parts of your argument will the negative side attack? What claims will they make? By looking at your case from your opponent's viewpoint, you can probe your arguments for weaknesses.

Arguing Against the Affirmative

The negative side usually wants to preserve the status quo. So it argues against change in general. The negative side always argues against the specific changes proposed by the affirmative side.

Creating a disadvantage

A traditional strategy of the negative side is to argue that there is a disadvantage to enacting the plan advocated by the affirmative side. In other words, the plan would only make the problem worse or create new problems. In either event, staying with the status quo would be a better course of action.

There are three components to a disadvantage: link, impact, and uniqueness. The link says the plan will cause consequence X. The impact says that consequence X is bad. And uniqueness says that consequence X won't happen if the plan isn't enacted.

That's kind of abstract. So here's a real-life example from Shawn. The affirmative side advances a plan to eliminate the car tax in California in order to improve the economic climate. The negative side argues that the plan has a major disadvantage. Link: Eliminating the car tax will bankrupt the cities in the state. Impact: Bankrupting the cities will make the state's economic climate even worse than it is now. Uniqueness: Cities won't go bankrupt unless the car tax is eliminated. The plan to eliminate the car tax uniquely causes these mass city bankruptcies.

"The disadvantage allows you to divide the world of the plan from the world of the status quo," explains Shawn. "Everything is great in terms of link and impact if we stay with what we've got. The plan makes a change which causes X to happen which is bad."

Launching a counterplan

What if the status quo is really as bad as the affirmative side claims? How do you defend a lousy status quo against the affirmative side's plan for change? Easy. The negative side proposes its own plan. Then you argue that your counterplan is the best solution to the problem. Specifically, it's better than the plan offered by the affirmative side.

By conceding that the status quo is unacceptable, the negative side essentially changes the nature of the debate. Instead of a fight between the plan and the status quo, it becomes a fight between the plan and the counterplan.

A counterplan is subject to the same proof requirements as the affirmative side's plan. The negative side has to show that its counterplan actually addresses the problem and that the plan will work. (See "Arguing in the Affirmative" for more information.)

Attacking a stock issue

The affirmative side must prove all three stock issues (significance, inherency, and solvency) in order to make its case and win the debate. That means the negative side can win if it successfully attacks any of those issues.

Here's how to attack each stock issue:

- ✔ **Attacking Significance:** The negative side argues that the problem identified by the affirmative side doesn't exist or that the problem is so minor, it's not worth discussing.

- ✔ **Attacking Inherency:** The negative side argues that the problem will be solved without the change proposed by the affirmative side. The status quo is already solving the problem but needs more time to complete the job.

- ✔ **Attacking Solvency:** The negative side argues that the affirmative side's plan won't solve the problem: The plan won't work because it's ill-conceived; the problem has multiple causes and the plan only eliminates one of them; the plan is impractical; or the plan fails to account for barriers to its implementation. You get the idea.

Want to really sock it to the affirmative side? Ask them to quantify how much of the problem their plan will solve. (They probably won't say 100 percent because the evidence doesn't usually support that claim.) After they give a number, you can chip away at it until it gets smaller and smaller.

Examining other lines of attack

Here are a few more ways to attack arguments advanced by the affirmative side:

- ✔ **Attack the evidence:** See if the evidence really supports the claim being made. For example, a study might find that a drug cures colds in people who have a certain blood type. That doesn't mean that the drug cures all colds. Look for restrictions in the evidence.

- ✔ **Attack the qualifications of the evidence source:** Go back to our study of the drug that cures colds in people with certain blood types. Who did the study? What are their credentials? If the affirmative side doesn't state the qualifications of its sources, then the negative side should demand them.

- ✔ **Use a turn:** A *turn* is like a judo move in debating. It redirects the force of your opponent's argument back against your opponent. For example, the affirmative side claims that its plan creates an advantage. The negative side "turns" the argument by saying not only would the plan not create an advantage, it would create a disadvantage.

For example, the affirmative side argues that implementing its plan to lower drug prices would help reduce the number of senior citizens living in poverty. The negative side turns that argument saying, not only would it not lower the number of senior citizens living in poverty, it would raise the number of senior citizens who can afford to abuse drugs.

Kiss My Rebuttal

The rebuttal period is the pressure-cooker part of the debate. You've got much less time to speak than during the constructive periods. You've got to advance your arguments while simultaneously defending them from attack and attacking your opponents' arguments. To many audience members, your performance during the rebuttal will determine whom they view as the debate winner. Follow these guidelines to come out on top.

Providing an overview

The biggest difficulty of rebuttals is dividing your time wisely to cover the most important arguments. The typical rebuttal speech lasts only six minutes. So it's common to begin with an overview. The overview recaps the main points made by you and your opponents; and it highlights why your side should prevail. "You use the overview to frame the debate in your favor," says Shawn. "You compare your package of arguments with your opponents' package and put your spin on it." The overview should take about ⅛th (or a little less) of the time you have for rebuttal. So a six-minute rebuttal would include an overview between 45 seconds and one minute long.

Giving a roadmap

After giving an overview of your rebuttal, you should state specifically how you'll proceed with the rest of your time. This is called giving a "roadmap." You say something like, "In order to prove that my overview is correct, I'm going to discuss this argument and that argument and then the final argument in the remainder of my rebuttal." The roadmap makes it easier for the audience to follow your arguments. It also helps ensure that you make your case in an organized, logical manner.

Going line by line

The line-by-line refers to keeping track of the arguments made by your opponents and responding to each of them. This "line-by-line" response in the rebuttal ensures that you answer all the relevant arguments raised against your position. It's particularly important if you're not the last speaker. "The nightmare is when you complete your rebuttal and the last speaker begins by saying you've made a big mistake," says Shawn. "That you never answered a major argument." Proficiency in line-by-line prevents that from happening.

Pre-empting opposing arguments

Pre-emption refers to defending your case against opposing arguments before the arguments are made. It's like giving your side an inoculation. When your opponent makes the arguments, they have no effect because you've already weakened them. Pre-emption is particularly important when you don't have the last speech of the debate. Because your opponents will have the last word, you've got to anticipate their arguments and defuse them in advance.

Avoiding repeating evidence

You don't have enough time in the rebuttal to repeat evidence word-for-word that you've already given earlier in the debate. You can refer back to the evidence. You can even highlight key words of it. But you should spend your time explaining the importance of your arguments rather than supporting them.

Attacking counterplans

If the negative side has offered a counterplan, then the affirmative side must attack it in rebuttal. Remember, the counterplan must prove the same stock issues as the affirmative plan. So a natural line of attack is to argue that the counterplan has no solvency — it won't solve the problem. The affirmative side can also argue that the counterplan creates a disadvantage. It will cause harm that wouldn't occur by following the affirmative plan. The affirmative side can also argue that the counterplan doesn't preclude using the affirmative plan. Both plans can be enacted.

Beating Your Opponent, in Six Different Ways

Throughout history, philosophers, lawyers, and teenagers have devised strategies for winning debates. Here are a few techniques that will help you triumph over *your* opponents.

Paying attention to structure and organization

A big mistake made by many beginning debaters is collapsing arguments into each other. "The argument begins as one thing, and then becomes another argument and the two sort of meld together," says Shawn. "And the debaters forget that there were two distinct arguments."

"If you're making multiple arguments you don't want your opponent to be able to reduce them to one argument because then it's simpler to answer," Shawn explains. By paying attention to the structure of your arguments you can keep them differentiated throughout the debate.

The more separate arguments you make against your opponent's position, the more difficult it is for your opponent to move through each of those items.

Managing your time (and your opponent's)

Managing time in a debate is critical because you have such a limited amount of it. That's why making multiple arguments and making them efficiently should be a key part of your time management strategy. The more arguments you make, the more pressure you put on your opponents because then they have to spend more time responding to your arguments than developing their own.

Two techniques are commonly used to increase the number of arguments that can be advanced in a limited time:

1. **Speak quickly.** Many debaters will speak much more quickly than their normal rate of conversation. This allows them to advance a greater number of arguments. While this technique will work with an audience of trained debaters, it's not effective with an audience made up of the general public. (Like the audience for a debate between political candidates.) A general audience will find the rapid rate of speech annoying and alienating.

2. **Word economy.** The other way to advance more arguments in a limited time is to use fewer words. "Distill what you want to say into the shortest possible phrases," says Shawn. "Simple and concise phrasing is the key to word economy." Much of this can be done while preparing for the debate. Make your arguments out loud and keep rewording them until they're in the tightest form possible.

The decision whether to use a quote or paraphrase (See Supporting an argument with evidence earlier in this chapter) can also be influenced by word economy. If a long quote can be paraphrased in a very short form, it will take less time to say and give you more time to introduce other arguments or evidence.

Practicing

It sounds obvious, but the people who need to do it the most, tend to do it the least — experts. "Experts know their content down to the smallest detail," explains Shawn. "That's why they don't think they need to practice much for debates."

Big mistake! The expert understands the material but the audience doesn't. "During the debate, it becomes obvious that the audience can't follow the expert's arguments," says Shawn. "So the expert ends up spending a lot of time explaining one little point. And he never gets to all the substance he really wanted to cover."

Shawn's advice: Practice translating the content of your major arguments into language your audience will understand. That will help you avoid the need to keep re-explaining yourself to get a point across.

Establishing your arguments early

The substance of your argument should be established during your constructive speech. That's where you want to provide the bulk of your evidence. Then in the rebuttal you can focus on attacking your opponent's arguments and polishing your own.

Common Logical Fallacies

A fallacy is an error in reasoning. Debaters like to point them out when made by their opponents. Here are some of the most common fallacies that occur when people argue with each other. (The Latin ones sound really cool to drop into conversations.)

Anonymous authority: The authority supporting the argument is not disclosed.

Appeal to authority: The "authority" cited isn't really an authority.

Argumentum ad Baculum: Appealing to the threat of force.

Argumentum ad hominem: Attacking the person instead of their argument. (My personal favorite.)

Argumentum ad ignoratium: An argument is true because there's no evidence against it.

Argumentum ad lips hoc buttocksia: Arguing that your opponent can kiss your butt. (OK, I made that one up.)

Circular argument: The argument's conclusion occurred earlier as one of its premises.

False analogy: The two objects being compared are more dissimilar than similar.

Inconsistency: One person advances two propositions that contradict each other.

Popularity: Everyone believes it so it must be true.

Post hoc ergo propter hoc: Arguing that if Event A occurred before Event B, then Event A caused Event B.

Red herring: Irrelevant issue thrown in as a distraction.

Straw man: Misrepresenting and weakening an opponent's position and then attacking the misrepresented position.

Unrepresentative sample: The sample doesn't reflect the characteristics of the population it's drawn from.

Avoiding repeating arguments

You have a limited amount of time to make your case. Repeating arguments just eats up time that could be better spent making new, additional arguments. When you repeat arguments, you just help your opponents. Because you give them fewer arguments that they must respond to. If an argument is important, say so and explain why. Don't keep repeating it.

Losing battles to win the war

Keep the big picture in mind as you make your case. A skillful debater will concede minor points to opponents rather than run out of time without answering major arguments.

Chapter 19

International Speaking

Most people wouldn't drive a car if they didn't know what the controls were or how to operate them because there's a good chance they would wreck. They'd hurt themselves, the car, and the people around them. But many people will give a speech to an audience from a different culture without knowing anything about them. And that can be just as dangerous.

If you know nothing about your audience's culture, it's more likely you will unintentionally offend, insult, or upset them. Your speech will be a wreck. And you'll hurt yourself, your cause, and your audience. Unfortunately, the damage to your relationship with your audience is sometimes harder to repair than a broken car. So, consider this chapter your insurance policy to make sure your world doesn't collide with anyone else's and do irreparable damage.

Discovering the Culture of Your Audience

How do you find out about another culture? Ask a member of that culture. Most people are delighted to talk about their ethnic or national background. And if you tell them what you plan to say, they can help you omit anything potentially offensive. They can also give you a window into the mind of your audience. Then you can shape your speech in a way that your audience will enjoy and appreciate.

For example, several years ago I gave a speech to Filipino insurance sales representatives in Manila. Fortunately, I had a friend from the Philippines who vetted my entire speech. He told me which references were too U.S.-centric and wouldn't be understood. And he provided a lot of information about the culture, history, and politics of the Philippines. So I was able to make some specific references to people, places, and current events that were relevant to the audience.

What if you don't have a friend who can guide you? Find someone who can. Do you know someone with a relative in the country where you'll be speaking? Do you know someone at a university or college? Many institutions of higher learning have professors from foreign lands. Do you know someone who works for a multinational corporation? Find out if they can get you in touch with someone from the country where you'll be speaking. And don't forget to ask the person who arranged your speech to provide some help.

Don't assume you know about a culture because you know the popular stereotypes. Just watching television shows or movies won't give you an in-depth understanding. Find out what the culture is really like. You'll spare yourself a lot of embarrassment.

Crafting Your Message

In the sections that follow are some important rules to keep in mind when you're preparing to speak to an audience from another country or culture.

Keeping it as simple as possible

The time for brilliant rhetorical flourishes, witty turns of phrase and complex message structures isn't when you're addressing non-native speakers of your language. Give them a break. Keep your sentences short. Keep your vocabulary as simple as possible. And provide very clear transitions that let them know when you're moving from one point to another. This will increase the chances that you communicate rather than confuse. (This *doesn't* mean that you should talk to them like they are two-year-olds.)

Quoting someone from the audience's country or culture

Every country and culture has its heroes. Authors. Artists. Scientists. Statesmen. Pick a native who is admired by your audience and quote that person in your speech. This will communicate that you went to the trouble of discovering something about your audience's culture, and it will be perceived favorably.

Don't just force in a quotation. Tie it into a point that you're making. Otherwise, you'll appear to be pandering to the audience.

Adapting substance and style to cultural needs

European audiences prefer more depth than a U.S. audience. This cultural difference affects both style and content of a speech. "In the U.S., audiences prefer speakers who are passionate about their topic," says Allen Weiner, president of Communication Development Associates. "They like speakers who are energetic — move around a lot and use a lot of gestures. In Europe, audiences regard high energy as a sign of shallowness — that there's too much effort going into style and not enough substance. If you're too upbeat in Europe, you're perceived as not having enough depth."

The distinction also plays out in content. Europeans prefer more detailed evidence in a speech — numbers and statistics. In the U.S., audiences like anecdotal evidence. "Give them stories in the speech and numbers in the handouts," Allen advises.

Keeping it as short as possible

It can be tiring to listen to a speech in your native language. So figure it's even more tiring to listen to a speech in a non-native language. That's why you should keep your speech as short as possible. If you have a lot of content to deliver, consider scheduling break periods for your audience.

Using worldwide examples

Do all the examples and references in your speech come from your own country? If so, you risk appearing pompous and arrogant when you're speaking outside your country. Find some examples from elsewhere in the world. Or at least acknowledge that such examples exist. (You just didn't have time to research them.) You don't win over foreign audiences by implying that your country is superior to theirs.

Remembering there's more than one America

People from the United States like to refer to themselves as Americans. This annoys people from countries in Central America and South America. They're also Americans.

Avoiding humor

What makes something funny? Although one could write a dissertation on this subject (and many have), the short answer is that much humor is rooted in cultural values. So something that's funny in one culture may not be in another. Unless you're very familiar with the culture, using humor is usually a mistake; avoid it unless you're sure it transcends cultural boundaries (see the sidebar "Emergency Laughs"). No one may get your joke, or even worse, they may find it offensive.

Getting rid of idioms

Every language has colloquial expressions that cause confusion if translated literally. Avoid them. Actively search for them in your speech and eliminate them.

Take the phrase "born with a silver spoon in his mouth." A speaker of American English would understand that to mean a person who was born into a rich family. But speakers of other languages might think it refers to a freak with a unique birth defect.

Even among English speakers, idiomatic expressions can cause confusion. If a British woman says to "knock her up" at nine o'clock, a British man would know she means to wake her up at nine. A U.S. male would think she wants him to impregnate her at nine.

Emergency Laughs

When Martin Gonzalez Bravo worked as a marketing executive for Hewlett-Packard, he gave speeches to audiences around the world. And he'd always begin the same way: "I'm glad to be here. I've only been here a few days, but I'm already picking up your language." Then he'd say the following phrase in the language of his audience: "A life-vest is located beneath your seat in case of emergency."

"No matter where I went, they always laughed," says Martin. "It was a great way to break the ice."

Everyone knows the line from the safety card on an airplane. And that's how Martin would learn it. "The safety card is always written in several languages," he explains. "So on the plane to wherever I was going, I'd memorize the line in the language of that country." He'd also write it down and ask local country co-workers to make sure he was pronouncing it correctly after he arrived at his destination.

Martin agrees that using humor when speaking to an audience from another other culture can be risky. But he says his line works because it transcends cultural boundaries. "Anyone who has ever ridden in a plane will get it," he notes.

Losing the jargon and acronyms

Jargon and acronyms are confusing enough when you're talking to native speakers of your language. They're even worse when you're talking to non-native speakers. If you have to use jargon, make sure you define it for the audience. And explain what acronyms stand for. But avoid both whenever possible.

Using appropriate sports metaphors

Baseball metaphors are great in the U.S., Japan, and a handful of other countries. But most countries in the world don't play baseball. Or football. If you're going to use sports metaphors, use them from sports that are popular in the country where you're speaking. Hint: soccer is probably the most popular sport in the world. (And if you mention it in England, remember to call it football.)

Getting the numbers right

If you're talking about money or measurements, convert your numbers into the system used by the nation where you'll be speaking. And remember, most of the world uses the metric system.

Being cautious about holiday references

A holiday in one country is not necessarily a holiday in another country. And some holidays have the same names but different dates and meanings. For example, more than one country has a Thanksgiving. But the stuff about pilgrims and Indians applies only to the United States. And while every country has a fifth of May in its calendar, only Mexico celebrates Cinco De Mayo. It's *not* a holiday for other Central American countries.

Getting graphic

It would seem like a good idea to use visual aids with lots of graphic symbols when you're speaking to a foreign audience. But often it's not. Although some symbols are used most places around the world (men's and women's restrooms symbols), many are culture specific. For example, a piggy bank would mean savings to an audience from the United States. But in some countries it would merely indicate a disgusting animal. And a thumbs-up image — meaning approval in some countries — is offensive in others. So make sure that the graphic symbols you use mean what you think they'll mean to your audience.

Coloring with caution

Another potential pitfall with visual aids is color. The problem is that different cultures assign different symbolic meanings to colors. For example, in western cultures white is associated with purity and weddings. In Asian cultures, white is associated with death and funerals. Red symbolizes rage in the United States. But it's a color for happiness in China. So find out what colors symbolize for your audience before you make your visual aids so you won't paint yourself into a corner.

Making magnificent handouts

Handouts are good when you're speaking to people who are not native speakers of your language. A written summary of your remarks will help them understand and recall more of your message — especially if the handouts are in their language. But make sure the translation is correct. And that it doesn't offend any of the cultural sensibilities of your audience. Ask someone from that culture to review your handouts before you give them out.

Watch out for the following:

- ✔ **Dates:** Use the format of the country where you'll be speaking. In Europe, 12/8/90 means August 12th 1990. In the United States, it means December 8th 1990.

- ✔ **Phone numbers:** Don't forget to include the country code as part of any phone listing. And remember that "800" numbers that provide toll-free calls in the United States don't usually apply in other countries.

- ✔ **Money symbols:** The $ sign is used in connection with several different currencies. For example, do you mean Canadian dollars or U.S. dollars? Indicate what country the $ refers to by adding a prefix such as US$ for U.S. dollars or C$ for Canadian dollars.

Adapting Your Delivery

When you're speaking in the international arena, just having a carefully prepared message isn't enough to ensure success. You also have to deliver it properly. That means adapting your style to the cultural requirements of your audience. Check out some general rules to keep in mind in the following sections.

Getting there ahead of time

Not just to the room where you'll be speaking (although that's a good idea). Get to the country where you'll be speaking far enough ahead of time to compensate for jet lag and to adjust to the time zone.

Projecting humility

The best way to win over audiences from any culture is to project the fact that you care for them and are really interested in them. You're really happy and honored to be there with them. In contrast, the opposite approach — arrogantly communicating that the audience has lucked out by being in your presence — is a big turnoff.

Talking the talk

It's almost a cliché for a speaker addressing an audience that speaks a different language to start by saying a few words or a sentence in that language. (Typically, it's something like "I'm happy to be here today" in whatever language is native to the audience.) This gesture shows that the speaker tried to learn a little of the audience's language.

If you're only going to learn one line, save it for the end. If you've established a connection with the audience, ending with a line in their language really cements the relationship. End by saying, "Thank you for being here with me today" in their language.

If you want to open with a line in the audience's language, learn how to say, "I'm sorry for not knowing how to speak your language." It's much more effective than a greeting like, "I'm happy to be here today." (See the preceding rule regarding humility.)

Eating their food

If you're speaking at a lunch or dinner meeting or any other event where food is involved, you have to eat some. You can tell people of another culture that they're great, you love them, and they're wonderful. But if you don't eat their food, they won't believe you. You have to eat what they're eating. (That's why politicians always get themselves photographed shoveling in souvlaki, or burritos, or matzoh ball soup when they speak at events held by various ethnic groups.) So unless you have a specific dietary restriction due to health or religious reasons — *bon appétit.*

Speaking slowly

Slow down. If you're not speaking to native speakers, don't speak at your normal rate. Give them some time to mentally translate what you're saying. (But don't slow down so much that you're insulting. You're not talking to children.) Elongating your pauses between sentences should be enough.

Interpreting reactions

Don't assume you're doing well or badly based on your own culture's typical reactions to a speaker. Other cultures can react quite differently. For example, in the United States, an audience that takes notes indicates that the speaker is doing well. But in Japan, the audience will take notes to be polite — even if the speaker is terrible. Some cultures show approval of a speaker by applauding, others show respect by remaining silent.

Just as you should know what the audience's reactions mean in their culture, you need to know how they may interpret *your* body language. So be very careful with the body language you use in your speech. A harmless gesture in one culture can be highly offensive in another. See Chapter 12 for specific examples.

Following protocol

Outside the United States, protocol often assumes a much more important role in the speech-making process. Speakers are sometimes expected to give and receive gifts or recognize dignitaries in the audience. If you don't want to risk offending your audience, find out the traditions and rituals that they expect you to follow. The person who arranged your speaking engagement should be able to help you with this.

Working with foreign voltage

If you're planning to use visual aids such as PowerPoint, make sure that your equipment conforms to the electrical standards of the country in which you'll be speaking. It sounds obvious. But a lot of speakers forget. Just go to a search engine on the Web and type "voltage converter" plus the name of the nation where you'll be speaking. You'll find out exactly what you need to know.

Chapter 20

Virtual Meetings: Phone, Video, and Web

In This Chapter

▶ Discovery a virtual meeting to meet your needs

▶ Getting ready for a virtual meeting

▶ Working the virtual meeting

▶ Teleconferencing like a pro

A virtual meeting includes any kind of conference where people don't meet face-to-face. They can meet via telephone, video, or over the Web. Virtual meetings sometimes include sharing audio and video data, documents, or other types of information. It can be highly interactive or primarily a one-way transmission.

In order to get the latest information on virtual meetings, I spoke with Kare Anderson, an expert who has spoken at numerous virtual conferences. A former journalist, Kare is now a professional speaker who talks about specific ways to communicate and connect to create more opportunity with others.(You can learn more about her at www.sayitbetter.com) Together, we've outlined what you need to know to make your next virtual meeting a successful one.

Choosing a Type of Virtual Meeting to Hold

Many criteria influence your decision regarding what type of virtual meeting will best suit your needs.

Some factors you should consider are interactivity, number of attendees, and type of information to be discussed. You can choose which type of meeting best fits these needs by examining the following short descriptions of each type of virtual meeting:

✔ **Audio conferencing:** Audio conferencing refers to a meeting in which attendees can hear each other but they cannot see each other or exchange non-oral data, although such data can be mailed or e-mailed ahead of time. Such meetings work best with smaller groups, are usually conducted over the telephone, and are useful if complicated visuals aren't necessary or if attendees are uncomfortable with more technical types of virtual meetings.

✔ **Video conferencing:** Video conferencing refers to a meeting in which attendees at various locations can see and hear each other. It allows the use of visual materials such as charts and graphs. Video conferences can be conducted in studios that are specially designed for that purpose or over the Web with streaming media. Many corporations and larger businesses with multiple locations have their own permanent video conferencing set-ups. Such meetings are best if watching body language is important or you need to communicate complex data. Video is also preferable if you want to make sure that all attendees are paying attention.

✔ **Web conferencing:** Web conferencing commonly refers to a meeting conducted over the Web in which attendees can receive and transmit video, audio, and data such as documents and PowerPoint slides. A small number of people can work on a project together, called *Web collaboration,* a large group of people can receive a one-way transmission of information, called *Web casting,* or several people can log onto a Web site and view a seminar or other event, called a *webinar.*

The ability to archive Web conferences is one of the reasons they are growing in popularity. They can then be played back on-demand at a time more convenient for people who could not attend the event. Some companies also break Web conferences into smaller segments and use them as training modules.

✔ **E-mail meetings:** An e-mail meeting involves the exchange of e-mails in real time between meeting attendees. It allows attendees to share documents, graphic files, and other information that can be attached to an e-mail message. E-mail meetings are useful for communicating information, but wide-scale interaction is difficult.

Just knowing what each type of meeting is doesn't factor in other important considerations, such as technology, budget, and meeting goals. See how those factors may impact the meeting you choose by reading the following sections.

Avoiding technical difficulties

The type of virtual meeting you choose to hold will depend on the technology you have available and the level of technology that you want to involve. Kare recommends choosing the lowest technology that will allow you to accomplish your meeting goals. "The more complex the technology, the more things can go wrong," she notes. "The lower the level of technology, the more people can participate."

Make the following considerations before you decide what type of technology to use:

✔ **Participant experience:** The human factor can play a major role in deciding what type of technology to use for a virtual meeting. If most of the attendees are familiar with audio conferencing but not Web conferencing, you need to take that into consideration. It doesn't automatically mean you shouldn't go with Web conferencing, but it does mean that you'll have to provide a lot more guidance to the attendees.

✔ **Bandwidth:** If you're planning a meeting over the Web, then bandwidth will be a major concern. Video requires more bandwidth than audio. And you've got to make sure that each attendee has the minimum bandwidth required to receive the Web conference properly. Otherwise you may have some attendees who receive the communication clearly and other who receive nothing. Check with the person or department responsible for running the technological aspects of the meeting to make sure that bandwidth is sufficient.

Use a telephone line to connect attendees for the audio portion of the Web conference. This will lower their bandwidth requirements and provide clearer sound.

✔ **Connection:** The kind of connection each attendee has can make a major difference in connectivity. Dial-up connections will be the worst, and may prevent folks dialing in from also accessing the audio (if they only have one phone line to share between the computer and voice communications). DSL, cable modem connections, and network connections are preferred.

Transmission speeds on the Web can vary greatly depending on the day and time of your meeting. If possible, plan your meeting for days and times have less traffic over the Internet.

Fitting the meeting into your budget

If budget constraints drive your choice of meeting, then an e-mail meeting is the least expensive. In fact, if all attendees have access to e-mail then the meeting costs nothing. On the other extreme, a video meeting involving several locations can become quite costly, especially if you need to rent video facilities for each location. In between these cost extremes are Web-based meetings supplemented by the telephone.

Factoring in your meeting goals

The purpose of your meeting will play an important role in determining what type of virtual format to choose. Here are some common meeting goals and factors to consider:

- ✔ **If your goal is to arrive at a group decision:** Group decision-making requires a lot of interaction. Ideas are discussed, opinions exchanged, and consensus achieved. These types of activities usually require a lot of interaction. That's why you should have at least two-way audio capabilities for your meeting. At a minimum that means telephone conferencing. It could also include Web conferencing or video conferencing. Holding the meeting solely by e-mail would be too slow and frustrating.

- ✔ **If your goal is to sell a product or service:** Many sales and marketing experts consider visual information to be an indispensable part of the sales process. Prospects want to see what they're getting and who they're getting it from. And sales people want to "read" the expressions of their prospects. So full-scale video conferencing is ideal for this type of meeting. An alternative is Web conferencing with two-way visual and audio communication.

- ✔ **If your goal is to train people:** Training meetings are well-suited for Web conferencing. The training information can be directed to meeting attendees as both visual and audio data. Upon completion of training modules, attendees can ask questions via telephone or e-mail. An alternative is a unidirectional video conference. The trainer performs in a studio and is broadcast to television monitors where attendees are located. Again, attendees can ask questions via telephone or e-mail.

✔ **If your goal is to announce information:** This meeting, centered on one-way communication, can be accomplished through e-mail. Just send the announcement to everyone who is supposed to get it. If the announcement is very important and you want to be sure it's received properly, you can choose a format with greater interaction such as a conference call.

Preparing for a Virtual Meeting

The key to a successful virtual meeting is the same as the key to a successful face-to-face meeting: preparation. Consider the following guidelines to ensure that you're ready for *your* virtual meeting.

Applying non-virtual rules

It's important to remember that a virtual meeting is still a meeting. So many of the basic rules for holding an effective meeting apply:

✔ **Identify the purpose for meeting:** Make sure you know why you're having a meeting, or else cancel it. No one wants to attend yet another meeting, virtual or otherwise, that has no real purpose. Identifying the purpose of your meeting is critical for knowing how to conduct it.

✔ **Provide materials in advance:** Essential to making any meeting run smoothly, providing materials in advance of your virtual meeting is one of the keys to making your meeting a success. Following are some common materials you may want to advance to meeting participants:

- **Agenda:** Whether a meeting is virtual or not, distributing an agenda to attendees beforehand makes the meeting stay on track and run smoothly. The agenda should indicate the goals of the meeting and the order of the speakers. Having a list of speakers makes it easier for meeting attendees to follow the proceedings, especially in virtual meetings such as audio conferences where the speakers will not be seen.

- **Support material:** Providing support materials such as speech notes and outlines in advance also helps attendees get more out of the meeting. These can be sent easily and cheaply through e-mail.

- **PowerPoint slides:** For meetings held on the Web, it may be smarter to distribute PowerPoint slides beforehand rather than using PowerPoint during the meeting.

- **Contact information:** A list of all attendees' names, phone numbers, and e-mail addresses should be distributed so that they can reach each other if there is a technical problem.

✔ **Check the room:** It's standard advice to check the meeting room in advance of the meeting. You want to make sure that it meets your needs: Check to be sure that it's big enough, that there are enough seats for attendees, that the room layout is conducive to discussion, and that there are electrical outlets available for audiovisual equipment if needed.

Considering virtual-specific factors

Because of the differences between virtual meetings and face-to-face meetings, you need to consider the following special factors:

✔ **Timing:** Unlike an in-person meeting, a virtual meeting can span several time zones. You need to take this into consideration when scheduling the meeting. If possible, hold the meeting during normal business hours for all the attendees. Be aware of when attendees at various locations usually take breaks or eat meals. Try to plan a meeting time that is convenient for all the attendees.

✔ **Technology:** Make sure that all attendees have the equipment necessary to participate in the meeting and that they know how to use it. Test the equipment beforehand. Then test it again. If the equipment doesn't work, the meeting doesn't work. Have a back-up plan ready in case the equipment fails during the meeting. (Will you call everyone? E-mail everyone? Shout out the window?) If they're using a phone to connect with others, they need to make sure the line doesn't have the call-waiting feature, or that call-waiting is temporarily disengaged.

✔ **Appearance:** If you appear on screen via a Web or video conference, then you should consider how your appearance will affect your message. Here are a few ways to improve your electronic appearance:

  - Wear a conservative outfit that doesn't draw attention away from your face.

  - Wear pastel colors rather than bright colors because pastels broadcast better.

  - Avoid striped, checked, or patterned clothing.

  - Make sure your clothes contrast with your background colors.

- Use a solid-color background.

- Remove objects from the background that will distract your audience, such as pictures, posters, etc.

Participating in a Virtual Meeting

Participating effectively in a virtual meeting means adapting to a situation where many of the people with whom you're interacting are not physically present. That can seem strange if you're the type of person who likes to shake hands and slap backs. Here are a few rules and tips to ensure you perform well with your virtual comrades:

✔ **Keep it as short as possible.** Many people think meetings are a waste of time. And those are the meetings where you can actually see each other face-to-face. Virtual meetings have the added burden of requiring the use of phones, computers, or other technology. So keep your virtual meetings as short as possible. You can also break them into segments. Instead of watching a streaming video for 15 minutes, break it into three 5-minute segments.

✔ **Make it as interactive as possible.** Even large virtual meetings can achieve a relatively high degree of interactivity if you plan for it. Software that allows polling can provide instant votes from any number of attendees. Or just ask questions and tally e-mail responses.

✔ **Encourage participation.** One way to increase interaction is to encourage individual participation. At smaller meetings, begin by introducing each attendee and asking that person to say hello. At a minimum, make sure that whenever people speak they identify themselves.

✔ **Ask for responses.** The simplest way to encourage participation is to ask attendees for responses. This is also a useful way to find out what they really think. (Unless everyone in the meeting is simultaneously televised, it's not possible to read everyone's body language in a virtual meeting. And if it's an audio conference you can't read anyone's body language.) To make up for a lack of visual cues, speakers should frequently ask attendees for responses, using questions, such as "Is there anyone who doesn't understand?" "Does this make sense?" "Do you agree?" "Would you like to hear more about this?" Don't assume that silence means acceptance.

✔ **Develop a protocol for questions.** Large virtual meetings often provide limited interaction by allowing attendees to phone in or e-mail questions to the speaker. Here's the problem. Time only permits some of the questions to be answered. So how does the speaker decide which questions to answer? "The person running the meeting should provide a rationale," says Kare. "Otherwise attendees will perceive the process to be unfair." She advises stating how many questions were received, how many will be answered and how the decision was made. "You can say something like, 'We tried to pick the most diverse ones so that there's one question from every type of category that was asked,'" Kare suggests.

✔ **Take time to build relationships.** People who attend face-to-face meetings build relationships by arriving early or staying late and chatting with each other. This type of bonding is good for any group that meets on a regular basis. If the meeting is virtual, you can create rapport by beginning or ending with attendees talking about non-work related items. Have attendees tell the group something about themselves. This is an especially good tactic to kill time while waiting for everyone else to dial in.

Taking in Tips for Teleconferences

One of the most common virtual meetings is the teleconference. It's relatively cheap and it employs a technology that's widely available and universally understood — the telephone. Your next teleconference will be more effective if you use common courtesy as well as a colorful voice. So, keep the following ideas in mind:

✔ Speak clearly.

✔ Keep your answers short.

✔ Put your phone on mute when you're not speaking.

✔ Identify yourself and your location when you speak.

✔ Indicate when you're finished speaking.

✔ Explain any extraneous noises (people moving around the room, etc.).

✔ Repeat any questions you're asked before you answer them.

✔ Don't hog time.

✔ Pause so another person can speak.

✔ Reserve complex questions for e-mail unless you need an immediate response.

✔ Use emotion in your voice rather than speak in a flat tone.

✔ Use metaphors and similes to create word pictures for attendees.

New words for new meetings

The rapid expansion of technology that has created new kinds of virtual meetings has outpaced our ability to describe these meetings. Old concepts just don't apply. Many of the situations that arise in meetings held over the Web or phone defy explanation with existing language. So as a public service, here are some new words to use for common virtual meeting problems and events:

bandwither: the Web connection dies because there's not enough bandwidth

f-mail: an e-mail message that's laced with expletives

interactuary: a professional who predicts the level of interaction that a virtual meeting will achieve

teleconspire: when two or more people arrange in advance to gang up on someone in a teleconference

virtualpha: a dominant personality who takes over a virtual meeting by hogging time and not giving anyone else a chance to speak

wetbinar: first-time test of a marketing seminar delivered over the Web

Part VI

The Part of Tens

The 5th Wave   By Rich Tennant

In this part . . .

*H*umor can be a useful tool in public speaking, so, in this part, I show you lots of simple ways to use humor in a speech even if you can't tell a joke. And to make you feel even more secure for your next speech, I give you a list of things to check before you speak.

Chapter 21

Ten Types of Humor That Anyone Can Use

● ●

In This Chapter

▶ Personal anecdotes

▶ Nine other simple types of humor that don't require comic delivery

● ●

*H*umor is a powerful communication tool. It can gain attention, create rapport, and make a speech more memorable. It can also relieve tension, motivate an audience, and enhance your reputation if it's used appropriately. Can't tell a joke? Don't worry. You have lots of other options for incorporating humor into your speech.

Using Personal Anecdotes

A personal anecdote is a story based on a real experience — yours or someone else's. It's a story about something that happened with friends or relatives. It's a war story from work. It's an incident that occurred at school or home or anywhere. It's your life. These stories provide an absolute gold mine of humorous material for any speech. And here's their best feature — *you can tell them*. You've already been telling them for years. So you don't have to worry about delivery.

Instead of telling these stories for no particular reason while conversing with friends or acquaintances, use them for a purpose: Use them to make a point. What follows is an example from a commencement address given by Alexander Sanders, Jr., when he was Chief Judge of the South Carolina Court of Appeals. His daughter, Zoe, was among the graduates.

> I am reminded today of something that happened when Zoe was just a little girl. When she was three years old, I came home from work to find a crisis in my household. Zoe's pet

turtle had died. And she was crying as if her heart would break. Her mother, having coped with the problems of the home all day, turned that one over to me to solve. At the time, I was practicing law and serving in the Legislature. Frankly, it was a problem a lawyer/politician was not up to solving.

The mysteries of life and death are difficult, if not impossible, for the mature mind to fathom. The task of explaining them to a three-year-old was completely beyond either my confidence or experience. But I tried. First, I made the obvious argument that we would get another turtle to replace the one that died. We would go down to the pet store and buy another one just like the one who was gone.

I got nowhere with that argument. Even at three years old, Zoe was smart enough to know that there is a certain nontransferability about living things. A turtle is not a toy. There's really no such thing as getting another one just like the one who died. Zoe's tears continued.

Finally, in desperation, I said, "I tell you what, we'll have a funeral for the turtle." Well, being only three years old, she didn't know what a funeral was. So I quickly proceeded to expand on my theme. You see, I was employing the typical lawyer's tactic of diversion. If you can't win on the issue at hand, take off on something completely beside the point.

"A funeral," I explained, "is a great festival in honor of the turtle." Well, being only three years old, she didn't know what a festival was either. So, I quickly proceeded to explain further. And, as I did so, I began to depart from the lawyer's tactic of diversion and engage in the politician's prerogative of outright lying. "Actually," I said, "a funeral is like a birthday party. We'll have ice cream and cake and lemonade and balloons, and all the children in the neighborhood will come over to our house to play. All because the turtle has died."

Success at last! Zoe's tears began to dry, and she quickly returned to her happy, smiling self again. Now, happy. Now, joyous. At the prospect of all that was going to happen. All because the turtle had died.

Then an utterly unforeseen thing happened. We looked down, and lo and behold, the turtle began to move. He was not dead after all. In a matter of seconds, he was crawling away as lively as ever. For once, a lawyer/politician was struck dumb for words.

I just didn't know what to say. But Zoe appraised the situation perfectly. And although this happened more than 20 years ago, I remember what she said as though it was yesterday. With all the innocence of her tender years, she looked up at me and said, "Daddy," she said, "Daddy, let's kill it."

The judge used the story to make a point about the lengths to which parents will go to make their children happy. But it could also be used to make points about knowing your priorities, analyzing a situation for maximum advantage, and learning that appearances can be deceiving. Or any other point that you can think of!

Analogies

An analogy is a comparison between two objects or concepts. A funny analogy makes the comparison in an entertaining way. And analogies don't require comic delivery because they're so short.

Following is an example from a speech about regulatory reform given by Eugene Ludwig, former Comptroller of the Currency of the United States: "Being a regulator these days is a lot like being the nearest fire hydrant to the dog pound. You know they'll have to turn to you in an emergency, but it's sure tough dealing with those daily indignities."

Now I admit that funny analogies are difficult to think up yourself, but you can use other people's analogies in your own speeches by switching some of the facts. The analogy about the regulator and the fire hydrant is a perfect example. It could apply to a secretary, a manager, or anyone who feels that his or her work is important but not respected. So, anytime you come across a funny analogy, write it down and file it away. You can never have too many at your fingertips.

Quotes

Funny quotes provide an easy way to get attention. Call it the cult of celebrity. Call it a fascination with the quoteworthy. Whatever you want to call it, the phenomenon remains the same — as soon as an audience hears a famous name, it perks up. If the famous name is followed by a really funny quote, then you've got them. (At least for a few seconds. But in today's computer age, that's a long time.)

This funny quote was used by Richard Lidstad, retired Vice President of Human Resources for 3M, in a speech about success:

> Second, you need to know that I don't consider myself an intellectual. I don't know everything. That's not all bad, however, since President Dwight Eisenhower once said, "An intellectual is a man who takes more words than necessary to tell more than he knows."

Cartoons

Even people who insist that they can't tell a joke admit that they can describe a cartoon that appeared in a newspaper or magazine. I see people do this all the time. Someone joins a gathering of coworkers taking a coffee break. The conversation turns to some business topic, and the person describes a cartoon from *The Wall Street Journal* that relates to the discussion. The coworkers laugh, and the conversation continues. If you can do this (and I know you can), you can use cartoons to make points in a speech.

One of my favorite cartoons is a picture of two shipwrecked survivors standing on a tiny island. One of the survivors is holding a bottle that floated onto the shore. He looks at the note that was in it and says to his companion, "It's from your alumni association." I can use this cartoon to make points about relentlessly pursuing an objective, finding what you're looking for, and how you can run but you can't hide.

You can even describe an entire comic strip in your talk — if it makes a point. The next quote shows how Professor James V. Schall of Georgetown University's Department of Government used a *Peanuts* comic strip in a speech titled "On Wasting the Best Years of Our Lives: Christianity Is a Religion of Joy."

> Sally and Charlie Brown are seen standing by a telephone pole waiting for the school bus one morning. Charlie is gazing down the empty street while in back of him we hear Sally exclaim, "Someday there's going to be a monument here, and you know what will be on it?" Charlie continues looking down the street in silence. Sally continues to explain. It will read, "This is where Sally Brown wasted the best years of her life waiting for the school bus. . . ." Finally, Charlie turns around to look at her with some considerable perplexity as she describes what she would proceed to do with the wasted time. She would have "slept another ten minutes."

Clearly, Sally did not think sleeping another ten minutes each school day morning constituted a waste of her time. The question of whether we are "wasting our time" by sleeping or waiting for school buses, however, is one of considerable interest if we think about the issue of human priorities.

Definitions

Funny definitions are extremely easy to use. Just pick a word or phrase from your speech and define it in an amusing way. Here's an example from a speech to the Ag Bankers Association given by Dale Miller when he was President and CEO of the Sandoz Crop Protection Corporation: "A cynic once defined a farm as an irregular patch of nettles bounded by short term notes."

Here's another example from a speech by Norman Augustine, former President and CEO of Lockheed-Martin: "I bring you greetings from my hometown, 'America's Most Confused City,' Washington, D.C., which I have occasionally referred to as 'a diamond-shaped city surrounded on all four sides by reality.'"

Want a formula for inserting funny definitions into your talk? Try the old "dictionary bit." You pick out a word or phrase that you look up in the dictionary and then state the meaning. Here's an example from a speech about biotechnology given by Richard Mahoney, former Chairman of the Monsanto Company:

> For those six weeks I spent splicing genes in the lab, the scientists presented me with a certificate, designating me an official "journeyman in gene splicing." I was quite pleased, until I looked up "journeyman" in the dictionary: "An experienced, reliable worker, especially as distinguished from one who is brilliant."

Where do you find funny definitions? Most "treasury of funny stuff for public speakers" type books contain them. Just look in your local library or bookstore. Trade journals and professional magazines are also good sources. These types of publications often have a humor page that includes amusing definitions related to their readers' occupations.

Abbreviations and acronyms

An abbreviation is formed by combining the first letters of a series of words. Two familiar (but boring) examples are IRS (Internal Revenue Service) and the accounting principle known as LIFO (Last In First Out). Funny abbreviations are much more entertaining.

You can make abbreviations funny in a variety of ways. The simplest way is to change the meaning of the underlying words. For example, PBS usually refers to Public Broadcasting System, but that's not how Daniel Brenner, former Director of the Communications Law Program at the UCLA School of Law, used it in a speech about the information revolution: "I've just come from a meeting of the Corporation for Public Broadcasting in Washington. Public broadcasting has its own problems. Most people think PBS stands for Plenty of British Shows."

Acronyms (abbreviations that form a word) can also be used in a humorous way. You can make up funny ones by abbreviating a funny phrase. Here's an example from a speech about corporate ethics given by William Dimma when he was Deputy Chairman of Royal Lepage Limited: "Ten or 15 years ago, corporate ethics was a MEGO topic . . . My Eyes Glaze Over . . . but not today and not likely ever again."

Another way to add humor is to redefine a negative word by making it an acronym for something positive. I recently heard an engineer use this technique after his department was referred to as a bunch of nerds. He said that NERDS stood for "Nouveau Engineering Research and Development Stars."

Signs

Have you ever seen a sign that made you laugh? They're all over the place these days. The "You Want It When?" sign posted in a secretary's cubicle. The "Mistakes Made While You Wait" sign hanging by a bank teller's window. The "Your Failure to Plan Does Not Constitute an Emergency on Our Part" sign taped to the wall of a printer's shop. All of these are potential material for a speech. You just describe the sign and where you saw it. Then tie it to a point.

Here's an example from a speech about health data given by James O. Mason when he was Head of the U.S. Public Health Service:

> I was driving through a small town in Maryland the other day when I saw a sign on a home/office that said, "Veterinarian and Taxidermist." Underneath in very small letters it said, "Either way you get your pet back." I thought if we collected data and analyzed it that way, we all would be successful. Everyone would have the data they needed to get the decision or policy done in a way that they wanted it done.

Laws

We live in a world of laws — civil laws, criminal laws, scientific laws. But no matter where we live, all of us answer to a higher law — Murphy's. That's the famous law that states that anything that can go wrong, will go wrong. This "mother of all laws" has spawned quite a brood. You can find entire books of Murphy-style laws, which is good because it means you can probably find a law that fits your subject matter. Why bother? Because funny laws provide a simple way to add humor to a speech.

Here's an example from Norman Augustine, former President and CEO of Lockheed-Martin:

> I have recently branched out from the rather narrow confines of laws governing aerospace management to promulgating the more general laws of nature. My latest endeavor in this arena has been the law, derived from a considerable base of empirical evidence, that "Tornadoes are caused by trailer parks."

Greeting cards

Would you like free access to easy-to-deliver material developed by highly paid humor writers? Then walk into your local card shop and start browsing. Birthday cards. Anniversary cards. Get well cards. You name it. What was once a field devoted to solemn sentiments is now dominated by mirthful messages. And you can adapt them easily to almost anything that you want to speak about.

Here's an example from a commencement address by David Magill, Superintendent of the Lower Merion School District in Pennsylvania:

> Pictures and dreams have a lot to do with each other and they both have a lot to do with graduations. Just a couple of weeks ago, I stopped in a local card store to buy a graduation card for my nephew. I spent some time reading the messages and many of them said something about dreams. Here are some of the samples:
>
> "The challenge is high, the dream bright and new. The world is out there and it's waiting for you. Reach for it all. Dare to dream, dare to try. No goal is too distant, no star is too high!"
>
> "Wishing you success as you follow your special dream and happiness when it comes true. Lots of luck always."

And then there was my favorite. On the front of the card it asks the question, "A Cash Gift for the Graduate?" Open the card and it says, "Dream On!"

Bumper stickers

One of the great breakthroughs in the history of public speaking occurred with the invention of the car. It provided a fantastic new source of material — bumper stickers.

From stickers concerning driving (Forget world peace — visualize using your turn signal.) to stickers offering self-insight (I just got lost in thought. It was unfamiliar territory.) and general advice (Be nice to your kids. They'll choose your nursing home.), wisdom previously limited to great minds became available to the masses.

Here's an example from a speech about public education given by Bob Chase when he was President of the National Education Association:

> Everyone is for change in the abstract. But when you challenge people to change in real, substantive, concrete ways, it's a different story. Then people avoid change. They stall it. They fight it. I love the bumper sticker that says: "Change is good. You go first."

And if you don't want to look for bumper stickers, you can also find funny lines on T-shirts, coffee mugs and just about any other object that has a printable surface.

So there you have it. There's help for the humor-impaired. If you can't tell a joke, you can still tell a personal anecdote, make an amusing observation, quote a funny line, or employ many other simple types of humor. Any of them can enhance your next speech.

Chapter 22

Ten Things to Check Before You Speak

. . . .

In This Chapter

▶ Arranging the room to your benefit

▶ Anticipating equipment problems

▶ Eliminating distractions

. . . .

You prepare a fantastic speech. You run it by your colleagues. Everyone says it's pure genius. Can't miss. You're going to be great. The big day arrives and you're psyched. You take your incredibly cool slides and go to the site of your speech. The audience applauds as you enter the room. But you wish you were dead. The podium you requested isn't there. Neither is the microphone or the slide projector. And the way the room is set-up, half your audience couldn't even see your slides anyway.

Rather than being stuck on stage without the right equipment, you should maximize your chances of giving a successful speech by taking care of the following *before* you start talking.

Sound System

Is there a sound system and does it work? Make sure that the volume is adjusted so that everyone in the room can hear you. *Test the microphone in the location where you'll actually use it.* I learned this lesson the hard way. Just before a speech to a group of Defense Department managers, I tested the microphone while standing in the front of the room. It worked fine. But I didn't go behind the podium where I'd actually be speaking. Big mistake. When I started my speech, the microphone erupted in screeching feedback. Great way to begin, right? Turns out the culprit was a metal sprinkler nozzle in the ceiling over the podium.

Make sure that you know how to work the microphone. Do you know how to turn it on and off? If you have a microphone stand, do you know how to adjust it? Different microphones pick up and broadcast your voice in different ways. Play with the microphone until you get a good idea of its range.

Podium

Is there a podium or lectern? And is it the right size? The *right size* is whatever suits your purposes. Do you want the audience to see you? Then make sure you're taller than the podium or that you get a box you can stand on behind the podium. Are you afraid the audience will throw things? Get a podium that's high and wide. In either case, make sure that the podium has a light that's in good working order — especially if you're going to darken the room for slides. You can't get the audience to see the light if the podium leaves your notes in the dark.

Audiovisual Equipment

You can't check slide or overhead projectors too many times. After you get your slides or overheads focused, walk around the room while one is projecting on the screen. Can it be seen from everywhere in the room? Overhead projectors often block the view of people seated in line with them. If that's the case, try to project your overhead higher up on the screen — closer to the ceiling. And definitely use a screen. It shows your slides or overheads much better than a wall. Many slide and overhead projectors come equipped with a spare bulb. Make sure you know where it is.

If your visuals are in PowerPoint, make sure there will be a computer available with the PowerPoint software, and a way to get your speech file into it (or, better yet, bring your own laptop). Make sure the right cables are with the projector (power for the projector and the right connector cable for the computer). If you're using video, be certain the right equipment to show the video is available, and that the video is easily seen and heard by all members of the audience.

Lighting

Test the "house lights" to see if they work and how the light fills the room. Find out if you can adjust their level of brightness. If they're adjustable, take advantage of this feature — especially if you're using slides.

While slides require that you turn the lights off, if your slides are easy to see, you can show them with the lights turned down but *not* off. A small amount of light makes a tremendous difference in your interaction with the audience. They can't go to sleep under the cover of darkness.

Human Equipment

If people are operating equipment for you, make sure that they know what they're doing. You don't need an Einstein to work a slide projector, but it does require a minimal level of competence. Also, make sure that you know who to contact for help with minor and major catastrophes — a light bulb burns out, a microphone breaks, or your podium is destroyed by a UFO.

Electricity

Where are the electrical outlets in the room? Do you have enough of them to run your equipment? Are they two-prong or three-prong? Do yourself a favor. Always bring an adapter and an extension cord (and perhaps a power strip). You'll be glad you did.

Restrooms

Definitely check the restrooms. Where are they located? Do they have paper towels available? Is there an adequate supply of toilet paper? Do the toilets work? This may sound trivial now, but it can become very important. You never know when you'll need a restroom in a hurry — especially if you're nervous.

Seating Arrangements

When it comes to seating, three basic considerations apply to any type of speech in any type of setting.

- ✔ First and most important, can everyone see you?
- ✔ Is the seating comfortable — both physically and psychologically?
- ✔ Is the arrangement of chairs suited to the size of the room, the size of the audience, and the purpose of your speech?

In considering these factors, start with the room. Will you be in a banquet room? A conference room? A large meeting room? An auditorium? The room establishes the parameters for seating. Next, will the audience be seated at tables? If so, will they be round tables or rectangular tables? After you have this information, you can arrange the seating pieces like a jigsaw puzzle until you get the picture that you want.

Within the boundaries established by the room and furniture, you can arrange seating based on the size of the room and your purpose. Chairs arranged in a semicircle provide a more informal atmosphere. This arrangement puts you directly in front of each audience member. It also allows all the audience members to see each other. If the audience is more than 30 people, the group is probably too large for a single semicircle. In that case, you can stagger a second row of chairs behind the first row. Now you have a double semicircle where the second row looks between the shoulders of the people in the first row. For large groups or a more formal atmosphere, I recommend classroom style seating in rows.

If you're speaking at a breakfast, lunch, or dinner meeting, the audience will probably be seated at round tables, which means that half of them will have their backs to you when you begin to speak. Factor this in when you begin your speech. Leave time for them to turn their seats around to face you.

Potential Distractions

If you're speaking at a restaurant, hotel, or office building, chances are there's a nice view out the window of the meeting room.

That's bad news, because you want audience attention focused on you, not the view. What can you do? First, try to speak in a room that has no windows. If that's not possible, make sure that the windows are covered with drapes or curtains. What if they have no curtains? Improvise. I've seen speakers hang tablecloths over the windows — anything to eliminate the competition of the view.

Another big distraction is noise. It provides direct competition with your message. If you're speaking at a grazing function — a breakfast, lunch, or dinner — don't start your speech until the waiters have cleared the tables. The clatter of dishes is an intolerable distraction. Unfortunately, due to "time problems," your contact may insist that you begin speaking before the meal is concluded. Try this tactic. Suggest that the waiters serve dessert and disappear. They can clear the dessert plates *after* you finish speaking. You start talking as soon as the waiters leave the room. The noise of people eating dessert while you're speaking is a drag, but it's a lot better than trying to speak with waiters running around the room.

How to Get There

Do you know exactly where you're giving your speech, how to get there, and how long it takes to get there? Well, find out. It's amazing how little consideration people give to these basic concerns. You knock yourself out preparing a killer talk, and then you blow it by going to the wrong ballroom. It's not enough to know the hotel. You need to know the *exact* location. Why? Because by the time you get to the correct room, you're frazzled and possibly even late. The time you were going to spend getting used to the room and psyching yourself up is gone forever.

Related concerns are traffic and parking. Don't plan your timetable on some general notion of how long it takes to get to the meeting site. Plan specifically for the time you'll be traveling. Maybe it generally takes 30 minutes to get there. If you have to travel during rush hour, it's going to take longer. Plan for it.

Then you have the whole parking thing. Is it my imagination or is it taking longer and longer to find a place to park? (Except for certain parts of California where people are, like, into creating their own space.) You need to know in advance where to park. Hey, you're the speaker. Tell them to give you a special parking spot at the meeting site. You deserve it.

Index

• *N* •

FOR DUMMIES®

A world of resources to help you grow

TRAVEL

0-7645-5453-0

0-7645-5438-7

0-7645-5444-1

Also available:

America's National Parks For Dummies
(0-7645-6204-5)

Caribbean For Dummies
(0-7645-5445-X)

Cruise Vacations For Dummies 2003
(0-7645-5459-X)

Europe For Dummies
(0-7645-5456-5)

Ireland For Dummies
(0-7645-6199-5)

France For Dummies
(0-7645-6292-4)

Las Vegas For Dummies
(0-7645-5448-4)

London For Dummies
(0-7645-5416-6)

Mexico's Beach Resorts For Dummies
(0-7645-6262-2)

Paris For Dummies
(0-7645-5494-8)

RV Vacations For Dummies
(0-7645-5443-3)

EDUCATION & TEST PREPARATION

0-7645-5194-9

0-7645-5325-9

0-7645-5249-X

Also available:

The ACT For Dummies
(0-7645-5210-4)

Chemistry For Dummies
(0-7645-5430-1)

English Grammar For Dummies
(0-7645-5322-4)

French For Dummies
(0-7645-5193-0)

GMAT For Dummies
(0-7645-5251-1)

Inglés Para Dummies
(0-7645-5427-1)

Italian For Dummies
(0-7645-5196-5)

Research Papers For Dummies
(0-7645-5426-3)

SAT I For Dummies
(0-7645-5472-7)

U.S. History For Dummies
(0-7645-5249-X)

World History For Dummies
(0-7645-5242-2)

HEALTH, SELF-HELP & SPIRITUALITY

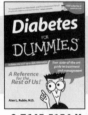

0-7645-5154-X

0-7645-5302-X

0-7645-5418-2

Also available:

The Bible For Dummies
(0-7645-5296-1)

Controlling Cholesterol For Dummies
(0-7645-5440-9)

Dating For Dummies
(0-7645-5072-1)

Dieting For Dummies
(0-7645-5126-4)

High Blood Pressure For Dummies
(0-7645-5424-7)

Judaism For Dummies
(0-7645-5299-6)

Menopause For Dummies
(0-7645-5458-1)

Nutrition For Dummies
(0-7645-5180-9)

Potty Training For Dummies
(0-7645-5417-4)

Pregnancy For Dummies
(0-7645-5074-8)

Rekindling Romance For Dummies
(0-7645-5303-8)

Religion For Dummies
(0-7645-5264-3)
